The Four Noble Truths

The Four Noble Truths

A Guide to Everyday Life

Lama Zopa Rinpoche

Edited by Yeo Puay Huei

Wisdom Publications
199 Elm Street
Somerville, MA 02144 USA
wisdompubs.org

Library of Congress Cataloging-in-Publication Data
Names: Thubten Zopa, Rinpoche, 1945– author. | Huei, Yeo Puay, editor.
Title: The Four Noble Truths: a guide to everyday life / Lama Zopa Rinpoche; edited
   by Yeo Puay Huei.
Description: Somerville, MA: Wisdom Publications, 2018. | Includes bibliographical
   references and index. |
Identifiers: LCCN 2017048508 (print) | LCCN 2017050858 (ebook) |
   ISBN 9781614294092 (ebook) | ISBN 9781614293941 (pbk.: alk. paper)
Subjects: LCSH: Four Noble Truths.
Classification: LCC BQ4230 (ebook) | LCC BQ4230 .T49 2018 (print) |
   DDC 294.3/42—dc23
LC record available at https://lccn.loc.gov/2017048508

ISBN 978-1-61429-394-1   ebook ISBN 978-1-61429-409-2

22 21 20 19 18
5 4 3 2 1

Cover and interior design by Gopa&Ted2, Inc.
Set in Adobe Garamond Pro 11/15.3.

Wisdom Publications' books are printed on acid-free paper and meet
the guidelines for permanence and durability of the Production Guidelines
for Book Longevity of the Council on Library Resources.

♻ This book was produced with environmental mindfulness.
For more information, please visit wisdompubs.org/wisdom-environment.

Printed in the United States of America.

Please visit fscus.org.

CONTENTS

EDITOR'S PREFACE

SIMPLE WORDS to illuminate the Buddha's profound teachings are rare. Experiential teachings on the Buddhadharma are rarer still. Over a coffee table conversation at Malaysia's Kuala Lumpur airport, Kyabje Lama Zopa Rinpoche suggested I attempt a book on the four noble truths based on his teachings over the years. I hesitated. After all, Rinpoche not only teaches the Dharma but also *lives* it. Further, what has Rinpoche taught in the past forty-five years that was *not* the four noble truths? To fail in accurately compiling Rinpoche's teachings on the entire Dharma would be to belittle this precious lama's life and lifework. I believe Rinpoche saw through my hesitation. He whipped out his dice, did a quick divination, and offered encouragement. I am deeply grateful.

This book consists of Rinpoche's experiential teachings given over a span of forty-five years. Nothing about Rinpoche's actions is ordinary. Everything about his being is interwoven with Dharma.

At the end of each chapter are stories or anecdotes from the life of Kyabje Lama Zopa Rinpoche. Most are from the journals of Ven. Roger Kunsang, the devoted monk attendant and secretary to Rinpoche for almost thirty years. Some are from lamas and senior students who witnessed events firsthand. This generous sharing of factual accounts offers glimpses into Rinpoche's daily life and a taste of the lived experience of Dharma.

I offer special thanks to Geshe Tenzin Zopa, whose conversations with Rinpoche on the need for *yigchas* (study textbooks) of Rinpoche's teachings somehow led to the suggestion of this book. I am hugely grateful for the generous help of Dr. Nick Ribush of the Lama Yeshe Wisdom Archive, his team, and the many diligent transcribers who have produced thousands of pages of documented teachings by Rinpoche.

I especially thank Steve Wilhelm and Mary Petrusewicz, who masterfully edited this manuscript, and David Kittelstrom, whose kindness made the editorial journey less stressful than touted to be. The book is now humbly offered to the reader. Any mistakes, especially omissions, are mine alone.

Rajiv Mehrotra of the Foundation for Universal Responsibility of His Holiness the Dalai Lama and Ashok Chopra of Hay House Publishers India have kindly given permission to use the line drawing of the Wheel of Life from *The End of Suffering and the Discovery of Happiness: The Path of Tibetan Buddhism*, by His Holiness the Dalai Lama.

This endeavor is dedicated to the good health, long life, and fulfillment of all the wishes of my root guru Kyabje Lama Zopa Rinpoche; all my gurus; my center's resident teachers past and present, who have been my lamps on the path; and the family of Losang Dragpa Centre, Malaysia.

May all sentient beings be guided by perfectly qualified Mahayana masters and complete the path to enlightenment. May the Buddhadharma flourish. This dedication, prayer of dedication, and person are all empty and have no inherent existence.

Yeo Puay Huei
Kuala Lumpur, Malaysia

INTRODUCTION: WORKING WITH THE MIND

In essence the four noble truths say that we all naturally desire happiness and do not wish to suffer. . . . If we are to pursue our aspiration to gain freedom from suffering, we need to clearly understand the causes and conditions that give rise to suffering and strive to eliminate them. Additionally we must clearly understand the causes and conditions that give rise to happiness as well and actively practice them. Having established the framework of liberation in the four noble truths, the Buddha detailed the . . . steps along the path to enlightenment . . . how the principles of the four noble truths are to be applied in one's day-to-day spiritual life.

—HIS HOLINESS THE DALAI LAMA,
Essence of the Heart Sutra

HAPPINESS AND SUFFERING are part of our life experience, but they do not come from the external world. They come from within, from our own minds. Suffering springs from afflictions in our minds.

Until we understand the causes of suffering, no matter our intellect, education, or wealth, no matter the ordinary success we may have achieved, in the heart there is something missing, there is no real peace. The heart is hollow.

To transform our minds into one of happiness, we start by pacifying the mind, separating the mind from the causes of suffering. When this happens—liberation! And if we are then able to cease even the very subtle mental imprints of negative action, speech, and thought—enlightenment!

The process of inner transformation begins with understanding the nature of mind.

THE VALUE OF AN OPEN MIND

How wonderful it is to open our minds! With an open mind we're open to exploration, which is the opposite of being limited by a closed and rigid mind as hard as iron, stuck to old concepts. An open mind enables us to look for fresh meaning and a better life. It allows us to investigate, check, and analyze.

We need to freely investigate whatever is being asserted. We need to apply analysis, logic, and reasoning to whatever is being taught before accepting it, whether the teaching is Eastern philosophy, Western philosophy, a teaching by Guru Shakyamuni Buddha, or a subject explained by scientists.

Guru Shakyamuni Buddha said, "Examine my teachings well, the way a goldsmith examines gold, by cutting it, rubbing it, and melting it to see whether it is false gold, mixed, or pure."

In the same way, we should examine the Buddha's teachings or Dharma, using reasoning, analysis, and logic, but not blind faith. Only after we have done that should we consider accepting his teachings.

Therefore when we first read about the Dharma, we should not accept it without thinking about it. Questioning Dharma is what we are expected to do at this starting point. Emotionally clutching to words or the idea of Buddha in heaven brings little benefit. This is because when life gets tough and problems arise, we will have no inner understanding of the Dharma with which to support ourselves.

Thank you to everybody who is seeking happiness differently from how you have sought it before. This time you are freeing yourselves to open the door to liberation, the door of the great release, through understanding the inner, spiritual method to gain happiness. This is a key point because happiness is not found outside but within. Happiness lies within the mind. Whether we are talking about temporal or ultimate happiness there is no other way to find it except through developing the mind.

Looking back at our own life experiences we should ask: How does happiness arise? How does unhappiness arise? Do happiness and unhappiness really come from external causes or do they come from our minds? It may seem as if the external world is the source of enjoyment and of troubles. However, look more closely. The key is our inner lives.

The real source of happiness and misery, the principal cause of these experiences, is mind and how it views everything it encounters. A person who realizes this makes fewer mistakes in life, experiences more happiness, feels greater peace. Sometimes we hear it said, "Oh, you were in such good spirits this morning, yet you seem so low right now." This roller coaster of life happens because we have no control over our minds.

Those who train their minds experience problems quite differently from most people. Whether conditions are good or bad, people who train their minds remain stable and happy. Nothing brings their spirits down. Such is the value of understanding the mind, its qualities and its potential.

In the mountains where I was born, in the Solukhumbu district near Mount Everest, villagers often dry animal skins in the sun. This causes the skins to contract, dry up, and become stiff. Villagers use these skins to make shoes, barley flour sacks, and containers for cheese by first softening the leather by applying butter to it, then pressing and squeezing the leather with their hands and feet. Kneading the dried skin makes it flexible, and the villagers then can cut it up and make shoes, sacks, and other things from it.

On the other hand, nomads in Tibet use dry animal skins to wrap big blocks of butter, and those skins stay stiff. The nomads keep the butter wrapped inside the dried skins for long periods but do nothing else to the skins. Therefore the skins remain stiff, even though they have been in contact with butter for many years.

The massaged Solukhumbu animal skin shows how a mind hardened by negative thoughts can be softened and changed for the better by listening to the Dharma. However, the mind untouched by the application of Dharma is unyielding and of limited use, like the hard skins used by Tibetan nomads for butter stocks. A thick, hard, closed mind is of limited benefit. Endless difficulties arise for such an inflexible mind.

The Nature of Mind and Its Potential

What is mind? It is not the brain. It is a phenomenon that is formless, colorless, intangible, and whose nature is clear and capable of perceiving objects. Just as a mirror is able to reflect an image of an object, likewise the mind is able to perceive objects and reflect them.

There are two aspects to the nature of mind: There is the conventional aspect of mind that perceives and so on, and there is the ultimate aspect of mind that is called the clear-light nature of mind. We will discuss conventional and ultimate states later in this book, but for now it is useful to think of the ultimate aspect of mind as clear light in nature. Ultimate mind is pure in that it is not mixed with delusions or obscurations of any kind, and it is empty of inherent existence. This is the ultimate nature of mind or what is called the buddha nature, which lies within us all.

There is buddha nature in every sentient being's mind, no matter how many negative actions living beings have committed or how heavy their minds are with mistaken views.

This underlying buddha nature brings us hope because it means that if our clear-light mind meets favorable conditions, such as a teacher who reveals the path of virtue, we can take action to achieve the happiness of liberation and enlightenment. However, if our clear-light mind meets unfavorable conditions, such as nonvirtuous teachers or friends who divert us from spiritual cultivation, then mind degenerates. When this happens buddha nature is not lost, but the chance to experience happiness, realizations, and wisdom is severely delayed.

Think of a big gong. The potential for making sound is within the gong, but the gong needs to encounter the condition of somebody striking it for the sound to emerge. The sound does not come from outside or from somewhere else. The potential for sound is already within the gong. Sound emerges when the gong is struck by a gong stick.

Similarly, butter can be produced from milk. The potential for butter is there in the milk. Butter does not enter milk from somewhere else! It is already there. It is just a matter of meeting the conditions that can produce butter from milk. Therefore, as our minds have buddha nature, the potential for ultimate, lasting happiness is already within us. It is a matter of our creating the right conditions to accomplish that.

So you see there is always hope. Life is full of hope. No matter how many heavy negative actions we have committed, there is always the potential to be free from disturbing thoughts and obscurations, free from negativities, free from fears, and indeed free from all suffering. That potential is always within us. It is in our own hands. It depends on us.

Since life is full of hope, there is no need to be depressed. Even for those who have met the Dharma long ago but still endure so many obstacles in life and make so little progress in spiritual practice, the potential for total fulfillment remains possible. This is because of the clear-light nature of mind, the buddha nature within us. Problems and obstacles are temporary. The causes of problems can be removed.

THE BEGINNINGLESS MIND

Where does mind come from? Some people think that one's mind comes from one big, universal mind, which, like a planet, broke up into millions of pieces long ago, each of which found their way into our bodies. This concept in practice means that if all living beings' minds come from one big universal mind, it is then possible that when our postman's mind is broken up into pieces and somehow placed into our bodies, we all become our postman. It is very funny to consider.

There are others who believe that our minds come from our parents. Let us examine this view. Let us check this feeling of "I" and where it comes from. Why is it we have this sense of "I" without needing our parents or teachers to show it to us? This feeling of "I" has already been there from the beginning. What caused this? Did this feeling of "I" come from mother or father, or both?

If our sense of "I" comes from our parents, that sense should be like that of our mother or father or both, in which case all children would be just like their parents, except dwelling in different bodies! Parents would then be born from parents. We would be born from ourselves! Think about it. It would be interesting to investigate such a view.

We are born from parents, but our minds and our parents' minds are not in oneness. We have our own experiences and thus we have separate minds. This minute's mind came from last minute's mind. The continuation of today's mind came from yesterday's mind. This present year's mind continues from the previous year's, and that previous year's mind was the mental continuity of the previous year's, and so on. Each moment's mind is dependent on the one before. This is why it is said that mind is a mental continuum and beginningless.

Some people think we are born with a mind like a blank page, and that delusions in the mind come into existence later. It is not like this. From the very beginning of this life, our minds have not been free from suffering and delusions, including ignorance, attachment, and anger.

Did the delusions come from our parents? No. Our delusions did not come from our parents. Why not? Because our minds are separate from our parents' minds. Our previous lives' minds had delusions, and as the delusions were clearly not removed, the continuum of mind carried those delusions forward from life to life.

We all have noticed how different children can be from their parents in personality, intelligence, interests, and so on. Even when two children are born from the same parents, those children are often different from each other and different from their parents. Even babies display different habits and traits without being taught by parents.

No matter how much parents may try to educate their children similarly, differences remain between them. Some children are aggressive or cruel from a very young age, whereas others are gentle and kind. The principal cause of these differences is the imprints of previous lives on the children's minds.

Let us look at a child born with defective organs or senses. Even if we try to explain this situation by showing that this gene and that gene were not functioning properly, that only shows *how* the defect came about. It does not explain *why* this specific child had to face this specific condition leading to this specific defect.

The parents may have had several children, so why is it that this specific child had a gene complication? This has to be checked. Scientists may not have written books about past lives, but this does not mean there are no past lives. After all, we have no memory of being conceived in our mother's womb but that does not mean we were not born from a mother's womb!

Therefore merely not remembering past lives cannot be the sole reason for rejecting the idea of past lives. Our own experience is that mind is a continuum—from past to present, from present to future. We need to think this through and reason it out.

Some people remember their previous lives clearly, with details being validated by persons who knew the predecessors. This supports the concept of mental continuity from before the present life. For instance, years ago the late senior tutor of His Holiness the Dalai Lama told me that when he would introduce a Dharma subject to His Holiness as a young boy, the Dalai Lama would display a profound understanding of the subject. This was the case even when the tutor had not previously taught or spoken to His Holiness about the subject, or even thought about it himself!

Many people can remember their past lives, the people they met and the incidents that happened, without ever being told about them. When the truth of those remembered incidents are checked, they turn out to be exactly as those people remembered.

MIND AND THE PURSUIT OF HAPPINESS

In our daily lives whatever we do with our minds, our speech, and our actions leaves imprints on the mind. Every moment of thought, speech, and activity plants seeds within our mental continuum.

It is like shooting a video. When we make a movie, the image of the photographed object is captured by our device. When conditions come together, such as editing the video, connecting it to a projector, and switching on the projector, the image is projected. It appears and everyone can see it on the screen. In the same way, our actions create imprints on our mental continuum, which manifest when conditions ripen.

Our positive actions, also called good karma, leave positive imprints on the mind. When causes and conditions come together to bring a positive imprint into fruition, we might suddenly see something of beauty like blossoming flowers, or get a chance to partake in something we enjoy. We may unexpectedly come across a very good restaurant that serves delicious food. These are the ripening of past positive imprints left on the mental continuum, from past lives even zillions of eons ago.

It is useful to observe daily life with this understanding of how our actions leave imprints, which later become projected results. This is the basic Buddhist philosophy that all our experiences come from mind, which motivated our actions or karma and later ripened into experienced results.

While we have all done some positive actions, we have also, over endless rebirths, been controlled by the delusions of ignorance, attachment, anger, and pride. Our minds have long been habituated to these delusions, which then influence our actions. Long has our mental continuum carried these imprints.

This habituation is why we are not able to apply the Buddha's teachings all the time, even though we may be familiar with them intellectually. We cannot effectively apply antidotes to the delusions just when they are most needed. We often forget the teachings just when delusions arise. And yet the teachings are medicine for the troubled mind.

When we are sick—whether from a headache, stomach pain, heart attack, wounds, infections, a toothache—taking one type of medicine may stop one of the ailments but not all of them. If we're suffering from several illnesses, we need to see a doctor to get the appropriate prescription for each of the illnesses, and then take those medicines to recover.

It is exactly the same with our minds. We have various diseases of the mind, such as the illness of ignorance, of attachment, of anger, of pride, of jealousy, and of the varying gross and subtle mental afflictions. These bring mental pain, and specific remedies are needed.

For instance, when the mental sickness of anger arises, how does it appear and feel? Are we at ease when we are angry? No, there is no comfort, no joy. It feels like having a sharp blade lodged deep inside the heart. Our experience is similar with the mental affliction of pride, which feels as if a huge craggy mountain is stuck inside us, one so large it almost fractures our bodies from within. And when we are overcome with attachment we constantly feel anxious and uptight, as if something were pulling out our hearts!

Why are our minds so often disturbed and upset? This is because we have not realized that the principal cause of unhappiness lies within the mind. We have always assumed the principal cause of happiness is external, so we constantly try to manipulate our external environment to find happiness. When this fails we blame others and never think to look within, never try to develop our minds.

Even when we try to investigate our inner selves we do so with wrong understanding, which only brings more confusion. If we have never tried the Dharma path that brings ultimate happiness, we cannot actualize it. But we have the potential to do so by following the path that eliminates the root of all suffering, the afflictive emotions or delusions imprinted in our minds. When we succeed in uprooting these delusions, there will be no hindrance to lasting happiness.

Sadly we often sabotage our own pursuit of happiness. When someone suggests we read a Dharma book or listen to a Dharma teaching, pride or laziness overwhelms us. We think, "Oh, I already know that. I don't need to hear it again."

If we think this way we will feel lost when a crisis arises in our lives, even if we have read many Dharma books or received many teachings. We will feel defeated, as if we had never encountered the teachings at all. To make matters worse, we may blame or harm others, thinking that will get us what we want, while we fail at the real solution, checking and managing our own minds.

Physical sickness can be cured with the right medicine, but curing the inner disease of deluded thought is not so easy. Disturbing thoughts can incapacitate us, so we take pills to numb the pain or we try to go to sleep, hoping unconsciousness can relieve the mental agony for a while.

But these inner diseases cannot be healed by external medicine. Therefore we need to study the Dharma and use it to eradicate the inner illnesses that bring suffering not only in this life but also from life to life.

Do we have any real chance at happiness? Of course we do! Even though the nature of mind is presently obscured by the delusions, mind is not the same as those delusions, any more than sky is the same as the clouds that float within it. Clouds form due to causes and conditions, but they clear away when those conditions change. When the sky clears it allows sunshine through, giving nourishment to the earth and bringing enjoyment to many living beings.

As cloudy weather is temporary, the self-centered mind with its delusions and mistakes is also temporary. Neither is eternal. Obscurations of mind, like clouds, appear through causes and conditions, so both can be cleared through different causes and conditions. This mind can become free of delusion and secure lasting happiness.

In Tibet villagers put milk into wooden churns, ensure that all the conditions are right, and then diligently churn the milk. From that milk is produced rich, golden butter.

Just as milk contains the potential for butter, mind contains the potential for happiness. We can fully develop our minds by studying and applying the Buddha's methods and be then able to understand sentient beings' minds, know the most suitable methods to help them, and lead them to peerless happiness. As we pursue lasting happiness we can secure not only our own happiness but also the happiness of all beings. This is the potential of our minds.

It is amazing and unimaginably wonderful how we are able to benefit others with our minds! Our precious human body gives us the ideal opportunity to fulfill both our own aspirations and those of numberless living beings.

Mind Is the Creator

One of the fundamental points of Buddhism is that there is no creator other than our own minds. There is no creator who has a mind separate from ours. There is nobody outside who created the ups and downs of our lives except our own minds and our own actions, which have collectively produced the results we now face. Our entire life experience has been caused by the mental afflictions of ignorance, attachment, and anger, which then motivated our actions.

The whole world as we experience it comes from the mind and is caused by the imprints of positive and negative karma left on the mind. Our world, our perceptions, our experiences are manifestations of our karmic imprints that have ripened. We experience a human body, as well as happy feelings, suffering feelings, and neutral feelings, all because particular karmic imprints have ripened. In addition our aggregates—form, feeling, consciousness, discrimination, and compositional factors—that make up our sense of self all come from our minds and karmic imprints.

How things appear to us depend on these karmic imprints in our minds, which determine what the mind projects and how it labels things. Therefore we cannot trust outer appearances. It is the inner factor of the mind that is important.

The root delusion of ignorance refers to not knowing the ultimate reality of the "I" and the ultimate reality of the aggregates. The ignorant mind sees the aggregates performing functions and then imputes the label "I" on to the aggregates. It is a mere imputation, yet the mind believes there is a truly existent self or "I" right here.

Ignorance is the greatest of all superstitious thoughts, the king of all delusions, which blinds us from differentiating between the true "I" and the false "I." The seemingly true "I," sometimes called the conventional "I," is one that is merely imputed by mind to the base of aggregates but that is empty of existing from its own side. The false "I" is one that appears as inherently existent, as if existing on its own, as if not merely labeled "I" by mind.

If we put on unclean spectacles to look at the world, we will see the world as unclean. We may be able to see something of the world, but not accurately. Therefore while we see appearances all the time, those appearances are not true or correct.

After we wrongly conclude there is a truly existing I, the ego arises, the self-cherishing thought emerges, and from there emotional disturbances and mistaken actions flow.

The arising of anger is often based on believing someone else created problems for us. We think, "The problem I'm experiencing now came from that person." Our angry thoughts about harming others are rooted in believing someone else is the source of our misery and that those problems had nothing to do with our own mistaken actions. This belief is totally unfounded and incorrect.

Such angry thoughts illustrate our belief in an external creator as the source of trouble. Instead of realizing that our own minds led us to do negative actions that resulted in negative consequences, we mistakenly believe there is an external creator or harm-giver who made problems for us. The minute we realize we are the creator, that all problems come from us acting on thoughts influenced by delusions, there will be nothing external to blame, no person to blame, and therefore no basis for anger to arise against anyone.

These days we often hear the term *instinct*. Whatever a child does that is not taught by parents or teachers is termed "instinct."

In Buddhism we explain such actions as caused by imprints left by positive, negative, or neutral actions in the past. These actions left imprints on the mental continuum, which caused the child to repeat similar actions in the present, and which will continue to manifest in the future unless the imprint is removed. In this way, the cycle of actions goes on, reinforcing imprints giving rise to the same results.

As per the video analogy, we imprint images of people and events like a video recorder does. Then with the proper device we can project and view these imprinted images. In exactly the same way, the imprints of what we consider true existence that was left on our mental continuums cause us to project true existence on to everything we perceive. When we first meet an object, person, or situation, these form the "screen" on which our past imprints will project an image.

If we meet a person who does not give us what we want, our negative imprints immediately project on to this person the label "bad person." Right there arises the creation of a problem, an enemy.

Our positive imprints work in a similar way. Our virtuous actions leave positive imprints, so that when causes and conditions come together our minds project positive labels on to an encountered object, such as "good person," "helpful tool," or "fun." In other words, mind imputes existence. Mind is the creator.

Once we label someone "friend," we are kind to that person. If we label a person "enemy," we may refuse to help that person. If we label someone a "stranger," we become indifferent.

So you see that everything, including our perceptions and emotional states, is dependent on the mind's projections. Because of delusions and imprints, our minds label objects, persons, or situations "truly existent," and we then completely believe in our own labels.

From this we can see that the principal cause of happiness or unhappiness lies within our own minds. The mind discriminates between people and situations, labels them, and then believes in the labels as true existence. But these labels are not truly existent. They are merely labels. This is a very, very important point to understand and remember.

It is therefore crucial to understand the nature of mind, its evolution, and how vast its potential is. Through this we open ourselves to correct understanding of all of the Buddha's teachings.

Understanding the mind and its potential enables us to fully understand the four noble truths' explanation of the nature of suffering, its causes, the possibility of the end of suffering, as well as the remedies that secure the end of all suffering.

1 : THE TRUTH OF SUFFERING

The noble truth of suffering (dukkha) is this: birth is suffering; aging is suffering; sickness is suffering; death is suffering; sorrow and lamentation, pain, grief, and despair are suffering; association with the unpleasant is suffering; disassociation from the pleasant is suffering; not to get what one wants is suffering. In brief, the five aggregates of attachment are suffering.

—DHAMMACAKKAPPAVATTANA SUTTA

WHY THE BUDDHA TAUGHT SUFFERING FIRST

WHY DO WE travel to the east, to the west, or anywhere? Why do we busy ourselves with activity? If we check our minds, we discover that behind all our actions is our quest for happiness. Deep inside we are bubbling with dissatisfaction. No matter what reasons we give for our busyness, such as wanting to learn and experience new things, the primary reason is that we yearn for happiness and wish to avoid suffering.

Because of this we might decide to change our lifestyle, thinking, "I will be happier doing that or living in a different place." For instance, when we feel exhausted from life as an office worker, we might think, "Perhaps there is more pleasure living life in a circus." Then we join a circus. However, we soon discover that circus life also is suffering.

I have heard that life can be rather difficult for television comedians if audiences do not laugh at their jokes. The fear of not being successful is a suffering that weighs heavily on many people.

Some of us have changed our lifestyles many times in the hope of attaining happiness. However, if we take an honest look back at those lifestyles, we see how the nature of each of them was suffering. Before we engaged in those lifestyles they looked very attractive. But after we immersed ourselves in them, anticipated delight soon gave way to discontent.

Whenever we first meet someone—either a high-status person like a king or an ordinary person—we will exchange pleasantries and all may appear well. However, as the conversation progresses the new person gradually begins to talk about his or her difficulties. If the conversation continues for an hour, much more suffering is revealed. Discontent keeps surfacing. This is the nature of life as we presently know it.

Repeatedly experiencing dissatisfaction by circling in suffering is called cyclic existence, or *samsara*. Many people have the idea that samsara is a place, so they are in samsara when in a crowded city or a noisy market, but not in samsara if they are in the mountains or at a monastery. This is a big mistake.

Wherever you are, including on your death bed, you are still in samsara. Even when the mind is no longer in your body but is in the intermediate stage after death, the mind is still in samsara. There is no break time from samsara! Over beginningless lives there has not been one moment of release from samsara. Until we totally uproot ignorance we are stuck in samsara.

Your hair is also in samsara. Some people think it is easy, that they can shave off samsara! You cannot shave off samsara with a machine. Samsara is the continuity of the aggregates, which are caused by the delusions of ignorance, attachment, and aversion. To escape from samsara you have to stop continuously grasping the aggregates, which are caused by delusion and karma.

This is why the Buddha taught suffering first, followed by the cause of suffering. Without understanding suffering and the nature of samsara in all its forms, there would be no reason to be rid of it, let alone find the causes for it and pursue the method to eliminate those causes. There would then be no wish to follow the method to happiness—to realize great peace, the cessation of suffering—and consequently no liberation.

When a person feeling unwell visits a doctor and the doctor explains what sickness the patient has, the patient identifies the sickness as the cause of his suffering and develops an aversion to it. The patient learns about the cause of that sickness, follows the treatment that removes the cause of the sickness, and is healed.

In the same way, Guru Shakyamuni Buddha revealed the truth of suffering before explaining the cause of suffering. He did this because unless we recognize how suffering affects everyone we will have no incentive to investigate the cause of suffering, the second noble truth, and no possibility of ending suffering, the third noble truth. If we don't envision the cessation of suffering, also known as nirvana, we will remain chained to suffering in samsara.

On the other hand, if we understand that suffering is not eternal and that freedom and everlasting happiness is attainable once the cause of suffering is halted, we will aspire to achieve freedom. That aspiration inspires us to seek the method to achieve it. This method is the fourth noble truth of the path.

The four noble truths are Guru Shakyamuni Buddha's psychological method for us to break free from suffering and to attain everlasting happiness.

THE SIX GENERAL SUFFERINGS

The six general sufferings refer to the hardships faced by all living beings in samsara.

Nothing is definite

Until we are liberated from samsara we have to continuously experience the six types of suffering. I once met the mother of a rich Indian family who said to me, "Please pray for my daughter to get married." The mother was anxious for the marriage to happen and couldn't wait. I advised her that it was better to wait and be careful, but the mother continued to worry about her daughter's single status. People never think there might be problems. They only think about short-term results, in this case marriage.

There are two occasions in Nepal when one hears loud music playing: during weddings when musicians blow horns and play drums while transporting the bride and groom, and after people die when funeral processions transport bodies to cemeteries, again accompanied by the sounds of horns and drums.

Nothing in samsara gives satisfaction

The Rolling Stones described this perfectly when they sang "(I Can't Get No) Satisfaction." Alcoholics are plagued by dissatisfaction, so they drink in search of relief, yearning to derive some level of satiation, but are instead overwhelmed by discontent. It destroys them, their work, and their families.

A common experience is that we are never satisfied no matter how much we have. If we make $100 in profit, we try to make $1,000. When we're able to get $1,000, we're not content until we make $10,000. If we are able to make $10,000, we feel driven to make $100,000. It goes on and on like that.

There was a wealthy person in London who was in the car business. He bought a mansion with many rooms and he would sleep in a different room each night. I heard he ate poorly but drank something like sixty bottles of liquor in a short time. He was rich but found little satisfaction, so he became unhappy, depressed, and drank excessively.

The man thought the root of his suffering was his car business. So he asked his bodyguard to buy lots of toy cars, place all those toy cars in the fountain in his garden, pour kerosene on them, and burn them. He thought that symbolic act would remove his unhappiness. Never once did he think that his mind and its delusions caused his misery. His problem was attachment, not practicing contentment, always wanting more and more.

A completely opposite response came from Kirti Tsenshab Rinpoche, the great Tibetan master from whom I received many teachings and initiations, when his doctor diagnosed him with cancer. When the doctor asked Rinpoche what he thought, Rinpoche answered, "I am very happy to have cancer because this gives me the opportunity to practice *bodhicitta*, taking on all sentient beings' suffering and its causes." This response demonstrates complete renunciation of clinging to life for one's own benefit.

We have to leave this body again and again

Until we attain liberation from samsara, we are forced to be reborn again and again in samsara. We have taken the body of a butterfly countless times. We have taken a cat's body numberless times. We have been born as dogs from Tibet or dogs from England—dogs with flat noses, long noses, short tails, long tails—numberless times in beginningless rebirths. There would be no empty space left if all our bodies were collected. This is the same with all the human bodies we have taken.

There is not one type of samsaric body we haven't taken or experienced. Whatever animal we've been attracted to, such as horses, birds, spiders, or rats, we have taken such bodies numberless times. Those insects we are so scared of, which we think are so menacing and horrible, we have been born as those insects numberless times. We have taken birth as tigers and poisonous snakes numberless times. This is the horror of samsara.

We have to take rebirth again and again

This body of ours is from the sperm of our father and the egg of our mother, which in turn came from their fathers and mothers, so there is a continuation from long before. All this mixing of sperm and eggs from long ago becomes like a septic tank, like feces and urine and all the smells collected together. Our bodies are like that. In this way, we should think of our bodies like very old junk, so there is no reason to be attached to our bodies. If we are able to detach from grasping at our bodies, the mind can be free from the attachment that causes us to be reborn continuously in samsara and to suffer in samsara.

This continuity of taking birth is like the continuous sound of a puja trumpet, how the notes join one to the next. The shortcomings of taking birth again and again, the aggregates taking birth due to karma and delusion, continuously circling from here to the next life and the life after that, ought to make us weary of samsara.

We move from higher to lower in samsara

As we are reborn, we continuously move from higher to lower states. Unless we know how to remedy mistaken action and engage in virtue, we are unable to remain in the higher states, such as the human realm.

After death the state of existence changes and we take rebirth according to karma, possibly as a hell being, a hungry ghost, an animal, or a god. We constantly shift and change our realms of existence. In a previous life we might have been a king, but in this life we become a servant or a beggar. Even in just one life we can become beggars after a life of luxury. It happens.

We are born alone and we die alone

We are born alone with just consciousness coming from the prior life to this life. Whatever body we had for the prior life didn't continue. Only the consciousness came into this life.

When we die we die alone, leaving behind the body so that only consciousness, that mental energy, leaves to go to the next life. All the negative karma we have collected due to actions toward ourselves and others that are embedded in our consciousness will follow.

If those negative imprints are heavy, we will find ourselves reborn in the lower realms, where only we experience the terrifying results. Nobody comes to share it. No family member or friend joins us there, saying, "Oh, I will help share your suffering. You have too much suffering, so I will share the burden and I will take over some of your suffering." Nobody comes and we have to experience it alone. It's like that.

IMPERMANENCE

All sense objects, including one's life, people, and possessions, are all causative phenomena. This means that they come about from causes and conditions. They are in the nature of impermanence. They all get older, degenerate, and perish. They are simply unable to remain the same, second by second, minute by minute, hour by hour. Whether at a gross or subtle level, sense objects do not last.

When we do not realize how things are in the nature of impermanence, we hold on to the hallucination that these things are going to be with us forever. This is not the case. It is a mistaken view. Your body and life, other people's bodies and lives, this beautiful flower, that skyscraper, that highway, they are all changing and decaying every moment, but we often fail to notice this. Only when the change is at a gross level do we notice it, but in fact the change is continuous.

By forgetting to apply this understanding of impermanence to our daily lives, we tend to think that our possessions will always be useful and that the people we know will always be the same. There appears to be something concrete and permanent about these appearances. But in reality they are all changing, degenerating, getting old, day by day, hour by hour, minute by minute, second by second. What exists during the first minute no longer exists in the same manner in the next minute. It is gone. This is the nature of suffering.

One time, I think at the Milan, Italy, airport shop, I noticed a figure standing there and thought it was a mannequin, but it turned out to be an actual person! That shop had many well-dressed mannequins, so I thought this person was also a mannequin.

One thinks something is one thing, but it turns out not to be so. Large concrete buildings seem permanent, making us think they will always be there. But suddenly an earthquake happens and the building totally changes into a collapsed heap. Or the building could be hit by a bomb or a tornado, and what seems to be permanent can get completely destroyed. Suddenly it is gone.

Even this planet will one day be gone and nothing will remain, only space. Such is the nature of impermanence. Causative phenomena, the things that come about due to causes and conditions, are like dew. They can drop or evaporate at any time, cease at any time. Our own life can end at any time.

During a lightning strike at night we briefly see varied phenomena like trees and houses. There is a vivid appearance of things during that moment, but in a flash it is gone. It happened, then it is gone. In the same way, this life, family, friends, enemies, strangers, possessions, reputation, and sense objects all appear but will end. Gone. It is no different when you die. Life happened and it is gone. Understanding impermanence and recollecting it frequently helps us gain the right view.

Remembering impermanence helps us cut off clinging to this life and turns us toward renouncing samsara. This renunciation is a cause of happiness now and in future lives, and a cause of liberation. Recollecting impermanence helps us see the futility of the self-cherishing thought. It persuades us to practice great compassion toward all.

The advantage of reflecting on impermanence is that we become a guide to ourselves. It steers us away from wasting our lives through blindly following delusions and having to face their troublesome results. Merely thinking about how death can come at any time is extremely powerful in weakening delusions like attachment, anger, and pride. We become less petty and able to appreciate what we have.

If you want to destroy pride right away, use the impermanence of status and possessions as the most potent tool to destroy it. If you want to be relaxed and contented, simply remember impermanence.

When meditating on how death is inevitable, fear may arise. We can intelligently use this fear as an antidote to the toxic thought of worldly concerns. More than that, this meditation is like an atomic bomb that can break the chains of cyclic existence. In a single moment it quickly and utterly destroys the empire of delusions and unhappiness. Such is the efficacy of meditating on impermanence and death.

Once we have a strong experience of impermanence through deep reflection on the shortness of life and certainty of death, we will naturally become less attached to the shallow happinesses of this life. Instead we become more focused on making this life meaningful, on doing the virtue that easily brings joy. Our minds will gravitate toward a better path, especially at the time of death.

Think for a moment: If a man is moving the next day from his hometown to New York, his mind will be thinking only of packing up his things. He will no longer be concerned about his present accommodations, how to fix his oven, or how to make the place he is leaving more comfortable. His mind will be busy packing up the old things, preparing for life in a new place, and planning his new life. His mind will be occupied with preparations for the impending move.

In the same way, a person who realizes impermanence and the inevitability of death will no longer be fixated on this life and will instead put effort into preparing for the future and future lives.

DEATH

Intuitively most people view death as a great suffering. Many people are afraid of death and do not want to hear the word, even though death is around us all the time and will definitely happen to us.

Although death is part of natural evolution, many people reject knowing more about it. Even where there is Buddhadharma in a country and people have access to it to practice and to solve their life problems, they do not want to discuss death. They shy away from all reflections on death, and if someone talks to them about death, they shun the subject and may even get angry.

Yet when a sudden and terrible sickness strikes or they simply get older, they are filled with anxiety. As they approach the moment of death they feel desperate and fearful.

On the other hand, some seek to understand death just as they seek to understand life. They study and analyze samsara and meditate on its nature. Such people find the energy to practice Dharma, create merit, undertake purification, and realize the ultimate nature of reality. Through these pursuits they develop the mind that renounces samsara, generates compassion, and cultivates bodhicitta and wisdom.

People like this, when faced with the critical moment of death, experience very little stress in their minds. Instead of feeling afraid their minds are relaxed, peaceful, and confident. When highly realized lamas pass away, death for them is like a stroll in a beautiful park or like going for a picnic. Their death is pure ease and happiness. They experience death with their mind in a blissful state.

Even an ordinary person without high realizations can be comfortable, peaceful, and free from fear at the time of death. But to achieve this, such a person must have prepared himself by meditating on subjects that include impermanence, death, and samsaric sufferings, while living life ethically, engaging in virtue, and purifying negativities.

The cause of all anxiety at the time of death is the negative mind, which comes from living life with a self-grasping attitude of self-cherishing, heavily afflicted by ignorance, attachment, anger, and other delusions. In contrast, a person who lives life cultivating good-heartedness, generosity, and compassion will end life calmly and happily. At the time of death that person's body will end but the mind will be peaceful and joyful.

If death strikes us right now due to sudden illness or extreme conditions, do we have a method to cope with that? Do we know what happens after death?

Visualize yourself at the moment of death right now. Your dead body is lying still and cold on your bed. People are preparing to take your body out. Family and relatives are upset about how your dead body looks. Your body is then brought to the funeral home. You are alone. Visualize all these events as clearly as you can. Immerse yourself fully in this situation. This is what will definitely happen in the future.

If you are scared to visualize this right now, how will you handle your mind at your moment of death? Avoiding thinking about death will not help. Dharma understanding and meditation is intended to fortify you in death as well as in life, to stop the dangers of the negative mind from arising. Otherwise what would be the purpose of meditating on death? What purpose would any religion or spiritual system serve, if it does not help us know what to do at the time of death? If religion fails us at the time of death, then better to have no religion.

We can prepare to face death without fear by meditating on these three points in relation to death: death is definite, the time of death is indefinite, and only Dharma helps at the time of death.

Death is definite

Every human being experiences death. Death is certain, and for most of us it will happen while we're controlled by delusions and karma. Death will occur without us choosing it or wanting it.

If we throw a stone into the air, it will fall back without stopping in midair for even a second before it hits the ground. Just like this our lives rush along without stopping for even one moment. Just like this our lives finish.

Every second sees our life diminishing, bringing us closer to death. This is not being macabre. It is a fact. Ever since we were conceived in our mother's womb, we have been moving closer and closer to death. If we are young adults, we may think we have another fifty years to live. We see fifty years as a kind of concrete certainty. Yet in fact with each split second—the snap of a finger—our lives get that much shorter. Fifty years stretches shorter and shorter and then finishes, just like that.

As it is for an animal tied to a rope and led from the family farm to the butcher, death comes closer with each step. The animal, which also seeks happiness, has no idea it is being taken to be slaughtered. The animal's life is shortening, yet the animal remains unaware. In exactly the same way we are approaching death. Fifty years or a hundred years is nothing. Each is made up of a definite number of seconds and each second is passing.

Perhaps we think, "I will have a long life. I will live another eighty years because a palm reader told me so." This we cannot trust. No one can be sure. There are no guarantees. And what will happen after death? Presently our minds are completely dark on this question because we do not understand what will happen when the body ceases and consciousness leaves. This is the poor level of our knowledge.

For most of us it is certain that we will struggle at death instead of having a happy passing. Dying with a negative, deluded mind will lead to a difficult lower-realm rebirth. It has come to this because we have allowed delusions to dominate our minds and cause us to continuously engage in negative karma while we march toward death. We cannot waste any more time before doing something about this.

We may have met the Dharma, so let us focus on overcoming delusions and not waste our lives. If we check carefully, very little of our lives have actually become Dharma. Each day we are engulfed by self-cherishing thought. That is how we have squandered away so much of our lives.

The time of death is indefinite

Many people go to work, but some die on their way home. When a person goes to sleep he or she may never wake up. Some people start their meals but die without finishing their plates of food. Some go on trekking vacations but never come back. Others drive away in their cars and die before they return. Some are young and never become adults or see middle age because death occurs. Many die in their mother's wombs. Others go out for a game of football, but their lives end before they get home for dinner. Some people order new clothes but die before wearing them. Others start to read books but never finish them because death interjects.

Many people start projects without concluding them because they die. Many people go to war, and fight and die, without seeing their families again. Many start jobs but die before receiving their salaries. Many people even die before completing what they were saying. Many breathe in but die before breathing out. These are examples of how the time of death is indefinite.

Only Dharma helps at the time of death

When death occurs our body is no longer any help. Family, friends, and possessions cannot stop the passage of death. Even if we have shoes that can last one hundred years, at the time of death we have to go barefoot. Even if the country's best doctors surround our corpse, they can do nothing.

Nothing worldly can help. We have taken such great care of our body, more than we have cared for others. We have been willing to harm others for the sake of our body, but at the time of death we must leave our body behind. We cannot carry to a future life even the tiniest strand of body hair nor its smallest atom.

Good karma or positive deeds are the only things that are beneficial at the time of death and that can be carried to a future life. If you have practiced Dharma, if you have worked on overcoming the delusions, practicing the good heart, purifying negative actions, then the resultant positive imprints and good karma are the only profit that can be carried to the future life and enjoyed. Nothing else can be carried forward. No worldly profit can be carried to the future, only good karma and positive deeds.

Ordinary people pass through the moment of death with much fear and worry. Thus they die with negative minds, causing them to be reborn in the suffering realms. Instead we should journey through death without fear and die with a happy and calm mind. Only the Dharma can support our minds to be fearless in the face of death.

For highly realized lamas death is blissful, like returning home. As for middle-level meditators' minds, they are peaceful and happy at the moment of death. Even lowest-level Dharma practitioners experience little panic or distress at the time of death if they have tried to understand the Dharma and lived ethically. Experiencing death in any of these favorable ways depends on how we live and how sincerely we practice the Dharma.

As a person's death approaches and at the moment of death itself, the greatest hindrance is attachment. If the dying person's last thought is one of attachment, whether to family or to possessions, that person is less likely to experience a peaceful death and could be reborn in the suffering lower realms.

An analogy will help to explain this: To make bread dough we mix flour, water, and yeast. The yeast is activated by moisture when mixed with water and flour. The moisture, in contact with yeast, causes the dough to rise.

In the same way, when attachment is activated unease grows and a kind of tightness in the mind arises. This tightness is a great hindrance that arises painfully in one's mind. If this happens at the time of a person's death, even if that person had been creating some good karma in his or her life, this negative mind of attachment will activate whatever negative karmic imprints the person had accumulated and propel that consciousness into the suffering realms. Thus the nature of rebirth is closely linked to the final thought at the moment of death. The final thought acts like a catalyst that triggers the corresponding accumulated karmic imprints and steers the consciousness into its next realm of rebirth, be that higher or lower.

To prevent rebirth in the suffering lower realms we need to have lived virtuously, to have purified our negative deeds, and to have made our last thought a virtuous one. We might think, "Oh, I can do that. I know how to think of virtue at the moment of death."

But actually it is very difficult to do this. When an earthquake strikes or when a crisis unexpectedly happens, we are often unable to handle our minds. We cannot think virtuous thoughts at such times because our minds are completely seized by distress and fear. Therefore there is almost no chance of making our minds virtuous during the even-more challenging time of death unless we have been accustomed to living a virtuous life. Can we say we have lived our entire lives virtuously?

So you see, when death occurs it will be very, very difficult to say, "Oh, I can think virtuously." To make the mind capable of virtuous thought at death requires prior mind training. Mind training includes living daily life ethically, generating merit, and purifying negativities. In particular, it is helpful to meditate on the shortcomings of samsara, on impermanence and death, and on delusions and their antidotes, all of which help eliminate attachments. These are the most powerful daily meditations we can do to train our minds, to control our minds. At the time of death, at least remember Guru Shakyamuni Buddha, an object of virtue.

Which is longer, our present lives or all our future lives? The suffering we experience in this life is nothing compared to the suffering we will experience in our future lives. Therefore it is more important to take steps to stop future suffering rather than trying to alleviate only present suffering or suffering over the next five or ten years.

It makes little sense to focus on preventing a short period of present suffering rather than stopping all future suffering. Even if we wish to stop our present suffering, the most efficient way is through engaging in Dharma. It is highly worthwhile to focus first on future happiness because the end of this life and the start of the next are uncertain, while it is certain the future will be long. Death can happen at any time—maybe this year, this month, this week, tonight, after this hour is over, we don't know. For this reason, it would be sensible not to delay preparing for the ultimate happiness of future lives.

What happens after death?

What happens when we die? Does the mind get extinguished like a candle? It is not like this. Mind or consciousness, imprinted by delusions and karma, continues on. The mental continuum does not cease. Where the mind will be reborn is according to our karmic imprints. Gaining a happy rebirth depends on having created good karma in our preceding life, practicing Dharma, and having virtuous thought at the time of death.

However, if we have created negative karma and die with a negative mind of attachment or anger, we are headed for rebirth in the suffering lower realms. Forcing the mind to think virtuously at the moment of death is not possible. We need the training of a life habituated in virtue.

The Three Categories of the Suffering of Samsara

If happiness is what we seek, we have to eliminate suffering. In teaching the first noble truth of suffering, the Buddha was instructing us to examine our experiences closely to understand the nature of our present existence. The nature of the suffering of samsara can be understood under three broad categories: the suffering of suffering, the suffering of change, and pervasive compounding suffering, which is the fundamental suffering of samsara.

The suffering of suffering

The suffering of suffering is easy to recognize, as it arises from life's hardships. The problems of everyday life include pain, extreme heat and cold, unhappy feelings, sickness, worries, and meeting with undesirable objects, difficult circumstances, enemies, and harmful things. We are disturbed when we encounter even the smallest bug, fearing it will deny us a comfortable night's sleep. We worry about not having wealth, favorable surroundings, friends, status, and other objects of desire.

After we have acquired these things, after working incredibly hard for them, we soon worry and fret about holding on to them. We may feel mounting dissatisfaction with the objects we have acquired. We feel anxiety about acquiring more things and better ones, and about not losing the ones we have. This is the suffering of suffering.

The suffering of change

The category of "suffering of change" often takes the form of sense pleasures, which is why it's so hard to recognize them as a form of suffering. The nature of the suffering of change arises from the temporariness of sense pleasures, the inevitable change from pleasure to dissatisfaction. All forms of samsaric worldly enjoyments fall into this category, for instance the pleasure of eating delicious food and enjoying the sun at the beach. How is this so?

When we like a certain type of food we tend to eat more of it, seeking more pleasure. But soon enough we get tired of that food or even develop an aversion to it. Likewise when we feel cold and go out to sit in the sun for warmth, it feels good at first. But when the heat begins to burn we feel discomfort and need to move away from the sun. What was an enjoyment has become a source of discomfort.

If enjoyments were a true source of happiness, the more and longer we engaged in them the happier we would be. If delicious food were the cause of true happiness, then continuous eating from morning to midnight would bring unbelievable bliss and comfort. If we continued such continuous eating without break for a further month or one year, amazing, inconceivable pleasure would arise. We know this is not so. Since pleasure does not arise from continuous eating, it proves something is wrong in our belief that food is the source of true happiness. This test can be applied to any worldly enjoyment. If the nature of these enjoyments were not ultimately suffering, the pleasure derived from them would increase with repetition. But in fact the pleasure from repetition decreases, which requires us to reevaluate them as the true causes of happiness.

In reality what is happening is that a sensation we have mentally labeled as "pleasure" lasts only until the feeling of discomfort becomes noticeable. Only then do we label it "discomfort" or "suffering." So our labeling an experience "pleasure" or "suffering" does not depend on the object or circumstance; it depends on our minds and how the mind interprets things and sensations. When an experience like basking in the sun at the beach becomes uncomfortable at a gross and noticeable level, we label it "suffering"; when the discomfort is not yet at a gross level, we call it pleasure.

Apply this to the earlier example of continuous eating. When we began to eat it brought relief from the suffering of hunger and we labeled it "pleasure," but as the discomfort of continuous eating became gross and observable, we changed the label and called it "suffering." What was pleasurable had become plain suffering. This is the suffering of change. All that happened was that when one suffering stopped, another suffering began. This is the nature of samsara.

His Holiness the Dalai Lama once said, "Nowadays many people first aim to buy a TV and later a car and then an apartment. After some time those become insufficient. They get tired of these possessions, start to find fault with them, and begin to search for more and better things." You can see how the first possession one acquired with the expectation of contentment actually brought about the result of more dissatisfaction. It has no end.

Because death comes without choice, there is an end to this life, but the grasping at more and better things has no end. The dissatisfied mind knows no end. The initial pleasure of getting the desired object turns to boredom; the pleasure changes into dissatisfaction and unhappiness. This is how the suffering of change works. These samsaric, temporal pleasures not only fail to last but they also change into suffering. One suffering stops and without our noticing it a new suffering starts.

Samsaric enjoyments are labeled "pleasure" because we do not examine their true nature, which is the suffering of change. Those pleasures do not last. Pleasures decrease the more we engage in them. Pleasures simply do not endure. Unlike Dharma activities such as meditation, through which pleasure increases while perfect peace develops to the point of achieving enlightenment, samsaric pleasures fail in providing increasing happiness. Ignorance and attachment generate continual desire, leading to repeated actions that bring dissatisfaction and suffering in the end.

Whether we live like a king or like a beggar with nothing, suffering is experienced. Whether we live in a busy city or up in the quiet mountains, suffering arises. Whether our job is sitting for hours in an elevator going up and down, seeing nothing of the outside world, or whether we are pilots traveling to many countries, suffering arises. Whether we live alone or with others, suffering is there. Suffering will remain this way *until* we are liberated from cyclic existence caused by delusions and karma.

Due to our aggregates being contaminated by delusions over beginningless lives, when our five senses make contact with an object that the desiring mind labels as "attractive," attachment arises; when our senses engage with an object that the mind labels as "unfavorable," anger arises; and when the senses meet an object that the mind interprets as neither helpful nor harmful, indifference arises. Without studying the path of Dharma, which trains our minds to recognize delusions and to know what remedies to apply, we will remain trapped in samsara, doomed to experience suffering again and again.

The suffering of change is difficult to recognize because we mistake samsaric happiness for durable, real happiness and get deeply attached to it. We don't realize the nature of samsaric pleasure is suffering. We spend our energy and time and devote our bodies, minds, and lives to chasing after temporal happiness. If we fail to see the dissatisfactory nature of samsara, if we fail to reject the negative mind of delusion, lasting happiness will elude us.

Samsara is like honey smeared on a razor's edge. We may be drawn to the honey, but when we engage with it the razor cuts our tongue. Pursuing samsaric pleasures is far more dangerous than cutting our tongue. A wound can heal in a few days, but grasping at samsara can enslave us for eons. Grasping at samsara causes the mistaken mind to continually dominate, leaving in its wake endless lives of unhappiness and more unhappiness.

Pervasive compounding suffering

This third and most subtle from of suffering refers to the contamination of the aggregates due to uncontrolled delusions and karma. Our relationship with the aggregates, the five components that make up our sense of self (form, feeling, consciousness, discrimination, and compositional factors or karmic imprints), is conditioned by the delusions and karma imprinted on our minds. From the very first moment an ordinary being's consciousness enters a fertilized egg, the aggregates include the seeds of delusion. This is because the past life's aggregates likewise were contaminated with the seeds of delusion, which are principally ignorance, attachment, and anger.

If those seeds were not eliminated in a previous life, they continue to contaminate and influence the next one. The mental continuum is like a field planted with seeds of delusion and karma from one life to the next. This stream of causation is why we are born with ignorance, attachment, anger, and the other delusions.

The cause of true suffering is not the bare mind, the stream of consciousness. The cause of true suffering is consciousness overwhelmed by delusions and by their seeds. Whether we can free ourselves from suffering depends on whether or not we can remove these delusions. Therefore a choice has to be made: Are we going to control these delusions with the mind or are we surrendering our minds to the delusions?

The mindstream, the stream of consciousness, cannot be stopped or eliminated. Due to the fact that the delusions and their seeds are embedded in our consciousness, when we meet with an object that our minds label as "beautiful," attachment quickly arises. When we meet with an object we regard as disturbing, anger immediately arises.

When we meet a neutral object that neither triggers attachment nor anger, indifference arises. Therefore when our senses contact an object, depending on how the mind behaves under the influence of delusions, the mind labels the object as "truly existent" and resultant emotions arise.

While we may seem peaceful right now, if the person sitting next to us suddenly disturbs us while we are having a good meditation or an enjoyable time, anger will instantly arise just as if a burning match had been thrown into a barrel of kerosene. So it is with all the other delusions.

Ignorance and action or karma planted the seeds of delusion into our consciousness. If in a past life or this life we have created negative karma by criticizing others with anger, or by blindly saying harsh words with ill will, this karma will create the potential for us to repeat these actions as well as result in our receiving similar harm, such as being verbally abused and physically ill. These negative actions plant seeds of delusion in our consciousness, giving rise to mental suffering compounded by the physical suffering of sickness.

From this we can now understand that without this fundamental pervasive compounding suffering—the aggregates—we would not experience the suffering of suffering and the suffering of change. Even if we don't think about the past, we can easily see how our present aggregates are controlled by the unsubdued mind and karma.

A common experience is when we try to use the aggregates to practice Dharma, like meditating on the Buddha or on the teachings, and find that we often can't concentrate. Thoughts of boyfriend, girlfriend, enemy, or cheesecake arise, instead of the virtuous object of concentration. We might be surprised at ourselves and wonder, "How did this happen? Where did these distracting thoughts come from?" These thoughts come from our minds that are habituated with delusions and overwhelmed by them. Pervasive compounding suffering is the main suffering from which we need to be liberated.

When we say we need to renounce samsara, what do we mean? We mean that we need to end suffering. While this goal may seem too obvious to mention, it's also quite obvious we have not yet achieved it. To cease true suffering we must cease the cause, the delusions.

How quickly we can free ourselves from samsara depends on how we live our lives each day, on our spiritual practice. Our hardships will have no end so long as we offer victory to the delusions, in particular the ignorance that holds things to be truly existent, the attachment that fans our grasping minds, and the anger that inflames us to harm others.

How are we to eliminate these delusions? All these delusions originate from the root delusion of ignorance grasping at the "I" as independently and truly existent. So much negativity has been committed due to this mistaken belief in the "truly existent I." When this is completely eliminated all the other delusions will fall.

THE THREE REALMS OF SAMSARA

There are three realms in samsara: the desire realm, the form realm, and the formless realm.

Desire-realm beings seek pleasure from their bodies' contact with external sense objects through sound, smell, taste, or touch. They indulge in those pleasures and always yearn for more. Due to this, they generate negative karma, creating suffering in their own life and in future lives. The desire realm includes humans as well as five other beings: animals, demigods, gods, hell-realm beings, and hungry ghosts.

Form-realm beings, having seen the shortcomings of the desire realm, understand the nature of suffering and that sense pleasures are gross. Due to this understanding they generate detachment from worldly pleasures and seek peace through meditation, developing concentration that brings physical and mental bliss. However, danger remains for them if they become attached to the pleasant sensations of meditative concentration, because they will then be reborn into the formless realm, which is still bound to samsara.

Formless-realm beings have no physical form and are made only of consciousness. They see the suffering nature of the desire realm and understand the mistaken pleasure derived from meditation in the form realm. To avoid those traps they continue striving in meditation, approaching the higher levels of concentration of limitless space. At this point they see the shortcomings of limitless space and move further toward the stage of infinite consciousness. This progress continues as they realize the flaws of infinite consciousness, move on from there to the next stage of nothingness, and then finally reach the stage called the peak of samsara.

At this time there is no visible delusion operating within these beings' consciousness, no discernible anger or attachment. Because of this the consciousness mistakenly believes it has achieved liberation, nirvana. However, the apparent absence of delusion lasts only briefly because the imprints of delusion have not been eradicated, the renunciation of samsara has not been completed. When the karma to remain in this formless state finishes, the consciousness sees that it has to reincarnate again to the lower realms.

At this stage anger and doubt arise in the mind with the thought, "Alas, it is untrue that there is liberation. Liberation cannot be achieved." With that heavy thought, rebirth in the lower realm occurs.

From this progression we can see that liberation requires the absolute renunciation of samsara, which means renunciation of the desire realm, the form realm, and the formless realm. As human beings, we dwell in the desire realm, but we can examine our life experiences and relate them to the Buddha's teachings on the sufferings of the human realm.

THE SUFFERING OF THE SIX TYPES OF REBIRTH

A mind or consciousness that is under the control of delusion and karma has no freedom at all. Depending on the karma a mind has accumulated, it reincarnates into one of the six types of birth: hell beings, hungry ghosts, animals, humans, demigods, or gods. Reborn into one of those realms, the mind experiences all the sufferings associated with that realm.

Sentient beings, battered by delusion and karma, are continuously reborn into one of those realms without any break. They get no rest from the sufferings of samsara, especially from pervasive compounding suffering. They get no holiday, no vacation. They have suffered from time without beginning. If we think about this, our only choice is to feel compassion for all sentient beings.

Hell beings

There are eight major hot hells and eight major cold hells. They all have neighboring hells where the conditions are less severe but still consist of unbearable, incredible, extreme suffering. Hell realms are also experienced in the human world—perhaps in Los Angeles, in Taiwan, in big cities and small villages too!

Beings in hell realms experience intense suffering without relief. Beings that don't know the ultimate nature of reality and that aren't mindful of avoiding nonvirtues create negative karma to be born in the hell realms. The strong negative imprints left on the consciousness keep beings in the hell realms to bear indescribable suffering until the negative karmic seeds are exhausted.

When a sentient being dies, its habitual desire causes craving and grasping to arise. Some people crave warmth, but no matter how many blankets are placed on them as they approach death they don't feel warm enough as a great coldness descends. This craving for heat and warmth, combined with the unpurified negative karma committed in the past, propels their rebirth into the hot hell realms.

In the hell realms one's body burns just like the blazing hot fire of hell itself. One's hell body is huge like a long mountain range, making the suffering even more intense. Every atom of one's giant body is burning, like the great fire at the end of an age. One's skin feels severely infected, so that even the lightest touch brings extreme agony. One endures this suffering for an immeasurable length of time. From the viewpoint of a human life this suffering continues for billions of years until the karma to experience the hell state is exhausted.

Conversely, at the time of death one may feel very hot, which leads to craving and grasping for cold. The dying mind, imprinted by past actions and seized by grasping, wakes up in a frozen cold hell where howling winds cut deeply into one's skin until it cracks. Great birds plunge their metal beaks into the cracks of one's ruptured skin, feeding on the blood and flesh. More birds and fierce sea animals approach, slicing open one's body, digging into the liver, intestines, lungs, ribs, and brain. These creatures drink one's blood and eat one's flesh, while one is fully conscious but unable to stop the torment.

One is forced to experience this unbelievable suffering for billions of years. Such intense suffering is due to the karma of killing and the completed karma of committing nonvirtues.

Right now we have all the opportunities to purify negative karma, to avoid karma's terrifying results, to free ourselves from samsara, and to achieve enlightenment. We even have the chance to liberate other sentient beings and bring them to enlightenment. If we do not realize this amazing and precious chance to purify negativities and create positive karma, we will repeatedly be reborn into samsaric suffering. More than that, we will risk rebirth in lower realms like the hell realms, unable to achieve realization and bound only to horrific suffering. Repeatedly engaging in negative karma is even more terrifying than the hells because these actions cause countless rebirths into the hells of extreme sufferings.

Hungry ghosts

The beings of the hungry ghost realm experience the heavy suffering of hunger and thirst for hundreds and thousands of years.

Due to their karma they cannot die. Instead they just linger on, experiencing tiredness beyond description and the incredible suffering of never finding food or drink. After hundreds of thousands of years of intense hunger and thirst, they suddenly see food and drink in the distance and struggle to get there. However, they encounter many obstacles on the way, as karmic guardians block their passage. Their limbs feel like those of an old cripple who is unable to walk or crawl.

Hungry ghosts have bloated empty stomachs as huge as giant boulders, but tiny, thin limbs. When they finally reach the spot where they thought they saw food and drink, they realize that it was a mirage.

Instead of finding a pond of water they find a pool filled with pus, blood, garbage, and hair. The disappointment is heartbreaking and they wail in despair.

Even if the hungry ghosts try to drink, their mouths are so small, like the eye of a needle, that nothing goes through. Then even if they get a drop of liquid into their mouths, their necks are constricted with two to three knots, so they can't swallow anything.

Finally, if they are able to swallow a tiny amount of food, the hungry ghosts' stomachs are ablaze with inner flames, so that nothing satisfies them. Due to karma their suffering is long and extreme.

Animals

For animals the pervading suffering is the constant, unimaginable fear of being chased and eaten by other animals, with no real protection. Little shelter can be found from heat, cold, hunger, and thirst. Animals always fear captivity, torture, and harsh conditions, and are plagued by the danger of a painful death, with their ignorance intensifying these fears. Even an animal living with a good family is never totally free of this terror and fear.

Humans

Humans experience eight types of suffering: rebirth, old age, sickness, death, separation from attachments, encountering disagreeable objects, not obtaining desirable objects, and contaminated aggregates, that is, the suffering of this body created by delusion and karma. It helps to meditate on these eight sufferings to discover the suffering nature of samsara and to generate aversion toward it. Meditate on each of these sufferings as actually happening to us. They are not just happening to someone else. These sufferings are taking place on us, within us.

1. *The suffering of rebirth.* The teacher Asanga said, "The rebirths of all other beings are the same, even my upper rebirth. We are all born with suffering."

The womb is full of thick fluid, secretions and excretions, filthy odors, and innumerable germs. It is narrow, with many ridges and irregularities. The baby usually faces backward toward the *ka-ka* (Tib. excrement), a product of the mother's food, liquids, and spit. Above the baby are the mother's intestines, containing stale food and bile. The baby feels all kinds of filthy dark things moving close to its body, it suffers from acidic and sour foods, hot and cold liquids, spicy or sweet heavy food, too much or too little food, coarse or greasy food. When the mother moves, runs, jumps, or sits too long, the baby suffers. The baby feels pain when the mother is near a fire or wears tight clothing. Even the baby's own posture makes it feel as if a stick ran through its body. At the time of leaving the womb karmic air pushes the baby's head down, its legs up, and its arms inward. The hip bones are compressed toward each other. The body feels like a raw wound and turns blue, like a large object forced with difficulty through a too-small opening that only grudgingly yields.

The baby is born covered with partly dried and partly sticky secretions and excretions. The lips, throat, and heart are dry. When the baby's skin contacts the external atmosphere it feels as if brushed with thorny plants. The baby suffers like a cow with its skin peeled off and cries because it is suffering intensely.

The suffering of rebirth into ignorance: The seed of ignorance in the mental continuum enables it to continue exerting influence life after life.

The suffering of rebirth into a suffering realm: Rebirth into the desire realm, or the form or formless realms, inevitably brings the sufferings of old age, sickness, and death.

The suffering of rebirth into a deluded state: In samsara the negative mind of ignorance, attachment, and anger gives rise to perceptions of objects of beauty, ugliness, and indifferent appearance, respectively. These in turn cause the body and mind to become unsubdued, agitated, and discontented, and suffering is thereby experienced.

2. *The suffering of old age and decay.* The beautiful-looking body becomes increasingly decrepit with each passing year and loses its strength. As we get older we see and hear less and less distinctly, we lose the power of the senses.

We lose enjoyments. Aging brings less and less satisfaction with objects or material pleasures. It also impairs digestion, reducing our enjoyment of favorite foods.

We lose the power of the mind. As we age we forget names, places, ideas, and so on.

We worry about the shortening of life and the approach of death. Without Dharma, old age is like a rotten orange with no beauty outside or inside. Old age is full of worms and bears a taste of sorrow.

3. *The suffering of sickness.* When sickness strikes, our bodies become exhausted and we are unable to use our bodies and minds as we wish. Our enjoyment of the beautiful objects we are attached to becomes limited, and we have to endure undesirable foods, treatments, and medicines.

4. *The suffering of death.* From the moment of birth life moves toward inevitable death, which invokes fear and anxiety to the uncontrolled mind and body. Instead of bringing release from suffering, death only brings more hardship. Repeated meditation on impermanence and death is thus very important.

5. *The suffering of separation from beautiful objects and attachments.* During our entire lives and at life's end we suffer from separation and the fear of separation from loved ones, enjoyments, and possessions.

6. *The suffering of encountering disagreeable objects.* Aversion arises from encountering ugly objects or an enemy, or from experiencing a catastrophe or a crisis.

7. *The suffering of not obtaining desirable objects.* We suffer from not getting what we seek or not obtaining satisfaction from possessions.

8. *The suffering of this body created by delusion and karma.* Taking the form of this body with delusions causes suffering even in future lives because we continue to commit negative acts, which will bear similar results in the future.

This samsaric body experiences all the present life sufferings, including old age and death.

The suffering of suffering, like physical pain, is experienced.

Changeable suffering, in the form of pleasures that do not last, happens because the body is controlled by delusion and karma.

Pervading suffering exists merely because the aggregates exist. We are born in the nature of suffering, we decay and then perish.

Therefore the eight sufferings—human rebirth, growing old, sickness, death, separation from what one likes, encountering what one dislikes, not getting what one wants, and contaminated aggregates—are all in the nature of suffering. On top of this, even if we find a desirable object, we don't gain lasting satisfaction from it.

Dissatisfaction is constant, one of the biggest problems for humans. Both poor people and rich people suffer. Wealth, power, and status bring the worry of losing them, and the struggle for reputation never ceases.

I have friends who are world-famous singers. They have achieved great recognition, but along with fame comes worry about losing their reputation. Any day could bring the loss of reputation, the loss of fame. It is plain to see that while they enjoy wealth, fame, and even health, they have little peace of mind.

Wealthy people are often dissatisfied because they are tortured by yearning for more, by wishing to be wealthier than others, and by fearing that the wealth and status of others will diminish them. These people can be deeply distressed.

No matter how rich a person may be, even decked with gold jewelry from ears to toes, if you converse with such persons you soon hear their problems. In samsara whatever lifestyle you have, suffering is there. Only when you practice Dharma is there no suffering. In anything else we do, there is suffering. This is not to depress you! These are observable facts.

Going to the mountains is suffering. Going to the beach is suffering. Whatever worldly activity you engage in will soon reveal its basic nature of suffering. Some people envy those who appear to have everything— renowned singers, rich businessmen, famous soccer players—but it is all suffering. A man who was featured in *Time* magazine, regarded as one of the most successful persons in the world on account of his wealth, also spoke of his experience of suffering. He was afraid to walk about freely and preferred to stay indoors, hiding like an endangered animal, afraid of being kidnapped.

Therefore even what we call the pleasure of wealth is in the nature of suffering. This body with its aggregates contaminated with delusions is in the nature of pervasive compounding suffering.

Demigods

One of the main sufferings of the beings of this realm is their relentless jealousy toward the god-realm beings who have greater riches, which leads to constant battles with them. The demigods lose every battle with the gods and lose everything. They bear the extreme pain of seeing their possessions and companions taken away, and their limbs are cut and burned. Yet they cannot control their jealousy, and this drives them to continuously battle the god-realm beings, only to repeatedly endure the same tragic fate.

Desire-realm gods

The worldly gods live a life of sense enjoyment, and their wealth is a billion times greater than we can imagine. Yet as they are still in samsara, they have to endure suffering in the form of the five signs of death when their karma to live a god-realm being's existence finishes. Due to their life of luxury and sense pleasures they have no interest in cultivating Dharma, and thus steadily use up the past karma that enables them to experience their opulent god-realm existence.

At the time of death they hear sounds that foretell their impending demise. They are able to see their next rebirth, always a lower-realm rebirth.

Seeing this lower-realm rebirth brings them great sorrow and terror. As god-realm beings approach death their radiance declines, other god-realm beings shun them, and even the flower garlands they wear begin to fade. God-realm beings ordinarily do not sweat, but when death nears they begin to sweat and smell. As god-realm beings experience the signs of death, they suffer mentally far more than hell beings suffer physically.

Beings of the form and formless realms
Some people meditate deeply on the suffering nature of the desire realm. They feel disgust toward the gross sufferings of the desire realm and generate detachment from the pleasures of the desire realm. They meditate to be free from the gross sufferings.

However, until delusion and its seeds are eliminated from these meditators' minds, even they are not free from samsara. As people strive at meditation they may achieve *samten*, the first of the four levels of calm-abiding meditation. The danger at this stage is that the meditator may view this calm state as something wonderful that will endure, bringing great happiness. Subtle clinging arises.

Those who practice concentration meditation (*shamatha*) with the attitude that yearns for the pleasure of meditative bliss can be reborn in the form realm. In the form realm they continue to meditate, but as time passes they get bored and develop aversion to the tranquility of the form realm. These meditators may then strive for the next level of meditative absorption for a better and longer life, believing this will bring more happiness.

From this we see that form-realm beings still cling to the pleasure of meditative peace. Samsara's subtle shackles are hard for these beings to recognize and those shackles remain unbroken. Their yearning for meditation's pleasure causes rebirth in the formless realm, which is still bound to samsara.

The highest of the four levels of the formless realm is called the peak of samsara. When meditators have not renounced their attachment to the bliss of meditation, they are drawn to the peak of samsara. Meditators who have not severed this delusion of subtle attachment are in great danger of mistakenly believing the meditative bliss they experience is nirvana itself. Eventually meditators realize this is not the case and experience great suffering of the mind, a heavy sense of futility, and the perilous denial that liberation is achievable. When meditators then exhaust the karma to remain in the formless realm, they die and are reborn back in the desire realm to again experience all of samsaric suffering.

To avoid this great waste of effort, a meditator needs to generate stable renunciation toward all of samsara, even the peak of samsara, and instead gain the wisdom realizing emptiness. Only then can the chains of samsara be broken and the path to liberation completed.

Do you remember the three main types of suffering in samsara? These are the suffering of suffering, the suffering of change, and pervasive compounding suffering.

Beings of the desire realm experience all three types of suffering. Due to their meditative endeavors, beings of the first three levels of the form realm do not experience the suffering of suffering, but they do experience the suffering of change and pervasive compounding suffering.

From the fourth level of the form realm up to and including the formless realm, beings there do not experience the first two types of suffering but still suffer from pervasive compounding suffering. Because their aggregates are still contaminated and pervaded by the seeds of ignorance and delusion, beings in the form or formless realm who pass away in that state are reborn back into one of the six realms of the desire realm after their karma to remain in those states is exhausted. Such beings continue to circle and suffer in samsara.

Therefore we need to wake up! Remaining in samsara is like sitting on the tip of a needle. There is not a single moment of real freedom. We, like all other sentient beings under the control of delusion and karma, circle without end in these samsaric realms and repeatedly experience all forms of suffering. Aren't we tired of this?

However, this suffering cycle can be stopped by the precious, optimum human rebirth that has the potential to purify all obscurations and to complete all virtues and realizations. This precious human rebirth has the potential for full enlightenment. It is most worthwhile to reflect on the human rebirth that we have.

PRECIOUS HUMAN REBIRTH: THE VEHICLE OF LIBERATION

Most of us shun the word "suffering." But do we think that if we bury ourselves in activity and avoid thinking about suffering it will go away on its own? If we do not regularly reflect on the suffering of samsaric realms and its causes, the distractions and numbness from our daily life could prevent us from using our precious human birth meaningfully. This human rebirth is the vehicle by which we can attain liberation from samsara and gain enlightenment for the sake of all.

Right now we do not see the value of human rebirth. We meet with daily life problems and immediately think our lives are troublesome and useless. This attitude arises from not investigating properly, with wisdom. Check and find the joy in this precious human rebirth.

An airplane is intended to fly in the air, not to be pushed through the jungle. Likewise in this precious human rebirth we have the potential to free ourselves and others from suffering and to attain lasting happiness. Thus we should not waste this life. It is in our hands to accomplish the goal of freedom. It is up to us to pilot our human potential.

When we want to travel to a destination, how quickly we succeed depends on our will, preparation, and resources. Likewise to reach enlightenment depends on our determination and strength of practice, which are well within our control. The fewer mistakes in our practice, the shorter time we need to achieve the goal of enlightenment. However, the practice must be pure, for purity provides a stable foundation.

What I am trying to say is that we should not be satisfied with merely gaining some form of short-term peace or with doing things for only this life's purposes. We should not do it just for that. We are capable of much more. If we want to achieve ultimate, everlasting happiness and liberation from the whole suffering of samsara, we need to attain the cessation of delusion and karma. Only then are we able to accomplish the great peace of nirvana.

Of course attaining liberation for ourselves is important, but even this is not the real purpose of our lives. The real meaning of life, the real purpose of living, is to make our life beneficial to other sentient beings for the long term. Addressing only the present-life needs of others brings them only short-term happiness. Being truly beneficial to others means bringing happiness to them for present and for future lives, and most important, to help them end all suffering and its causes, to help them achieve total liberation from samsara. This is an incredible endeavor.

Bringing happiness to others for the short term refers to giving comfort, shelter, food, clothing, and solving this present life's problems. These activities offer others some relief, but as the underlying samsara has not been dealt with, problems will return.

Therefore bringing happiness to other sentient beings for all future lives is much more meaningful. Offering real happiness to sentient beings is becoming their cause of happiness and helping them end delusions, and in that way liberating them forever. Imagine that. This service to others is extremely urgent because if we do not do this numberless beings will continue to suffer.

Unless the causes of others' suffering—the delusions imprinted on their mental continuum and karma—are removed, whatever we do for them will not spare them from endless hardships. They will repeatedly face the same problems, be they starvation, poverty, fear, sickness, sorrow, or difficulties.

That is why the Dharma, the method that removes all delusions, is so important. We need to help all beings remove these delusions, and of course this includes removing them from ourselves. This precious, optimum human rebirth, with its eight freedoms and ten endowments, has the ability to accomplish liberation.

The eight freedoms and ten endowments

Due to hardships we might be skeptical about the value of this human rebirth and say, "I have so many problems and so little help. What's so good about my human life?"

We might find nothing particularly worthwhile in our lives. Of course not all human rebirths qualify as the precious human rebirth, but it is useful to examine our own life in relation to the criteria for the precious human rebirth. These criteria are the eight freedoms and the ten endowments.

The first three of the eight precious human freedoms are to not be born (1) a hell being, (2) a hungry ghost, or (3) an animal. In such lower-realm rebirths, moments of even temporal happiness are few. But worse than that, there is no opportunity or freedom to pursue the spiritual path, to practice the Dharma.

The next five are freedom from being born (4) a long-life god, (5) in a place where Buddha has not descended, (6) in a place where there is no Dharma, (7) without complete faculties like intelligence, and (8) with wrong views. If we're free of these five unfavorable conditions, we can connect with the Dharma, understand it, and begin our journey to liberation from samsara.

Here are the ten endowments of a precious human rebirth:

The first is to be born as a human being with the eight freedoms and other endowments.

The second endowment is to be born in a country where Buddhism is present. If we are born in a place where there is no Buddhism, it means there will be no fully ordained monastics and thus no opportunity for us to take ordination vows. Why is this important? Ordination and precepts highly discipline the mind through vows, called *dompa* in Tibetan. These vows protect the mind from negative actions, keep it away from delusions, and give it freedom from negativities.

Ordaining as a monastic is a fruitful way to practice the Dharma. As monastics increase so will Dharma teachings. Monastics upholding ordination and precepts encourage us to practice morality purely.

We are extremely lucky if we are born in a country where there are ordained monastics. Some may think ordained persons have nothing to do with ordinary society, that ordination is only an ancient tradition or custom. In truth a person who receives ordination is very fortunate because keeping monastic vows is a quick way to be released from suffering and to attain enlightenment. Just the presence of monastics in one's country is fortunate because people observing monastic precepts support us in our efforts to combat delusions and help us perform positive actions.

The third endowment, to be born with perfect faculties, is a great advantage. We need these faculties while cultivating the spiritual path in order to learn, contemplate, meditate, investigate, and analyze.

To be free from having committed any of the five heinous offenses is the fourth endowment. These five are: killing a Buddha, an arhat, our mother, or our father, or causing a schism within the ordained community. If someone commits any of these serious negative acts without purifying them, the resulting heavy karma will bring great hardship and obstacles while cultivating the path.

The fifth endowment is having faith in the Dharma and the three divisions of the teachings. These three are the sutras, which explain the path and help us to develop concentration; the vinaya, which details the precepts and ordination; and the Abhidharma, which explains the evolution of mind and of the universe.

Being born in an era where the Buddha has appeared and has given teachings on the path to liberation and enlightenment is the sixth endowment.

The seventh endowment is to have been shown and taught the teachings of Buddha.

The eighth endowment is to be born at a time when realized practitioners are alive, when there are experiential Dharma teachings in the world. Our present gurus received teachings from prior gurus, in an unbroken lineage tracing back to Guru Shakyamuni Buddha. If there were no practitioners with experience of the teachings in their own minds, something vital would be missing. It is not enough for the teachings to exist only in books. Practitioners must possess realizations of those teachings to be able to guide others.

Meeting others who follow the Buddha's teachings is the ninth endowment, because pure practitioners of the Buddha's path support sentient beings on the path to enlightenment.

Our future enlightenment and overcoming all suffering depend on our minds. If we don't look into ourselves, we will spend countless eons without finding the solution to our problems. Just as sentient beings can be their own worst enemies, they can also be their own best friends on the spiritual path.

The final or tenth endowment is receiving the kindness and compassion of others. For instance, we have a compassionate guru from whom we learned the Dharma and family or friends who support our spiritual efforts by providing us food and conditions for practice.

In Tibet the lives of Dharma practitioners used to be conducive to practice because people had great respect for anyone who observed the precepts or did retreat. Benefactors with faith offered practitioners food and help, so those practitioners were not distracted by struggling to meet their temporal needs. These days this kind of support has become more difficult to obtain. But nevertheless we are fortunate to be born in a period where practitioners continue to receive support through the kindness of others.

The rarity of a precious human rebirth

An analogy from the text *Liberation in the Palm of Your Hand* explains how rare it is to gain a precious human rebirth. Imagine a wide ocean with a golden ring floating on the surface. At the bottom of this ocean lives a blind tortoise. It swims deep in the ocean and surfaces only once every hundred years.

What would be the chance of this blind tortoise swimming to the surface and randomly placing its head into that golden ring? Almost no chance, you would say.

The story is a metaphor for the difficulty of obtaining a precious human birth. The golden ring signifies the Buddhadharma. The blind tortoise represents sentient beings that, due to ignorance, are blind to Dharma wisdom. The tortoise swimming aimlessly at the bottom of the ocean represents us and how we wander in samsara for eons. The tortoise rarely swimming to the ocean surface illustrates the difficulty of lower-realm beings gaining higher rebirth in the human realm.

The tortoise finally placing its head in the ring reflects how hard it is to secure a precious human rebirth with all the eight freedoms and ten endowments.

We meditate on the sufferings of the samsara realms, in particular the lower realms, to gain clear understanding of those unhappy states and how there is no freedom to practice Dharma there. We should feel the suffering of those beings beyond words. We should understand profoundly what it is to be ignorant, not knowing about mind, not realizing how much bad karma can be created and with such terrifying results. If we can think in this way, the meditation will be very effective and beneficial for the mind.

We meditate on these eight freedoms and ten endowments to realize how fortunate we are as human beings who have come into contact with the Dharma. With this realization the mind will become joyful at engaging in Dharma and invigorated in overcoming the delusions, making liberation and full enlightenment achievable.

Unfortunately, even though we have received such an optimum human rebirth, we often fail to use it well because we don't realize its potential. Practicing Dharma does not appear urgent to us because we do not recognize the sufferings of life and of the various realms. We do not value the freedom we have to escape from suffering nor the tools we have to accomplish this.

Instead we often seek happiness through external means. We travel, indulge in sense objects, take vacations, swim in the sea, climb mountains, lie under the sun, and ride the waves on surf boards. While we rely on external methods to gain happiness, we cannot deny the feeling deep within us that something is missing.

Right now this human rebirth qualified with the eight freedoms and ten endowments is indeed precious. It is unbelievably precious. Let's not waste a moment of it.

The moments to practice Dharma during this lifetime are limited because death is certain and the time of death is uncertain. Death can happen even today or in the next minute. Since what we want is happiness and what we do not want is suffering, abandon the causes of suffering and practice the causes of happiness, which are virtue and Dharma.

The very first thing to do is to make sure we are not reborn in the lower realms. We need a higher rebirth, the best of which is a precious human rebirth, if we are to continue practicing the Dharma to actualize the path. But just winning a higher rebirth in samsara is not sufficient, because it is still samsara. Therefore, resolve to use this optimum human rebirth as the vehicle to gain freedom from samsara altogether and to achieve the ultimate happiness of enlightenment.

Remember always that achieving liberation just for oneself is not enough. Numberless beings are struggling and suffering, and the purpose of life is to benefit others. Therefore aspire and think, "I must achieve enlightenment so as to benefit others, to free all living beings from suffering and its causes and bring them to full enlightenment." Think this way all the time, OK?

Here is a tip to achieve balance in life: Whenever we find ourselves feeling too lazy to reflect and act on the teachings or too excited about worldly enjoyments, remember death can come at any time. Whenever we feel depressed or discouraged, remember our precious human rebirth. This is how to balance our minds.

I hope it is now clearer why the Buddha chose to teach suffering first when he taught the four noble truths. If we do not recognize all the forms suffering takes, and the suffering nature of samsara, we will not seek freedom from it.

Instead we will wander blindly in samsara. We will repeat our mistakes and never find the lasting happiness we yearn for, never actualize our potential for enlightenment, the source of joy not only for ourselves but for countless living beings.

ANECDOTES FROM THE LIFE OF KYABJE LAMA ZOPA RINPOCHE

Endless compassion to goats

A goat is standing by a butcher shop near Kopan Hill in Nepal, tied on a very short leash. It is waiting to be killed by the butcher. I am not sure if it is aware it will be slaughtered very soon. Rinpoche asks the jeep to stop as soon as he sees the goat. It is a nice-looking young goat, brown colored with spots all over it.

The negotiations start immediately with the shopkeeper. How much does he want for the goat? The shopkeeper discusses it with his friend in the shop and we settle on 8,500 rupees (about US$119) for the goat, the cost of a cheap cell phone.

The man explains they will get another goat because they have a commitment to supply meat for the weekend. Rinpoche immediately starts negotiating for the second goat. I wonder to myself how long this will go on. We settle on the price for the second goat. Then we drive off to Kopan nunnery and the two goats are brought to the nunnery soon after. Rinpoche blesses both goats before releasing them in the compound. They look happy!

Since we have arrived back in Nepal Rinpoche has saved ten or eleven goats from the little butcher shop at the foot of Kopan Hill. At the nunnery a Nepalese man helps take care of the goats. A similar animal sanctuary operates further up the hill at Kopan monastery.

Blessing a cockroach

We were having a meal in Bangalore, India, when Rinpoche jumped up from his chair and ran to the center of the restaurant. He got down on his knees and quickly tried to protect the cockroach from the waiter who was about to crush the cockroach with his foot!

The cockroach got away and we were all after it. It ran under Rinpoche's foot and Rinpoche stood still, keeping it just under his sandals, protecting it and reciting mantras. While this was happening, we explained to the puzzled six or seven waiters that we were just trying protect the cockroach and bless it.

Saving even the smallest ant

"I can't move," said Rinpoche.

"Why?" asks the physiotherapist (who is attending to Rinpoche since his stroke).

"Ants! I will tread on the ants," Rinpoche replies from his bed at Kopan monastery, Nepal.

So starts the debate between Rinpoche and his physiotherapist Rajesh, who doesn't understand why Rinpoche is so concerned about treading on one or two ants while he is doing his exercises. Rinpoche gives Rajesh a brief explanation about the suffering of sentient beings and the need for compassion toward all, which Rajesh accepts.

We all chip in to gently remove the ants, and only then does Rinpoche continue with his exercises.

Big prayers for a small dog

We are in a car and take the back streets through Varanasi, India, to avoid the road construction. The lanes are narrow, busy, and full of different activities.

We come across a wounded puppy. Rinpoche stops the car and we all pile out to see the little dog. The puppy is lying still on the road and appears to be dead. The mother dog is nearby and in a very pitiful condition: skinny, limping and howling, seemingly upset about her dead puppy.

Rinpoche starts to recite mantras over the pup, in the middle of the road. We try to keep the busy traffic from running us over. Passersby are very curious as to what is happening. In this part of the world a dead dog doesn't carry much value, so it's interesting for them to see this. The mother of the puppy is frantic, howling, and confused. Rinpoche continues to pray over the pup.

On another day, while on another journey, we screech to a halt. Rinpoche has spotted a buffalo that looks about to die and wants to recite mantras for it. The locals say the buffalo was hit by a truck a few days back and had been left on the side of the road since then. Rinpoche spends time blessing the buffalo and we feed it some water.

Advice for liberating animals

Animals have been reborn in samsara over countless lives, and just like other sentient beings have been our mother, father, brother, sister, or a loved one. Numberless times they have cared for us, protected us, borne hardships for us. Because they died and changed their bodies, we cannot recognize them, as we are not omniscient. Yet it does not change the fact that they showed us great kindness over many lifetimes.

Animals suffer tremendously but they cannot express it. They hurt but cannot explain it. So it is incredibly good to help them and to repay their kindness. The center in Singapore has liberated at least two hundred million animals.

Sometimes I ask people with cancer to participate in animal liberation practices by sending in their names and by helping to buy animals that otherwise would be killed. Some people who did this recovered from the disease.

Reciting short prayers to animals is very beneficial because it leaves imprints on the animals' consciousness. As the animals hear the prayers, much negativity is purified and positive imprints are placed on their minds. These imprints will help them to a good rebirth, where they might find the opportunity for Dharma practice and to eventually attain enlightenment.

2 : THE TRUTH OF THE CAUSE OF SUFFERING

....

This origin of suffering as a noble truth should be abandoned.

—DHAMMACAKKAPPAVATTANA SUTTA

DELUSIONS AND KARMA

THIS IS the big question: What is the cause of all suffering? From where does suffering come?

Our minds have been sleeping comfortably in samsara, although perhaps not as comfortably as sleeping in American hotels (I'm joking). From creatures so tiny they can be seen only through microscopes to the largest beast in the jungle or the most famous person in the world, all living beings are conditioned by suffering or dissatisfaction (Skt. dukkha).

Even a king with great power has no choice but to suffer through samsara. It's therefore vital to recognize the true cause of suffering if we are to be rid of it.

Everything exists and occurs for a reason. We might think our problems are caused by outer enemies who harm us, who cheat us, who carry weapons, or who have horns growing from their heads.

The true enemy is not any of these externals but instead lives in our minds and manipulates us. The true enemies, the true causes of suffering, are delusions and karma.

Delusions are the mental afflictions of ignorance, attachment, and anger, those negative emotional mind states that disturb us and destroy our peace. These mind states in turn move us to commit negative action or karma, which inevitably leads to suffering. These delusions are internal states of mind. Therefore real perfect peace depends on recognizing the delusions and the problems they cause through karmic action, and then taking steps to stop them.

Running away to the mountains or to the moon is only a change of place, an external thing, which will not cut off the inner source of our problems. We have to check within ourselves. Through understanding the delusions and karma and how they cause suffering, we are able to open the door to solutions.

We might think, "What's the point of meditating on suffering or reciting mantras? It would be better to do chores, help out at the hospital, or travel to a war zone to alleviate starvation."

We might think it is silly to meditate instead of participating in worldly but helpful activities. This view arises because we have not adequately thought through the evolution of suffering. It is a product of thinking, but not thinking deeply enough. It is only thinking about a person's hunger at this moment. We are not thinking beyond that.

We are not thinking about the source of that starvation, those diseases, those conflicts, those relationship problems. We are just looking at the surface of suffering, wishing to address the symptoms of suffering, without digging deeper to find the root of suffering. Therefore we conclude that our only solution is to give medicine or food to relieve those symptoms.

Of course, we should offer whatever help we can. The motivation to unconditionally help others in these worldly ways is undisputedly kind; it comes from a good intention. But remember, after worldly relief is delivered, suffering again rises like a towering blaze to torment the very same beings. We thus need to provide a long-term solution. We need to free all living beings from harm and from suffering forever. To do this we need to get to the cause of all problems and cut off suffering at its root. What living beings need is to be entirely freed from misery. There is no way for this to happen other than to first identify the causes of suffering and then to eradicate those causes.

It is not sufficient to merely help others recover from a headache, stop their hunger for a while, or give them shelter for a season. That is something, but it is not enough. Just offering temporal happiness is not sufficient. As long as we do not help others to become free from the true causes of suffering, from delusions and obscurations, even if we give them medicine and food, the underlying causes of woe will remain and more suffering will be coming their way.

If we are suffering from poisoning, we must identify the type of poison causing our misery before we can expel it and alleviate the suffering. If, for instance, we smell something foul near us, such as *ka-ka*, and we want to be rid of the stench, we must first find the cause of the smell. After we identify the source of the smell, we can clean it out.

If we don't find the cause of the smell, it will not help to merely wish it weren't so or run around rearranging our surroundings or blame others for it. These approaches are of no help. The most sensible strategy is to identify the cause. We can seek a remedy and apply it only when we understand the cause. Wrong understanding will produce wrong methods and wrong action, making life very complicated.

Delusion and karma are the cause of all suffering. There are six root delusions and twenty secondary delusions. We shall look at the six root delusions—ignorance, attachment, anger, pride, doubt, and wrong view—and discuss their antidotes.

Root Delusions and Their Antidotes

Ignorance

Ignorance (Tib. *marikpa*) is the principal delusion, a negative mind from which all other delusions arise.

There are two types of ignorance. The first type is the mistaken view of a truly existent I, the erroneous thought that "I" exists from its own side. Related to this is the second type of ignorance, the ignorance of karma and how it functions.

Let's begin with the second type of ignorance. Not realizing the evolution of karma, how it comes about and how it operates, leads us to act in ways that cause us to be born in samsara again and again, experiencing all the problems of samsara. Ignorance of karma gets imprinted on our consciousness, which then causes other delusions to arise and influence our actions of body, speech, and mind.

Karmic imprints from such actions are then carried by the consciousness into the next samsaric life, whereupon, meeting the appropriate conditions, they ripen into results that are experienced. The ignorance of karmic formation causes us to be surprised, shocked, upset, and outraged when undesirable events happen in our lives.

Now to the first type of ignorance. It is the concept that views "I" and phenomena as independently arising and truly existent. We believe 100 percent that there is a real "I" inside our bodies. When we fail to analyze, we believe the "I" really exists from its own side and is not merely a label placed by the mind on a base of aggregates.

The five aggregates of a human being (form, feeling, discrimination, consciousness, and compositional factors or karmic imprints) are a collection of parts that forms a base. On this base we impute the label "I." The "I" is mentally constructed and empty of inherent existence. There is only the base of the five aggregates and the mental label "I" imputed to it. That is all. The "I" arises *dependently* on a mental label and a base; it does not exist independently or inherently.

So in reality the "I" is completely and totally empty of inherent existence. There is only a grouping of parts, with the rest of it merely labeled by the mind.

Another example is the aggregate of feelings, the mental factor that experiences happiness, suffering, and neutrality. Upon encountering an object or situation, depending on which other delusion, such as attachment or anger, is dominant in our mind at that moment, our mind imputes "feeling happy" or "feeling unhappy." Right after that moment of imputation, the imprints left on our mental continuum by past ignorance project the notion of "true existence" onto the feeling our mind just created.

From this we conclude the feeling is real and label it so. We mistakenly believe the feeling inherently exists. There is no awareness that our mind created the label.

This sense of a truly existent feeling is totally false, but we hold on to it as true. We do the same thing with our notion of a "truly existing I." Once our mind has placed the label "I" on the aggregates, we believe the mental label of "I" as true, as reality. Therefore instead of seeing the "I" as existing dependently, as merely a mental label on the base of the aggregates, ignorance mistakenly believes the "I" is independently, inherently, truly existing. Think about how much suffering we have experienced in relation to this seemingly inherently existing "I" and how much negativity we have committed on account of this "I."

Another example of how ignorance functions to give the false impression of true existence can be seen in the letter *A*.

Ignorance causes us to see the letter *A* as a real *A* existing from its own side. But all that is actually there are three lines placed in a particular arrangement. *A* is the mental label we learned to put on that base of three lines. If we investigate and search for where the *A*-ness is on those lines, we cannot find it. If we look for the characteristic of *A* within this slanting line or that horizontal line, we cannot find it. This proves that the appearance of a real, independent, truly existing *A* is a mental construct, one that is totally nonexistent from its own side, not existing independently on its own.

It is vital to thoroughly understand how ignorance, holding on to the concept of "true existence," dwells deeply in our consciousness, if we are to catch it and be rid of it. All delusions originate from the root of ignorance, grasping at "I" as truly and inherently existent. The point is that there is no "truly existent I" on these aggregates, there is only a "merely labeled I" imputed to the aggregates.

We might say, "So what? What is the problem of regarding the 'I' as truly existent?"

The problem is this: Once we see the "I" as truly existing, attachment to it immediately follows. We want happiness for ourselves, for this seemingly real "I," and we are prepared to do all sorts of things to get that happiness because the happiness of this "I" is more important than the happiness of others. We grasp at the four desirable objects of gain, comfort, good reputation, and praise. When we do not get what we want and instead experience loss, discomfort, bad reputation, and criticism, we immediately feel unhappy, angry, and even depressed.

Any interference with what "I want" triggers resentment, causing harm to ourselves and to others. When some form of recognition is given to us, pride about this "I" balloons from within, resulting in unbelievable disregard for others and deepening ignorance further. When friends or neighbors do better than us, unease builds up in our hearts. Jealousy is awakened. Clinging to status and to life itself, mistaken views such as "I will cease when this life ends" create disturbing views about death and about reality.

All our life problems arise because we believe there is a real "I" right here. This ignorance that believes in an inherently and truly existing "I" is the root of all suffering and emotional distress.

Because we selfishly guard this "I," once we finish one package of problems another bundle of trouble comes our way! The deluded "I" is never satisfied. The myriad sufferings of life are painfully endured because of this, then death comes, followed by rebirth in the six realms. All this flows from our mistakenly believing in the "I" that exists from its own side. Completely convinced of the false "I"'s existence, we make it the focus of all our daily actions of body, speech, and mind. Holding on to false beliefs cannot lead to true happiness.

Therefore if we can eliminate this grasping at the truly existent "I," we will sever ignorance from its very root and be free from all suffering once and for all. It would then be impossible for ignorance to ever arise again, leaving no room for the other delusions to function and to disturb us. Just as the sun rises to dispel all darkness, as we analyze how this seemingly existing I has come about, we will discover how we have been gripped by this dangerous delusion all this time.

When we recognize delusion and apply the antidote seeing the falsity of the truly existent "I," when we understand that "I" is only a mental projection on to a base of aggregates (and the aggregates are likewise a product of mental imputations), the mind will immediately feel lighter, freer, more spacious. Persevere in this contemplation and gradually the dark, negative mind will be dispelled. The negative mind will simply stop.

Why do we fear death? This fear arises because we believe the so-called real and truly existing "I" is going to die, is going to cease. But the fact is that although the body will end, the mind will not. Mind is a continuum. Until we eliminate this ignorant belief in an inherently existing "I" we cannot break free of samsara, we cannot achieve liberation or enlightenment. This ignorance has been cheating us our entire life. It has been deceiving us since beginningless rebirths.

To cut off ignorance we need to study, analyze, and meditate on the teachings in order to develop special insight into the true nature of the "I," how the "I" is empty of true existence. Even though we might think we have now understood that the "I" is not inherently existent, the next moment criticism is hurled at us, a solid sense of an inherently existing "I" will arise again to get angry and retaliate at the critic. When we gain the wisdom that directly perceives emptiness, ignorance and its seeds will be uprooted and vanquished. Only then will we be rid of samsara and its oceans of suffering. The wisdom realizing emptiness, when combined with the altruistic intention to liberate all sentient beings that is bodhicitta, will enable us to collect extensive merits, complete the *paramitas*, or perfections, and thereafter achieve enlightenment.

When ignorance is purified or expunged other delusions cannot survive. Without the earth there would be no basis on which buildings, living beings, and nonliving things could exist. Likewise if there were no ignorance there would be no platform for the continuation of the rest of the delusions—of attachment, anger, pride, doubt, and mistaken view.

Ignorance is the most dangerous thief of all. It robs us of the realization of the true nature of reality, it cheats us of the attainments of the mind, such as seeing the past, present, and future, and it especially denies us the attainment of everlasting happiness, of enlightenment. How does it do this? Ignorance deceives us about the true nature of things and the evolution of karma, which in turn causes us to commit negative actions that bring about painful consequences. In this way, ignorance robs us of happiness and blocks us from wisdom.

We have suffered over countless lives because these two types of ignorance—ignorance of the nature of reality and ignorance of the mechanics of karma—have caused us to blindly run around in circles and create causes for endless misery and suffering. But be encouraged! Ignorance is not permanent. It can be completely eliminated because it is a hallucinated conception.

Suppose we enter a dark room and, upon coming through the door, we see a snake coiled up on the bed. What is actually there is a coil of rope, but due to insufficient lighting we mistakenly believe it is a snake. Completely trusting the appearance of a snake to be true, we get frightened and run out screaming and scaring others. Instead of running we should first switch on the light to see what is there and whether it is really a snake or not. Once the light is switched on we will see it is just a bundle of coiled rope.

Right there the hallucinated concept of "snake" vanishes. We are able to clearly see what does not exist there and what exists there. In the same way, the truly existent "I" does not exist. What does exist is merely the mental label "I," applied to the aggregates. By using the light of Dharma wisdom, we realize the truly existent "I" is hallucinated and does not really exist.

The principal cause of all suffering, which is ignorance, is created by ourselves. We could say we are enemies to ourselves. However, enlightenment is achieved through our own efforts to subdue our minds and overcome the delusions, which brings perfect peace and enlightenment.

Therefore we can be our own perfect guide. There is no external thief of our happiness. Unhappiness and suffering are created by ourselves when we allow ignorance and the other delusions to influence our actions. In other words, we could say, "I started the whole experience of suffering by following ignorance. The entire evolution of suffering, from its causes to its suffering results, is the fault of my ignorant deluded mind."

Understanding this evolution is really crucial because from this understanding we begin to discover ourselves and know where we are at the moment. We can think, "Every time I suffer enables me to discover who I am, to become aware of my own mind and situation, to understand my evolution."

This understanding brings a sense of inner calm. It will prevent us from being angry all the time and blaming others for our hardships, because we realize our role in our unhappiness.

When a person comprehends the evolution of suffering and the destructive impact of delusions imprinted on consciousness from long before, he realizes that he alone is responsible for his problems and he alone is his own rescuer. He unveils the treachery of the delusions and begins to find the energy to eliminate those delusions by following the path of virtue. He becomes less agitated in the face of troubles and is able to muster the courage to persevere in practice.

On the other hand, the person who chooses not to think through the evolution of suffering and is content to remain ignorant and a servant to delusion lives a life of frustration and confusion. Instead of examining how his own ignorance has brought about problems, he accuses others, condemns situations, and does things that compound his suffering and the suffering of others. His mind becomes attached to his personal aims and he is willing to injure others to obtain those aims. He has no interest in breaking the cause of suffering—ignorance—because he does not realize it is there and because his negative mind has become habituated to doing whatever it likes to get what he wants. Inevitably more problems and more suffering pile up on this person. There is a big difference between these two types of persons—which one are you? Check this carefully.

It is therefore clear that without destroying the ignorance within our minds, no matter how much we try to destroy our outer enemies or change our external circumstances, the problems will continue. On the other hand, if we pay more attention to eliminating delusions that are cunning inner thieves of happiness, our troubles will subside. To conquer our inner enemy of delusion is to end all outer enemies and suffering.

Antidote to ignorance

How do we overcome ignorance? We need to cultivate the wisdom realizing emptiness. This is the direct antidote to ignorance and cuts it off at its root. Realizing emptiness requires consistent effort at meditating on how the appearance of a truly existing "I" is a mistaken perception, and how the true nature of "I" and all phenomena is that which dependently arises and is empty of inherent existence.

Attachment

Clinging only to the happiness of this life is the cause of recurring problems and confusion. For instance, people in a household sometimes quarrel over insignificant things like what to eat for breakfast. One person desires pancakes and the other person wants bread. Even if each of them thereafter consumes what they want every morning, the problem of attachment won't cease. The clinging mind will seize new objects to latch on to and argue about. So these persons throughout their entire lives will find their dissatisfaction unquenched. Then without solving that problem, life passes and death comes.

On the basis of ignorance, attachment arises. Attachment is a particularly slippery delusion. It is not easily recognized as a delusion because it acts as if it is helping us gain some form of happiness. For instance, when we look at a new watch, our ignorant view first sees the watch as a truly existent watch in front of us. This view activates attachment, which then makes the object more attractive than its reality warrants, exaggerating its qualities.

Attachment makes us see only the appealing qualities of the watch. Other delusions such as pride, for instance, may also be at work, persuading our attached mind to want to possess this watch, thinking it is sought after by many people.

When attachment arises within us there is the feeling of merging with the desired object, like a thorn going inside the flesh. The mind absorbs into the object of attachment, and we start to feel we do not want to be separated from that object; we want to have it with us all the time. This is how attachment latches on to the desired object and emotionally relates to it. This is how attachment becomes deeply rooted. We can examine how attachment operates in our own daily lives through the workings of the eight worldly concerns.

The eight worldly concerns

The object of desire in itself is not the problem. Having possessions and wealth is not the problem. The problem is the mind that clings to the wealth. Having a friend is not the problem, but the mind that clings to the friend makes having a friend a problem. The mind of desire and clinging is what attachment is all about, and it makes having these four commonly desired objects—material possessions, comfort, good reputation, and praise—problems for us.

The eight worldly concerns are wanting gain and possessions but not loss, wanting comfort but not discomfort, wanting a good reputation but not to be put down, and wanting praise but not criticism. We use so much of our time and energy chasing after these eight worldly concerns.

Let us investigate them more closely.

Wanting material possessions and not wanting to be separated from them. Due to our attachment to gain and material things, when they are not forthcoming we become unhappy. Dissatisfaction rises swiftly. There would be no problem if we had no attachment to these things in the first place. But the worldly concern of wanting gain makes our lives like a roller coaster going up and down, sometimes almost giving us a heart attack!

When we do not get what we want, feelings of discontent and resentment arise. When we get the material things we want we feel momentary happiness, but we soon find ourselves wanting more. If we really check, the nature of the mind of so-called happiness is not really happiness, in the sense that a mind that clings to a material gift is neither calm nor effortlessly delighted. Instead it is kind of an uptight mind, wound up like a knot, threatening to unravel at any moment. The attached mind is not a relaxed, comfortable mind. It is constantly squeezed by grasping and by wanting more.

Whenever we do not get what we want disappointment strikes us first, followed by anger. Then we act according to our agitated minds, for instance, by making others unhappy by quarreling with them, by saying negative words, or even by breaking things. We do this through-out our lives. To make things worse the dissatisfied mind leaves heavy imprints on our mental continuum, imprints that are then carried for-ward into the future and into future lives, breeding more discontent. When we follow desirous clinging and the self-cherishing thought, a vicious cycle of misery is set in motion.

Clinging to comfort and disliking discomfort. We might be in deep sleep one night when our sleep is suddenly disturbed by a mosquito biting us. If we have a strong worldly concern about comfort, we will get very annoyed by this mosquito. We are instantly enraged by this tiny insect and remain upset all night. The next day, we complain all day long to family and friends about the mosquito, saying, "I couldn't sleep for hours last night because of that wretched mosquito!" Losing a few hours' sleep becomes the same as losing a million dollars. For some people small disturbances become huge disasters.

Clinging to good reputation and getting upset at the opposite. One of the painful problems of ordinary people is their attachment to repu-tation. Renouncing attachment to reputation is much more difficult than renouncing attachment to food and clothing. I have friends who are renowned in their fields of work but who constantly stress over their fame declining or being lost. Likewise there are people who yearn for the respect of others. If someone happens to overlook such a person or walks past them without offering words of respect, they take it as a great insult.

So much suffering arises from this particular worldly concern. High expectations and intense clinging to respect result in any failure to acknowledge such a person as synonymous with shooting an arrow straight into that person's heart. The stronger the grasping for reputa-tion and fame, the deeper the pain when one encounters the opposite.

Clinging to praise and getting upset at criticism. People may say to us, "What a good person you are, how generous, how kind, how intelligent, how wise," and the moment such words touch our ears our minds get shaken. Attachment to these words of praise inflates us like a party balloon. The mind becomes stuck like glue to those words, like a moth flying into melted candle wax, completely immersing itself in the candle wax—such is the mind that hears words of praise.

Attachment is exactly like this. The mind is stuck to an object of desire. The mind becomes unsteady, unsubdued, grasping for more pleasant words and unhappy at anything different. The problem is not with the words being said but with the mind that hears them, which is attached to sounds of praise and admiration.

Conversely, when someone criticizes us or complains about us, ignorance thinks there is something solid in each word, that those are truly existing words. Ignorance thinks there is a truly existing "I" being criticized and that the person saying those harsh words is a truly existing enemy. This immediately ignites our anger. Nothing can put out this fiery emotion. Our entire being becomes distressed when we are angry.

When we cling to possessions, comfort, good reputation, and praise, it shows we are attached to the happiness of just this life. That is why these four pairs are called worldly concerns. They activate our delusions and inevitably serve up dissatisfaction and unhappiness. Attachment is one of the great causes of samsara. It tricks us into thinking it is our friend when in truth it is our jailer.

So you see, we do not have to abandon or throw out the objects we enjoy or value. We just need to check our mistaken view of those objects and abandon our sticky clinging to them.

Antidotes to attachment

What are the techniques to overcome attachment? The Buddha prescribes several methods.

When attachment to body arises, the remedy is to meditate on the less-attractive aspects of the body. For example, think about how the body is in the nature of impurity, filled with blood, pus, and excrement. Through acknowledging these facts we gradually lose our attachment to the body. If we are attached to entertainment, think about how it drains our resources and distracts us from developing aversion to samsara. This lack of aversion to samsara keeps us enslaved and interferes with your spiritual progress.

Another antidote for attachment is to remember impermanence, to see all things as an illusion, as a dream. See yourself as in a dream, and all your possessions, your family, the people around you, as dreamlike and illusory. There is a big difference between a person who recognizes that everything in a dream is untrue and a person who believes a dream to be real. When you realize a dream is not real, nothing about it bothers you. You know that whatever happens in the dream is unreal and so it does not stir up strong emotions. Even if someone praised you in your dream, you are not attached to those words of praise when you awaken because you know it was only a dream. Likewise if someone criticized you in the dream you would not get upset with the critic, because it was only a dream, an illusion, a mere reflection.

As master Nagarjuna explained, life is like a bubble, like the flame of a butter lamp that moves with the wind and can be put out at any time. Nagarjuna said life is more transitory than a water bubble, as death can happen at any time. If that's the case, why cling to anything as if it were durable or permanent? Meditate on impermanence, because only then will the futility of attachment to things clarify. See all things and experiences as transitory, as illusion-like.

Each morning when we wake up it is good to meditate deeply, even for just a few minutes, on the wonder of awakening from sleep. The night before many people died. They went to bed with many plans about how to get more possessions, what to do tomorrow or next year, but by this morning their bodies were corpses.

We can do so much with this precious human rebirth. We are unbelievably fortunate to have awakened today with the freedom to practice Dharma and to use our life wisely.

Another remedy for attachment to an object is to investigate its true nature. If we can see that an object's beauty comes not from the object's side but from our mind's perception and labeling of it, we would be less likely to become attached to that object. Prior to investigation, we saw the object as inherently beautiful, as a self-existing object of beauty. But when we see the beauty is only our own mental label on an object, it's easier to break the attachment.

Whether we see an object as ugly, beautiful, or neutral is the result of our past karma. What we perceive comes from our mind and is the karmic reflection of our mind. We see the condition of our mind with all its imprints from past actions. We are attached to our own karmic projections! We cling to our own mental labels.

There is no inherently existing beauty, ugliness, or neutrality out there. The mistake comes when we believe thoughts such as the beautiful flower or wonderful holiday exist outside and did not come from our mind. This is the big mistake. This is so very important to know. Awareness of the reality of beauty will help us control attachment and gain mastery over the grasping mind. Meditate on it.

Whatever we perceive and wherever we are—walking on the road, sightseeing, experiencing events, people, objects, sky, clouds—practice the mindfulness that recognizes the true nature of things. Think, "This is the view of my karma. This is the projection of my karma. This is the result of my past karma. Beautiful, ugly, happy, unhappy, neutral; all are mere mental views, the mental projections of my past karma."

If we can't reflect as explained above, the simplest way to weaken attachment is to mentally change our object of attachment into a stone, a block of wood, or anything neutral that will not cause attachment to arise. This will deliver a blow to our strong clinging.

The less we cling to the eight worldly concerns, the fewer problems we will have. Less clinging means less fear, less pain, more delight. If we cut off clinging to this life, we won't be in crisis when we experience loss, discomfort, disrespect, or criticism. If we do not cling to the expectation that a friend will always be nice to us, or will always help us when asked, we won't be hurt when the friend does the opposite. Desire is very sneaky. It is virtually unnoticeable, yet we suddenly find ourselves trapped in its web.

Without the eight worldly concerns there will be joy in our minds, peace in our lives. There will be few ups and downs. The eight worldly concerns are one of our most serious diseases. This disease infects our entire lives until we apply the antidotes.

If somebody kills us while we are doing virtue, all that happens is that our consciousness moves on to another optimum human rebirth or goes to a pure realm. But if we cling to the eight worldly concerns, even if we live to be one hundred we will continue to experience problems and endlessly create causes for rebirth in lower realms. Therefore the eight worldly concerns are a greater danger to us and are far more harmful to us than the person who kills us.

A story about the famous Kadampa Geshe Ben Gungyal, who lived in a hermitage, shows the stealthy power of the eight worldly concerns.

One day Geshe Ben Gungyal received a message that his benefactor would be visiting him that day. In preparation for this visit Geshe Ben Gungyal cleaned up his altar and set out the best offerings. He then sat down to check his motivation and realized that he did all that simply to impress his benefactor.

Realizing this was a worldly concern and not Dharma, he stood up from his cushion, took some ash from his fireplace and threw it all over the altar, making a mess of it. Meanwhile he chastised himself with the thought, "Don't tell lies. Stay without being false, without being a liar."

When the great clairvoyant yogi Padampa Sangye heard what Geshe Ben Gungyal had done, he expressed his admiration and said, "In Tibet, as far as making offerings to the Three Jewels goes, Ben Gungyal's handful of ash is the best offering."

Padampa Sangye recognized that Geshe Ben Gungyal had seized his own worldly thought, had seen how that rendered his altar offerings impure, and had lost no time in rejecting the eight worldly concerns. This rejection is the best offering of Dharma practice to the Three Jewels.

Therefore whenever problems arise, if we can remember that the eight worldly concerns born out of attachment are the recurring source of our problems, we will experience problems with less intensity. Remembering the eight worldly concerns helps us to abandon this corrosive, clinging mindset. This is the basic psychology. If we use this method, adverse situations will not disturb us.

Anger

Anger is an emotion that ranges from violent rage to minor irritations and discomforts. It is not only about explosive outbursts but includes small aversions as well. No sentient being is free from anger. Hundreds of troubles come from the angry, dissatisfied mind. When there is strong desire or clinging, anger arises very easily. When someone does something that goes against our wishes, or interrupts our enjoyment of possessions, family, and friends, our mind becomes displeased and anger is triggered.

When a man feels craving desire for his girlfriend, he's likely to get angry when he thinks someone else also desires her. He thinks, "Oh, this man is eyeing my girlfriend." Paranoia arises. You know what I mean? Desire effortlessly gives rise to anger, then paranoia and much trouble. When we are in the state of anger, we immediately see an enemy right there.

This unsubdued mind of anger is extremely destructive. If we do not practice patience to pacify anger, once it arises it is very difficult to control. Anger puts our life and the lives of others in danger. Anger may lead us to harm or even kill our own mother, even though she kindly gave birth to us, worked hard to give us food and education, and provided us with enjoyment and opportunities.

When anger arises we hit out with whatever is available, like bottles, stones, knives, tables, or guns. If the angry person threw only cupcakes, that might be nice as the other person could at least taste them!

When anger arises, the mind goes completely dark and focuses on inflicting harm. Even if we had some understanding of Dharma, once anger arises the teachings on karma vanish or seem far away. Anger has a harmful nature that makes us automatically hurt ourselves and injure others too. It is an agitated, extremely sensitive, tormented state of mind. It is like having a long sharp nail pierced into one's flesh. The evolution of anger is such that even before it manifests outwardly, inwardly we are already unstable and forgetful about morality. Every muscle feels tight. The mind is pricked by a million thorns.

Anger is a terrible enemy, as it ruins our inner peace and inflicts harm on others. Therefore it is crucial to be able to control anger.

After twenty years of good relations, some couples suddenly get into crisis. One morning an angry explosion of emotion happens, and in those few moments everything is destroyed. Twenty years of companionship is demolished. Such is the destructive force of anger.

Some people think anger is like instant coffee that just happens and is no big deal. But even instant coffee has a cause. Instant coffee does not suddenly manifest in midair without any interdependent causation. Many conditions come together to produce a cup of instant coffee.

In the same way, anger has an evolution. We need to understand anger well and be conscious of its arousal, its causes, and its passage to completion, which is always damaging. Therefore before anger fully arises we need to recognize it and train to control it.

Some Western psychologists say it is good to express anger; they regard anger as an inner pressure that needs to be released to restore normalcy. But Buddhist psychology disagrees with this approach because if we regularly express anger the imprint of anger is reinforced and is buried deeper into our consciousness. Each time we express anger the imprint gathers greater strength in our mind.

This process is like generating electricity. The longer we generate electricity the more is produced and then stored, correct? Anger is similar. The more we engage in anger the more our minds are filled with it and the greater the danger to ourselves and to others.

By understanding how anger functions we can see its shortcomings, and we should strive to control it and ultimately eliminate anger's influence over us. To people who are frequently angry, I give this simple advice. Understand the disadvantages of anger to yourselves and to others and set up a strong determination that says "Today I am not going to get angry."

Determination has power. It is not Buddha's power or some other being's power. It is your power, your conscious power, your mind power. Use it.

Once this inner enemy of anger is destroyed all outer enemies vanish.

The great master Shantideva advised that while we cannot cover the entire earth with leather to protect our feet from rocky surfaces, we can cover our feet with shoes for the same protection. Similarly, when we protect our minds from the inner enemy of anger, all outer enemies disappear.

Antidotes to anger

How can we control and overcome anger? Whenever we label an object or experience negatively, "I don't like that" or "It's uncomfortable," the mind of aversion is there and anger is there.

To overcome anger we need to be convinced of its shortcomings, to understand that anger causes immediate unhappiness to ourselves and to others. Anger shakes the mind and causes us to commit all forms of negative behavior, which bring trouble to us in the short and the long term. Anger breeds conflicts. An unsubdued angry mind is incapable of wise decisions, and poor decisions create further problems. Anger can even make us commit suicide. One second of anger can destroy a thousand eons of virtue accumulated through generosity and offerings to holy beings. This is how destructive anger is.

It is rare to accumulate virtue, so the ability to destroy a thousand eons of virtue with one second of anger shows how potent anger is. This is why the dedication of merit is so important. It keeps anger from destroying merit accumulated from prior virtues.

Master Atisha had an attendant whom he brought to Tibet from India, and this attendant was incredibly bad tempered. Whenever people came to Atisha to discuss matters, the attendant would not make appointments and would make things very difficult for them. People used to complain to Atisha, asking him why he kept such a terrible person in his service, one who even turned some people away from the Dharma. But Atisha replied that this person helped people to accomplish their practice of patience.

Dharma practice isn't just about sitting on meditation cushions. It means subduing our own minds and taking care of others more than ourselves. The merit we create depends on sentient beings. When we see a little child doing something silly and dangerous like playing on the edge of a fast-flowing river, we would feel compassionate concern because foremost in our mind is protecting the child from danger. In the same way, when we see an angry person heading for suffering, we should feel compassion and try to help. While an angry mind remains, no one can experience happiness.

The antidote to anger therefore is the patience that understands the disadvantages of anger. The person who helps us practice patience is the person who agitates us, who is angry with us, who tries to harm or even kill us, and is generally the one whom we discriminate against and call enemy. Such a person gives us the opportunity to cultivate the antidote to anger, to gain realizations, and to progress on the path. So this person is actually doing us a great favor!

Bodhisattvas regard an angry, difficult person as a most precious jewel because they understand anger is driving that person to do harm. Bodhisattvas therefore feel great compassion toward that person because his harmful actions will never give him peace and happiness. Worse than that, his anger is making him commit actions that guarantee him more suffering in present and future lives.

An angry person may think his anger makes him strong, may believe that harming another will give him a sense of power and satisfaction. He is unable to see he is racing toward the deep pit of burning karmic coals.

If we saw someone walking along the street distractedly looking up at the sky, not noticing a deep hole in the road, we would not cheer him on. We would instead call out to warn him or rush out to stop him from falling into the hole. In the same way, instead of retaliating to anger with more anger, we should feel compassionate concern for an angry person. We should try to offer help.

Pride

When someone praises you your heart races, your emotional mind goes up and up. A person inflated with pride is like a pot turned upside down, unable to hold water. A prideful person cannot hold the nectar of wisdom.

A successful or wealthy proud person might think, "I am capable. I made my wealth. I am somebody great. I did it all by myself." Not for a moment does such a person think of the role other sentient beings played in his success, how all his wealth and enjoyment came from their kindness.

General pride comes from comparing ourselves with others. For example, a highly educated person may think he or she is more intelligent than those with little or no education, or may be proud of owning an object more beautiful or more expensive than those owned by other persons.

Double pride is the thought "I am superior to others" or "I am in a special group." Even within that special group double pride is the thought "I am the most special of all."

Pride of consciousness arises from the mistaken belief in a truly existent self, which in turn comes from lack of insight into the dependency between mental labels and the five aggregates.

The pride of having gained realizations comes from the thought "I have realized *shunyata*" when in fact our mind is nowhere near achieving the wisdom of shunyata, the wisdom realizing emptiness. This erroneous thought arises from wrong conceptions of shunyata, so we think that we have attained the perfect realization of shunyata and pride arises.

Some people think, "I already know this Dharma point or meditation, so I don't have to practice anymore." Thinking this way becomes a major hindrance to gaining spiritual realizations. Sometimes even though our realizations are not complete, when we observe some tiny little change or experience we conclude we have arrived at high realizations. This becomes a huge obstacle. It also makes us lazy and in danger of losing even that tiny little effect we had gained.

Those who meditate with a sincere mind for years and years, resolving to live in solitary retreat for as long as it takes to transform their minds, do not suddenly run out into the street announcing, "Hey, look at me.

I have gained realizations. I have received this experience." They never show themselves to be higher beings or more special than anyone else. They are always very humble. We never get the feeling that they have even a tiny bit of pride in their realizations.

Mistaken pride comes from misunderstanding a subject, for example, tantra. There are people who just read books on tantra. Such readers see words like "kundalini," read about male and female energies, and wrongly think the tantric path is about sexual intercourse between the male and female. They develop the pride that thinks "I am practicing tantra." This is a totally wrong view and wrong belief.

Antidotes to pride

There are methods to control pride. First we should reflect on whatever understanding of Dharma we have and ask, "Where did that knowledge come from?" If a virtuous teacher did not reveal the teachings, from where would we have obtained the clear understanding of Dharma we now have? This is the same with any form of knowledge. Without someone revealing it to us, we would not possess that knowledge.

Second, use the remembrance of impermanence and death to combat pride. Death is certain, while the time of death is uncertain. Nothing is definite. We may be part of high society today with wealth and friends, but in one minute everything can change. Right now we may be living in a beautiful apartment, lying on a soft bed, and enjoying every comfort. Suddenly death comes and we find our body on a red-hot iron ground surrounded by burning walls that are doorless and offer no avenue for escape. There is no way to get out until the karma to experience this suffering finishes. No matter how much we scream, this flaming iron house burns stronger, and we have nowhere to take refuge, no guide to help us.

One moment we were eating soft, delicious food, but suddenly death arrived. Now our own karmically created guardians are stabbing red-hot iron rods into our throats, pouring burning, molten iron into our mouths, burning our insides and tearing our stomachs apart.

Who knows? In a moment our situation can change into this terrible existence. Even right now it can change into that. How will our pride help us then? What is the point of having pride?

As a third approach we can control pride by reflecting on the short-comings of whatever makes us proud. For example, we may be wealthy, but being rich has its own problems. The more material possessions we have the more we worry about protecting them, and our grasping chains us more tightly to samsara, making us more miserly and narrow minded.

The best attitude is to think of ourselves as lowly, and in humble terms such as "There is only the ground and running river below me; there is no sentient being that is lower than I." If we can remember this, there is a chance for humility to take root, a chance to erode pride.

At the same time we should begin to cherish others by remember-ing their kindness. We should respect others, thinking they may have higher knowledge than us, knowledge we do not have. Look for special qualities other sentient beings have and feel joy over this. Even though sentient beings' minds are full of mistakes, if we are able to find some good quality in them, something positive about them each day, how wonderful that would be for us. It would be like finding a treasure all the time! In that way, there would be no chance for pride to arise.

Doubt

I began by mentioning that at the start of Dharma study it is good to have doubts, because we are beginning to investigate and analyze the Buddha's teachings. We are exercising the mind and developing our wisdom. Therefore this questioning mind that has doubts is fine. As we continue to study and meditate we will be able to remove more of the doubts.

Rather than living life in doubt and puzzlement we should put effort into studying, contemplating, and applying the teachings, to test the principles and to resolve doubts. It is very worthwhile to do that, so in that sense doubts can be beneficial.

There is little use in blindly holding on to concepts of great beings in heaven and do nothing more than that. One of the Italian students told me about his grandmother, who was a devout Catholic all her life, praying and going to church all the time. But when death approached she felt her prayers were unanswered, and in her dying moments she grabbed her rosary and flung it to the ground, expressing her sense of the futility of praying to God. She was suddenly seized by disbelief just when she needed the support of her beliefs at that critical moment.

This is dangerous and can happen to a person interested in the Dharma who does not understand how the Buddha guides. "The mighty ones do not wash away negative karma with water" means the unhappiness, hardship, and suffering of sentient beings cannot be washed away by the Buddha using water. The way that Buddha liberates sentient beings is not like that.

The Buddha does not eliminate the sufferings of migratory beings with his hands, like taking a thorn out of flesh. If the Buddha could eliminate ignorance and all the other root delusions and secondary delusions by washing them away, or pulling them out by his hands, he would have done so. He would have done this without any effort by sentient beings. We could simply wait for the Buddha to do the work.

If liberation was as easy as that, only up to the Buddha, all sentient beings would have been enlightened by now. This is because Buddha, in his infinite compassion for every suffering being, would have freed every being. Buddha has a billion times more compassion and loving-kindness for us sentient beings than we have for ourselves.

But the Buddha cannot transplant realizations like transplanting a heart. Instead the Buddha liberates sentient beings from all suffering by revealing the truth of suffering, suffering's cause, the possibility of the end of suffering, and the path or methods to end suffering. These are the four noble truths.

Therefore we need to know that as soon as we take refuge in the Buddha, Dharma, and Sangha, the ball is right back in our court and we have to do the work. The Buddha has done his work, has raised himself out of suffering, and has shown us the path so that we can achieve the same result. Whatever happens to us from this moment on is in our hands. That is right and reasonable. We can be our own best friend or our own worst enemy. It all depends on what we do.

Doubt as one of six root delusions refers to questions that undermine our ability to progress on the path. Even though we have encountered the Dharma teachings and studied them, we still think, "Maybe there is cause and effect, maybe not." We doubt karma, we doubt the ability of the Three Jewels to guide us to enlightenment, we doubt reincarnation, we doubt emptiness, always thinking, "Maybe there is, maybe not."

Doubt, without further examination and analysis, is very harmful because it denies us knowledge; it prevents us from deeply understanding the teachings, it prevents us from gaining realizations of the path. Doubt hinders our nirvana and enlightenment. If we ignore doubt without trying to clarify our understanding and resolve the doubt, we will end up in a state of perpetual doubt. This perpetual doubt is like a heavy stone hanging around our neck, a giant roadblock to full liberation and enlightenment.

But if we instead persevere in checking and analyzing the teachings, seeking clarifications from the learned ones, our realizations will become deeper and stronger. If we doubt, we should further investigate the subject we're in doubt about. However, intellectual and scriptural knowledge cannot alone cut off doubts. In addition, we need our Dharma practice to purify mental obstacles and obscurations created through previous negative actions.

If we do not purify our minds, doubts will continue despite good intellectual understanding of the texts or explanations by teachers. If we have heavy obscurations, doubts can arise over the simplest things. We may have faith in karma and so forth right this minute, but when some past negative imprint ripens and manifests into problems, we may find our minds shifting and changing. When that happens we may start to disbelieve the Dharma we have been studying and trusting. We lose all belief in reincarnation, karma, liberation, enlightenment.

In fact, to lift the mind out of doubt, purifying defilements is even more vital than studying the teachings. Without purification practices doubts will arise about the most basic Dharma points, let alone the more sophisticated philosophical points.

Therefore I think purification practices, prayers, and dedication of merit for the enlightenment of all beings are very important to do daily in addition to studying and meditating. When we complete the path to enlightenment and cease all gross and subtle defilements, not a single doubt will remain. The ultimate removal of doubts comes through the direct experience of actualizing the path.

Wrong view

Wrong view refers to the five wrong or false views. In Tibetan these are called *jigta*, where *jig* means "changing" and *ta* means "view," so that *jigta* refers to viewing the changeable aggregates as truly existing. Because of this view our efforts have not brought us to nirvana nor secured our release from samsara, no matter how much we practice. It is therefore crucial to know about the five false views in order to avoid them. They are:

Believing the changeable aggregates are the "I." The five aggregates of form, feeling, discrimination, compositional factors/karmic imprints, and consciousness are not permanent but changeable. Yet we believe, incorrectly, that a concrete, independent, truly existing "I" exists based on the aggregates, which false view causes the sense of "me" and "mine."

That is why when someone is nice to us we think, "Oh, how fantastic! This person has given me this and that. He is a friend because he helped me." We believe he helped the illusory truly existent "I." Due to this wrong view, clinging to self and our own happiness occurs and delusions like attachment, anger, and pride arise.

Extreme view of ceasing the "I." The second wrong view is *chetah*, the view of ourselves ceasing. From the wrong conception of the aggregates being the self-existent "I" arises the mistaken belief that when death happens the "I" will completely cease without any continuation. This is an extreme view. Believing in an "I" that ceases at death is a false conception. The body ends but not the mental continuum.

Heresy. Heresy here means the false view that there is no cessation of suffering, no cause and effect (law of karma), and no existence of the Buddha, Dharma, and Sangha. Heresy believes there are no realizations, such as nirvana or enlightenment, and believes there is no true nature of things, that is to say, shunyata or emptiness.

Holding the above three to be supreme. This is holding the three views discussed above to be correct and the most advanced views when in fact they are mistaken views.

Wrong view of discipline and mode of conduct. This one is interesting. Some people have a mistaken understanding of morality, by which they believe that certain austere disciplines make up a code of moral conduct that will release them from all suffering. An example is the practice of sacrificing animals, which is based on people's thinking that animal sacrifice will bring them to a paradise without suffering, when the truth is completely the opposite.

An example of the "wrong view of discipline" is when people persist in the wrong view of animal sacrifice and its harmful practice when there is no proof that sacrificing animals will bring them the desired result of paradise. As another example, some people think that merely washing one's body in the river will purify all negativities and bring liberation. Others believe that if they walk on a trident and that trident goes through the body, liberation will be achieved.

There is no proof that people will achieve the results they seek through these extreme methods, yet people hold firmly to them. In this way, these are said to be wrong forms of discipline and conduct, even though people holding these views regard this discipline and conduct as the best.

Underlying these five mistaken views is the ignorance that believes the "I," which is merely a label on the base of five aggregates, truly exists. Without the antidote of wisdom realizing emptiness, this ignorance cannot be extinguished.

The six root delusions of ignorance, attachment, anger, pride, doubt, and wrong view have been deeply rooted in our minds since beginningless lives. This explains why we think and act the way we do and yet we wonder why we meet so many problems in our daily lives! These delusions are the causes of suffering, and the antidotes are to be applied to overcome them.

KARMA: THE LAW OF CAUSE AND EFFECT

What do we do when we get sick? We look back at our past actions to see what we did in the morning, what we ate, and what we came into contact with. We know that without checking our past actions we will not be able to identify what caused the illness, nor will we obtain the cure. Worse still, we might get sick again. In the same way, any doctor attending to us will also ask about our past actions and medical history.

In this way we can see how, even in the ordinary world, it is useful for us to be aware of the past. Otherwise we will not be able to understand our present situation or how to solve present problems. If we remain ignorant about our past mistakes, we are likely to repeat them and suffer the consequences. This is basic logic.

In fact it is impossible to live without thinking of the past. Present thoughts come from past thoughts, and then become past thoughts of the future. Without understanding the past and all that happened then, there is no way to understand our present life and how it evolved.

The word *karma* means "action," and there are two types of action. First is action of mind or consciousness, which is intention or motivation. Second is action of body and speech that follows from intention. Through these actions of body, speech, and mind, seeds are planted in our minds that will bear future results.

If we plant a variety of seeds, including beans, corn, and potatoes, our field will bear this variety of crops. If we intend to grow only corn but plant a variety of seeds, clearly we will grow not only corn but crops from the other seeds we planted as well. Potato seeds will not produce corn; rice seeds will not produce barley. It simply does not work that way.

In the same way, whatever karma or action we commit—virtuous, nonvirtuous, or neutral—we plant different types of seeds and the results are according to the seeds. If we act negatively, positive results will not come, no matter how much we wish for good results. If we want happiness, we have to create its causes, which are virtues. If we seek happiness with all our hearts but indulge in nonvirtuous actions, only suffering will arise. This is definite. If we uproot a negative karmic seed through purification practices before it ripens into the unpleasant result, that result can then be averted. But if the seed is left as is, upon it meeting a conducive condition, the negative karmic seed will ripen into the experience of a negative, suffering result.

The word *karma* is often used these days. It is vital to understand karma in a complete way.

The four features of karma

Karma has four features: it is definite, it is expandable, we would not experience a result if we did not create the cause for it, and once it is committed it will not disappear on its own.

1. *Karma is definite.* It is certain that every action of body, speech, or mind will bring about a result. This is just as a seed planted in the ground will grow into a plant and bear fruit once it meets favorable conditions, so long as the seed is not eaten by worms or dug up.

In the same way, the fruits of positive and negative actions are definite. If an action is done with a negative mind and is not purified through Dharma practice, the negative result of suffering is inevitable. Similarly, action done with a virtuous mind will definitely bring happiness, unless the karma is destroyed by anger or by wrong view. Simply put, actions bring about corresponding results. However, those results can be avoided if the seeds are uprooted *before* they ripen into the results.

2. *Karma is expandable.* One tiny action will result in magnified results and multiple ones. Planting a single tree seed in conducive conditions will result in a tree with thousands of branches, thousands of flowers, and thousands of seeds. All these come from planting one small seed.

Of course we may not see the results of this one small seed in one season. It takes time for conditions to come together for germination. But when those conditions do, the result of this one small seed will be much greater than the seed itself.

By understanding how even a small action can produce results far exceeding the action itself, one understands how small good karmas or actions can bring about great positive results. Conversely, one should not be careless about small negative karmas, for they too produce great negative results. Do not be careless and do not be lazy.

3. *We would not experience a result if we did not create the cause for it.* It is enormously helpful to remember that all experiences are karmically caused. Without our actions that planted a karmic seed, a result would not arise.

A tomato does not simply appear out of nowhere. If we are holding a tomato it means a tomato seed was planted and the seed met good conditions, resulting in the tomato we hold. Without creating the cause for the tomato through planting its seed, there would be no tomato.

Therefore getting upset about our problems or blaming others for them is unreasonable because we created the cause for our own problems. Plant the seeds whose results we seek and remove the seeds of results we wish to avoid. If we wish to avoid problems, we should avoid creating negative karma. Whether we suffer or are happy is entirely in our hands. The choice is ours about the physical actions we take, the things we say, and the thoughts we have.

4. *Karma that has been committed and collected will never disappear on its own.* The karmic seeds of future results are never lost, even if the negative or positive actions are small. For eons the karmic seed could remain like a plant seed lying dormant in the ground until it is activated by conditions coming together. When that small karmic seed meets those favorable conditions, even after an incredible length of time, the seed will grow and the result will ripen.

Unless and until the seed is removed, the result is definite. Therefore whatever we experience now, the happy moments and the miserable moments, all came from past actions whose karmic seeds were not destroyed. Conditions came together and seeds ripened into whatever we now experience. Accumulated karma will not disappear by itself. As long as negative karmas are not purified by Dharma remedies, no matter how many eons pass we will encounter the suffering results. It is the same with virtuous karmas, which, no matter how small, will generate magnified results.

As an example of the fruit of positive karma: There was once a very poor artist in Solukhumbu who earned a living by carving the prayer *Om mani padme hum*, the mantra of Avalokiteshvara, on stone. People would request this carving for themselves and, instead of money, would offer food and wine as payment. Although the carving was his livelihood, he recited that mantra extensively and did so with goodwill toward everyone.

When the artist passed away his wife had him cremated. After the cremation she noticed that while his forehead bone was black from the burning, the mantra *Om mani padme hum* appeared etched into the bone in white. The wife offered that bone relic to a great lama meditator, who asked me to keep it in the monastery.

As an example of the fruit of negative karma: A dying villager was having much difficulty, so much so that a monk was called to the man's house to help him. The dying man was screaming a lot and gritting his teeth with his eyes wide open in fear. He kept screaming, "I am going to be killed! So many sheep around! They are attacking me!" He yelled this again and again with a very frightened face.

The monk inquired into this man's life and found out that earlier he had worked as a butcher in Tibet and had slaughtered many sheep. Because this heavy karma of killing had not been purified, he started to experience the suffering result of that negative karma just before death. He was terrified. His death was not peaceful and there were signs he would be reborn in the lower realms to fully experience the result of the negative karma.

Four factors for complete karma

Four factors must be present for complete karma to arise: intention, the object, the action itself, and the accomplishment of the intention.

Without all four conditions the karma is incomplete and the results will be lighter and different.

For the complete karma of killing there needs to be the intention to kill due to a delusion such as attachment, anger, or pride, and then there needs to be an object of our intent to kill. This object needs to be a sentient being that is alive and has a mind. Thus the full karma of killing requires an intention to kill, a sentient being to be killed, the action of killing, and the accomplishment of the intent—the death of the intended object.

If we die before the intended object dies, the karma of killing is not completed. While there is negativity, the completed karma of killing has not occurred. But when these four factors of intention, object, action, and accomplishment of the intent are present, the completed karma occurs.

Let us say we want a piece of animal fur. We go out to hunt. We spot the intended animal and, due to our attachment in wanting that animal's fur, we fire our gun and carry out the act of killing, so that the animal dies. We then feel pleased that our intention has been fulfilled. Right there arises the completed karma, the completed nonvirtue of killing, beginning the cycle that will bring us suffering results.

However, there are situations where all four factors of intention, object, action, and accomplishment of the intent are not present. For instance, we may kill an animal without intending to, which means that only some of the four factors are present. In such a case, the killing happened but the karma is incomplete.

Negative results from such a killing will follow but will differ from the results we would have experienced had all four factors been present. The differing consequences from complete and incomplete karma are seen in one's rebirth and conditions of rebirth. These are referred to as throwing karma and completing karma, respectively.

Throwing and completing karma

Throwing karma refers to a situation where all four elements of intent, object, deed, and accomplishment of intent are present when we do an action. The karmic result from that is to "throw" us into a birth within the suffering realms. The term sounds a little awkward but is a literal translation from the Tibetan term *penchey leh*.

In this context *pen* means like shooting an arrow. Throwing karma "throws" us into a specific realm of future rebirth. For instance, negative actions done under the strong influence of any of the delusions will throw us into a rebirth in the hell realms.

Finishing or *completing karma*, on the other hand, arises when all four factors are not present when we commit an act. Completing karma affects the conditions we experience in a future rebirth. For example, a person might knowingly fail to keep good ethics, but engage in generosity out of some feeling of unease at past deeds. The negative throwing karma of the deliberate breach of ethics will cause the person to be reborn in the animal realm, perhaps as a dog. But the positive completing karma of generosity (although done with some questionable motivation) will cause that person to be reborn in good conditions like living with a family that loves dogs and treats dogs well.

Right now we have been born human. This is due to the positive throwing karma created from our positive actions in past lives that have propelled us to a human rebirth. The pleasures we are now receiving are the finishing or completing karma of past virtuous deeds.

However, it should be understood that as we experience these pleasures, the past good karma seeds that make them possible get extinguished. Each time we are able to heartily eat and drink is the result of previous good karmas. While we are experiencing and enjoying these results of past actions, the karma to continue enjoying them is depleting. This is why even those who have no aspiration toward liberation and seek only a happy life still need to continuously engage in virtue.

Heavy or light karmas

Aside from the karma being complete or incomplete, the results from actions are also influenced by whether the nature of an action is karmically heavy or light. Whether a karma or action is heavy or light depends on the intensity of the thought that accompanies the action and the manner of carrying out the action. For instance, insulting a person with intense hatred will generate negative karma that is heavy from the aspect of thought. If a person kills a goat, but before killing it he starves, beats, and tortures the goat so it suffers for a long time, heavy karma is generated from the side of the action.

Another determinant of heaviness of karma is in relation to the object of our thoughts and actions. For example, insulting or beating people, such as our parents or monks or nuns, creates very heavy karma. Speaking to or looking at our gurus with anger and disrespect also creates heavy karma from the side of the object. Karma can also become heavy through repeated action, such as when we habitually gossip for no beneficial purpose. Such karma becomes heavy when neither remedy nor purification is applied.

Karmic results

It is extremely important to understand the four types of karmic results or at least have an idea about them. While both positive and negative actions generate results, given how easy it is for negative karma to arise in our lives, let us look at the four types of negative karmic results.

Ripened results. This refers to the realm where we are reborn. Completed negative karmas will cause us to be reborn in the lower realms as a suffering hell being, a hungry ghost, or an animal experiencing very heavy sufferings for billions of years until our negative karma finishes.

An effective preventive measure is to live according to vows. These can be lay vows, one-day eight-precept vows, or ordination vows, because they help us to change our way of doing things and to refrain from killing.

Results similar to the cause. The basic principle here is that if we have inflicted harm on others we will receive harm. Even if due to the ripening of some past positive karma we gain a human rebirth, the prior harm we inflicted may mean our lives are short, we die suddenly, we die in our mother's womb, or our lives are cut short by others or through suicide.

Possessed results. These possessed results are sometimes called environmental results. For instance, harming others may result in our living in a place where there are no resources, or a place that presents many dangers and no one to protect us.

Dangerous places could include regions where suitable medicine can't be found for illnesses, or places with forms of harm such as wars, aggressive people, fierce animals, or insects that sting. In some African countries weather is a major problem and people there suffer severe droughts or terrible floods, causing homes to be lost and crops to fail. In many places planted seeds are eaten by worms, burned in bush fires, or simply do not grow.

Result of repeatedly creating the causes of suffering. Even if we are born into a higher realm like that of humans, a previous negative habit, such as taking others' lives, can give us a taste for killing and thereby create fresh causes for suffering.

People who do not understand karma, and the karmic imprints on the mental continuum that move into future lives, use words like "instinct" to try to explain human behavior. They theorize the inclination to harm comes from the genes or from a brain disorder, but there is no proof of this. It is extremely helpful to understand how we repeatedly commit negativities due to imprints and the habitual harming of others.

Let us see how these four types of results play out for each of the ten nonvirtues, these ten commonplace actions that all of us have committed at some stage in our lives.

THE TEN NONVIRTUES

When examining karma, use the above four characteristics of karma to better understand life. In addition it is worthwhile to reflect on the ten nonvirtues, actions we take in our daily lives, often unconsciously.

The ten nonvirtues does not mean we commit only ten negative actions. However, focusing on these ten nonvirtues gives us some idea of our negative habits, the karmic seeds we continually plant. We need to recognize our negative actions before we can purify them, so we can avoid their suffering results.

Of the ten nonvirtues, three relate to actions of the body, four relate to actions of speech, and three relate to the actions of mind. The three nonvirtues of the body are killing, stealing, and sexual misconduct. The four nonvirtues of speech are lying, harsh speech, divisive speech, and gossip. The three nonvirtues of mind are covetousness, ill will, and wrong view.

Some of the nonvirtues are heavier in terms of karmic negativity, while some are lighter. Generally the nonvirtues of body and speech are heavy in negative karma in descending order, so that, for example, killing is heavier karma than stealing, and lying is heavier karma than gossip. However, the nonvirtues of mind are in ascending order, so that the heaviest karma is wrong view.

We might protest, "But I am a decent person. I have not killed anyone and I have done good deeds, so why should I be experiencing any suffering now?"

One reason is that even though we have created positive karma and done virtuous deeds, those deeds have not been perfect. To make any virtuous action perfect we need three elements: pure motivation, virtuous action, and dedicating the virtue for the welfare of all sentient beings. If any of these three are missing, the virtuous action is not that powerful. On the other hand, when we commit negative actions we tend to do those perfectly. We start a negative act with clear intention, we are clear about whom we intend to act on, we carry out the action willfully, and we feel satisfaction when we complete the act.

For example, if a bug bites us we instantly decide to end its life, seize it, and kill it between our nails. As the bug dies we experience satisfaction in the mind, thinking, "Ah, I've finished off this bug who irritated me." Our minds tend to work this way and thus our negative actions are karmically very strong.

Another reason is that planted seeds need time for conditions to gather before young shoots appear, let alone fruits. Likewise with karmic seeds.

A further reason we face problems, despite creating some positive karma, is that we erase the merit due to our limited control over our anger and our negative minds. We allow resentment or wrong view to arise strongly, which can destroy the virtue we just committed! Like a burned seed, the positive karmic imprint no longer can bring about a good result.

Anger and negative mind can render merits impotent and strip them of their potential to actualize into happiness. Even when we commit perfect virtues, the arising of the uncontrolled negative mind prevents the quick fruition of the karmic result. The negative mind can postpone a happy result for a long time, even one hundred eons. This depends on the negative action and also on whom or what we get angry at, or where we direct wrong view.

For instance, developing wrong view or an angry mind toward a person with higher spiritual realizations than ourselves will for a long time interrupt the result of happiness created by virtues. Since we're unable to know who is spiritually higher than ourselves, it is wise to not have negative mind toward anyone!

Whether an act is positive or not is not determined by an action itself. It is the thought or motivation behind the act that is important. If we do an action with pure motivation, that action will bring benefit to us; conversely, if our action is made with attachment or anger, the action will bring its own troublesome results.

There are, however, exceptions. For example, if we make an offering to a holy object like a Buddha statue or a stupa, which is the representation of the enlightened mind, then even if our mind is in a negative state while making the offering, through the power of the holy object the offering is still a positive action.

While motivation distinguishes virtue from nonvirtue, just pure motivation alone is not enough to ensure the action is appropriate. We also need wisdom. For example, you may wish to offer tea to your Dharma teacher but unknowingly offer contaminated tea that makes him sick. Although your motivation was good, you didn't have the wisdom to know the condition of your teacher nor the wisdom to discover the tea was contaminated. Therefore, both good motivation and wisdom are required for an action to be positive and appropriate.

It is helpful to regularly reflect on these ten nonvirtues to see how easily we slip into doing them. It enables us to recognize, "Oh, I have done this (a particular nonvirtue) before. Because karma is definite and expandable, I am now facing this trouble, which will not go away unless I purify the cause."

This approach can provide an explanation to our sometimes confusing lives. It shows us we have freedom of choice, and it encourages us to more seriously apply antidotes to the delusions. It alerts us to the need for purification, and it helps us avoid future repeats of negative actions.

Let us look at the four types of karmic results for each of the ten nonvirtues of body, speech, and mind.

Killing

- We are reborn in the hell realms.
- Even if we are reborn human, we are stricken by deadly diseases and have a short life span.
- We may be reborn in a country where conflicts and wars are common and where food and medicines are scarce.
- We become habituated to killing.

I visited New Zealand some time ago, and there was a news report on the problem of an unbelievable number of rabbits attacking crops and farmlands. This was due to the karma of the people. The authorities thought the solution would be to kill rabbits, but think for a moment—what is the connection between rabbits coming to eat crops and the people living there?

Some people thought that by killing the rabbits they could once again enjoy their property. But they needed to ask how this happened in the first place. By harming living beings we create the cause to receive harm. So if people have created the karma that results in rabbits attacking crops, it will happen. More killing is not the solution.

Stealing

- We are reborn in the hungry ghost realm.
- Even if we are reborn as a human, we will experience extreme poverty or frequent theft of our possessions.
- We are reborn in a country with much destruction and hailstorms.
- We become habituated to stealing.

Some people lose their things all the time or regularly have their things stolen by other people. When this happens to us, remember, "What I am experiencing is the result of my past actions of taking what does not belong to me."

Sexual misconduct

- We are reborn in the animal realm.
- Even if we are reborn a human, our spouse or partner will be hostile and unfaithful. Quarrels with loved ones will be frequent and even family members appear as enemies. There will be disharmony all around.
- We are reborn in a place that is dirty and smelly, filled with excrement, dirt, and garbage. Our environment and dwellings will be unhygienic and unpleasant.
- We will become habituated to sexual misconduct.

Even though we might not live in a filthy place, we might have to walk or drive past dirty places on the way to work, on the return home, or going somewhere. That too is the result of our past sexual misconduct.

Telling lies

- We are reborn in the animal realm.
- Even if we are reborn human, we are constantly accused and disbelieved by others, even when we speak the truth.
- We are reborn in a thorny place.
- We are habituated to lying.

Harsh speech

- We are reborn in the hells.
- Even if we are reborn human, we are subject to abuse and distressing words.
- We are reborn in a desert country of limited resources.
- We become habituated to harsh speech.

Many people live in places rife with prickly bushes and rough terrain, places that are difficult to get to or from and that offer little comfort. This is the result of past harsh speech.

Harsh speech is not just about negative, abusive words. It includes words that sound nice but that are intended to hurt another person's mind.

Divisive speech

- We are reborn in the hells.
- Even if we are reborn human, we are separated from loved ones and surrounded by untrustworthy, deceptive people.
- We are reborn in places with bumpy and cracked roads.
- We become habituated to divisive speech.

Saying things that cause relationships to break or that weaken already troubled relationships and create great disharmony and suffering are examples of divisive speech. This explains the heavy results.

Gossip

- We are reborn in the animal realm.
- Even if we are reborn a human, we have no credibility, discipline, or virtue in speech. No one respects anything we say.
- We are reborn in a place with reversed summer and winter seasons, where wells go dry.
- We are habituated to gossiping.

A result of gossiping is that in the place where we live trees do not bear fruit. Even when they do, the fruit does not appear at the right time or when we need it. The fruit may appear ripe, but when we pluck them we discover that they are unripe. Our fruit trees and crops lack stable roots and do not endure.

Covetousness

- We are reborn in the hungry ghost realm.
- Even if we are reborn human, we suffer constant discontent and failure in everything we do.
- We are reborn in an isolated area without help or resources.
- We are habituated to being covetous.

This grasping mind produces the heavy karmic consequences of poverty, so that whatever is precious to us declines. Each year our crops and our possessions decline. Year by year, month by month, our opportunities decrease. Therefore we should guard our mind when we go out shopping because attachment to sense objects displayed generates covetousness, leading us to buy those products with a grasping mind.

When you next go shopping be alert to these karmic dangers by renouncing samsara, and shop with the compassionate motivation to help sentient beings instead of acting solely for your own personal happiness. That way shopping does not become covetousness. It's best if we can shop with right view, contemplating how our minds create mental labels and how all things lack inherent existence.

Malice or ill will

- We are reborn in the hells.
- Even if we are reborn human, we are always in danger of being harmed.
- We are reborn in a place with only foul-tasting food.
- We're habituated to ill will.

Because of our ill will we experience karmic results including contagious diseases that are life-threatening, wars, and being bitten by snakes, scorpions, and stinging insects. When animals or insects bite us, reflect on how we're experiencing the karmic results of our past ill will toward others. Why get angry? The insect is just a condition, it did not cause our experience of discomfort. The bite and our unpleasant experience was caused by our earlier action, based on delusions.

I recall when the Indian town of Dharamsala was flooded with reports of the spread of a new life-threatening disease. His Holiness Dalai Lama advised people to sincerely pray to avert the disease, for the sake of all living beings. Many laypeople would go to the nearby McLeod Ganj stupa after their office hours to turn prayer wheels and recite the prayer of Lochama, a healing deity. The disease never became an epidemic in Dharamsala. Such diseases arise due to the past negative karma of ill will.

Wrong view

- We are reborn in the animal realm.
- Even if we are reborn human, we experience fear many times during our lives and our ignorance deepens.
- We are reborn in a place where no crops or fruit grow to nourish us.
- We're habituated to wrong views.

After analyzing all these karmic results, it's clear we should take great care to avoid the ten nonvirtues. Instead, we should carry out the opposite virtuous actions, and we will have a healthy and bountiful life and good relations with everyone, and will live in pleasant, gentle surroundings. Each day we should recognize how our life enjoyments came from our past good karma and our problems came from our negative karma. *We* created all of our life experiences. Our recognition of this fact will encourage us to abandon negative karma and to practice virtues, which are the basis of all happiness.

Steering clear of the ten nonvirtues is of much greater value than possessing many jewels. Material possessions never bring lasting happiness, realizations, or enlightenment. In fact in the hands of those lacking Dharma understanding and mindfulness, possessions cause further delusions, grasping, and suffering.

We need to be honest. Acknowledge our negative karma, purify it, and live our lives by following the path of ethics and virtue. Just as a rice seed can be burned or uprooted, the harmful seeds of delusion can be expelled by reflecting on the karmic process. This is why it is crucial to observe the law of cause and effect if we seek happiness and wish to avoid problems.

Dromtonpa, the great Kadampa master and devoted disciple of Lama Atisha, once asked his master, "What result will the actions created with ignorance, greed, and anger bring?" Atisha answered, "A rebirth in the suffering realms of a hell being, a hungry ghost, or an animal." Conversely, actions done purely, without ignorance, attachment, or anger, are the cause of all happiness.

Therefore renouncing suffering and overcoming the delusions is the actual Dharma, which becomes a field of all happiness in our present and future lives and the cause of enlightenment. Not harming others and doing things only to benefit them brings immediate happiness and peace to our minds. Life's problems simply fall away. Dharma is the medicine to stop all suffering.

Once a layperson yogi, with a family, discovered he had leprosy. His wounds had spread and he remained very ill for a long time. His own family became afraid of him and kept him in isolation. At first he got very upset at this situation. He was abandoned by his family and had no one to care for him. However, he then made a decision: "If I have to be out of the family, so be it. There is no need for me to be attached to anyone or angry at anyone. I will just live by the roadside, recite prayers for all sentient beings, and beg for food from people."

So he did just that. There was a cave near that road and he spent the first night there. That night he dreamed that a person came to him and placed him on a rock, under heavy rain. When the man woke up all the pus in his wounds had flowed out, leaving him wet but totally healed. His decision to renounce suffering and focus his mind on Dharma cured him and brought happiness to his life.

STORAGE OF KARMIC IMPRINTS

Where are all the karmic imprints arising from our actions of body, speech, and mind stored? They are stored in our minds or consciousnesses. The mind holds all the imprints, it warehouses all the karmic seeds and potential left by karma, by our actions. A seed's potential determines the growth of a good- or bad-quality plant. Similarly, all the imprints for samsaric happiness and suffering are contained in our consciousnesses or mental continuums.

All the imprints for rebirth are held in our consciousnesses, whether as a god-realm being or a human being. All the imprints for a suffering rebirth as an animal with little opportunity for temporal happiness, or as a hungry ghost experiencing the intense sufferings of hunger and thirst, or as a hell being enduring the heaviest sufferings of heat and cold are also held in our consciousnesses. The type of seeds planted is entirely up to us.

Craving and grasping act like heat and water by nourishing the germination of karmic seeds that we planted in our own consciousnesses, like cultivators in the field of karma. When the consciousness carrying an imprint joins to the next life, and if the next rebirth is as a human being, the consciousness enters the mother's womb, and when the child is finally born it is possessed of that imprint.

This is why the Buddha taught that every experience of living beings, of objects or situations, comes from our own minds that are carrying imprints. We should remember this every day, every hour, every minute of this life. Your body, from your head to your toes, has come from your own consciousness. There were external cooperative causes, such as our parents, but your existence came from your mental continuum embedded with the imprints you created in the past.

In this manner our bodies came from our own minds. All that is beautiful and desirable, all that is ugly and undesirable, all that is neutral and that we are indifferent to, everything that we encounter every day has come from our own minds. Remember the video and projector we talked about earlier? The video device's memory has many images recorded on it. With the conditions of a projector, electricity, and a screen, the filmed images can be seen. What is projected is completely dependent on what is captured by the device.

Likewise with the imprints on our consciousnesses. These imprints have been left on our consciousnesses by our actions. When these karmic seeds meet suitable conditions over time they get actualized and experienced. We call this the ripening of karma. When this happens we perceive an experience right there, which can be of a person, an object, or a situation, just like the video we see on the screen.

Therefore when we are in trouble or unhappy, blaming external circumstances is missing the point and is totally inappropriate. Just as without recorded images there would be no video to project, without the karmic imprint we ourselves planted there would be no experience to perceive!

Karma is an action that comes from a thought influenced by delusions and karmic imprints. Consequences follow. Every experience is born from karma. All the various worlds are born from karma. All good and bad appearances from birth until death, including how we perceive our own bodies and our worlds, come from the field of karma.

ALL APPEARANCES ARE KARMIC PROJECTIONS

A person's specific karmic vision is such that what that person sees is not shared in an identical way by others. For instance, in a hot country some people really suffer from the heat, whereas others enjoy the heat. Both experiences are karmic results determined by the individual's karma.

A person's experience does not depend on external conditions but mainly on the person's mind. One person's mind can be completely happy with a given situation while another person's mind is totally miserable. It is not up to the circumstances. It is up to the perceiver's mind. In this way, everything is created by mind, by individual karmic viewpoints.

Therefore our entire lives and experiences come from our own minds, so there is nothing and no one to blame. Whatever problem happens there is no one to blame except ourselves, the negative karma we created in the past that now compels us to perceive the situation as a problem. By following wrong conceptions and delusions we accumulated this karma, we created our own movies, our life experiences. There is nobody else to blame for it!

If somebody criticizes, harms, or even comes to kill us, there is actually no one to blame except ourselves. The appearance of this harmful person comes from our negative minds that caused us to commit negative karma. As for our enjoyments and people who respect and help us, they too come from our own minds, from the good thoughts and good karma we committed.

Can you now see why there is no reason at all to get angry at anybody and no reason to grasp at anything? Appearances come from our minds, they are our creation. There is no point in clinging to our own creations. We made them up and clung to them, and that has brought us countless problems.

Similarly, there is no reason to be jealous or proud. We can relate to all the other delusions in the same way. If we had not created the karma that left this imprint of ignorance, we would not now have all our relationship problems, failures, criticisms, and harm from others. We planted the seed, so why blame it on others?

Our turbulent minds steady when we understand through reason and analysis that we are responsible for all that happens to us, that it all originated from our actions influenced by the delusions imprinted on our minds. This understanding brings a form of peace to ourselves, and hence to others. It is a kind of relief because life's problems are no longer a mystery. We now know where they came from and how to get rid of them. This becomes the best reason to practice patience, which subdues anger that comes from the dissatisfied mind of attachment.

Some people may see a place as incredibly beautiful, while others may see the same place as ugly. If a hundred people look at a particular place, each person will have a different perception. This is due to differing karmic projections. All these various appearances come from our own minds. The perception we have of a person or a place comes from our own minds. Every hour and minute we see different things: trees, flowers, roads, people, and situations. Every single appearance or view comes from our own minds. Even the word "view" has to do with how our minds think.

All appearances are like dreams, and whether they are pleasant or unpleasant is completely due to the mind. For instance, an unpleasant experience may arise from unpurified negative imprints, which remained dormant until they met supporting conditions that actualized them into negative appearances or experiences. When this happens we see something negative, like someone harming us. Even if another person is not harming us, or indeed even if that person is an enlightened being, because our karma is tainted by negativity we will have a negative view of that person and we will have problems with that person.

Likewise, due to previous angry karmic imprints, when we meet a particular object that triggers aversion, anger arises because the seed of anger has not been erased. Even when a most beloved friend from whom we cannot be separated changes his manner of looking at us or speaking to us, right in that minute he can become an object of our anger. Previously we might have thought, "I will never get angry with him. How could I get angry with my best friend?"

But karmic seeds of anger can transform a once-favored object into something undesirable. The main point is that the negative imprint has not been removed. The second thing is that this undesirable appearance comes from our karma. Third, because we do not regularly practice patience, loving-kindness, and compassion, our minds are vulnerable to being overwhelmed by anger. Failure to apply antidotes to delusions, as and when they arise, constantly endangers our peace of mind.

Therefore strive to remove the negative imprints of delusions. Without them there will be no negative karma committed and no results of suffering to endure. Getting rid of delusions is a one-time solution. Without the imprints of delusions we experience no harm.

Ignorance, attachment, and anger bring about terrifying emotional states. They arise dependently on negative karmic imprints. Our perception of an object is solely due to our own minds. The basis on which we discriminate, whether we like something or not, comes from our own minds. This is the result of past karma, of our thoughts and actions. Samsara is created by the arising of delusions and by the actions that flow from them.

A doctor in Delhi who researched the causes of heart attacks found that many sicknesses are related to strongly negative minds that think other people are bad and frequently put negative labels on them. I am certain there are many people whose intense negative thoughts have brought on death from heart attacks.

Once we put a negative label on a person or a situation we whole-heartedly believe the label. From that moment, the person or situation represents something bad every time we encounter it. This then causes us upset and unease. We have forgotten that we authored that experience.

Walking meditation is very useful. We normally look at our surroundings when out for a stroll, but with walking meditation we look with a new awareness that what we see is our own karmic projection. Be aware of the six sense objects, and be aware of how our perception of every single thing we encounter—people, objects, flowers, places—are all influenced by our karma, our thoughts. This awareness that we are the creator of our own happiness and our problems is a pivotal point in Buddhism. No one else creates our happiness and suffering. We alone are responsible.

We now have an idea how suffering and the causes of suffering dependently arise. Once we have achieved the complete cessation of delusions and karma, it is impossible for suffering and the cause of suffering to arise again. Since everything comes from our minds, we need to be careful with this inner mental factory that never stops, use mindfulness to prevent negative thoughts from controlling us, and as much as possible keep our minds in virtue and infused with a positive attitude.

The essential thing is to have a good heart, to never harm others, and to benefit them as best you can. Consciousness and all the imprints it carries joined your past life to this present life and will join you to your next life. This process is more elaborately explained by the next discussion on the twelve links of interdependent origination, also known as the twelve links.

THE TWELVE LINKS OF INTERDEPENDENT ORIGINATION

How do delusion and karma cause life in samsara and its continuation in different bodies?

Over beginningless lives the imprints of ignorance have pervaded our consciousness. When we commit actions or karma out of ignorance, those actions leave an impression or seed on the consciousness. As the end of life approaches, craving and grasping arise, nourishing the karmic seeds. Craving is a deluded thought that does not want to be separated from the object. Grasping is a deluded thought that enhances craving, for example, grasping at the mistaken view of the truly existing "I."

Craving and grasping acting on karmic seeds give rise to becoming, generating the potential for actualization. Rebirth then follows. Life begins when consciousness enters the mother's womb. The fertilized egg is form, while name refers to consciousness, feeling, cognition, and internal phenomena. Due to name and form the six senses arise, which then make contact with others under the influence of delusion. From this contact deluded feelings arise, and then old age and death follow.

Delusions and karma are imprinted on consciousness and bind the mind to the body like a heavy sack tied to a person's back. When we cut off the burden of delusion and karma, the mind is set free. Only then do problems end. In order to sever the chain that shackles us to samsara, we must understand the process of the twelve links of interdependent origination.

In the *Rice Planting Sutra*, Buddha explained the twelve interdependent links in the evolution of samsara and how one is reborn in samsara. Ignorance is like the farmer who sows seeds in the field, while consciousness is like the field where various crops grow.

The karmic seeds imprinted on the consciousness are carried from life to life. Through a single tiny action we sow one small seed from which a huge tree comes into being, complete with trunk and thousands of branches and leaves. From one small seed can grow the Banyan tree, which in India can have so many branches that it covers many horse carriages placed under the tree for the shade. Consciousness carrying karmic seeds is like that. Craving and grasping act like nutrients to those karmic seeds, so they are made ready to produce results, to become the results. When the result sprouts it acquires name and form.

In this manner the three delusions of ignorance, craving, and grasping, combined with the two actions of compounded action and becoming, give rise to the seven results that are name and form, the six sense bases, contact, feeling, birth, old age, and death. All these results are of the nature of suffering. The seven results originated from ignorance imprinted on the consciousness, followed by compounded karmic action. For us right now, what is left of the seven results is death. Our aging started from our mother's womb, straight after birth. The only result pending is death.

We are presently in the stage of aging. Ignorance and its seeds operate within our consciousness while we experience the results of the twelve links, causing us to continue to create many karmic formations in a single day. This will bring future rebirth as different samsaric beings.

Just think of it. In just one day we can start multiple sets of the twelve links to be born as an insect, a hungry ghost, a hell being, a god-realm being, or a demigod. Most of the time we create the karma to be born as lower-realm suffering beings, which happens so easily. Therefore what causes us to circle in samsara are delusion and karma. Master Nagarjuna comments on this:

> Two of them derive from three,
> seven of them derive from the two,
> and from the seven, the three occur again.
> That is the Wheel of Life, and so it turns and turns.

Let us take a look at the drawing of the Wheel of Life, which explains the nature of samsara and the twelve links.

The Wheel of Life is always held in the mouth of Yama, whose figure symbolizes death. The Wheel of Life illustration shows how living beings are controlled by death and rebirth, living in impermanence and circling in the cycle of death and rebirth. The two pairs of limbs holding the Wheel of Life represent suffering and the cause of suffering.

The drawing of the twelve links appears in the outer rim of the Wheel of Life.

1. *Ignorance.* There are two types, ignorance of the nature of reality and ignorance of karma. When ignorance of the nature of reality ceases, ignorance of karma also ceases. Ignorance of karma (depicted by the blind man) arises from basic ignorance of the nature of reality.

2. *Karmic formation.* This is action under the influence of ignorance. Ignorance creates many kinds of karma, just as a potter makes many different kinds of pots.

3. *Consciousness.* Just as the monkey swings from tree to tree, consciousness goes from rebirth to rebirth, from the past life to the present life and on to the next. The journey of consciousness depends on karma. Consciousness or mind is the place where karmic actions leave impressions or imprints.

4. *Name and form.* This refers to the physical and mental aggregates of form, consciousness, feeling, discrimination, and compositional factors/karmic imprints.

5. *Six sense organs.* Due to name and form, these six senses come about. There are two aspects to consider: the six objects of the senses and the bare consciousness of each of the six sense organs.

6. *Contact.* When contact occurs and the six senses meet with their objects, perceptions of pleasant, unpleasant, or neutral arise.

7. *Feeling.* There are three kinds of feelings: pleasure that causes greed to arise, unpleasantness that brings about aversion and anger, and indifference that causes ignorance to arise.

8. *Craving.* After a being experiences pleasure and unpleasantness, craving arises from not wanting to be separated from the object of desire, or there is craving to be separated from the unpleasant.

9. *Grasping.* The grasping mind deepens craving and includes clinging to mistaken concepts like the "truly existent I." According to one story, once in ancient India there was a Hindu who through meditation remembered his immediate previous life as a dog.

Once he realized he had been a dog in his previous life and now was human, he mistakenly concluded he had to act like a dog to be born again as a human. So the man crawled on the ground and behaved like a dog. We can see how grasping is a delusion.

10. *Becoming.* This refers to the potential for actualization, or preparing for a result to manifest. The readiness for the next rebirth is fueled by craving and grasping.

11. *Rebirth.* The stage of becoming gives rise to birth. Sentient beings are born in four ways: through the womb, through the egg, through heat, and through intuitive rebirth, which doesn't depend on parents.

12. *Old age and death.* These are put together because old age and the passage toward death begin from birth. The signs of old age are not assured for everyone, because many beings die before displaying the signs of old age.

The quote from Master Nagarjuna is very effective to reflect on, as it shows how the twelve interdependent links work, how the cycle goes around and around. The two deluded actions are karmic formation and becoming; the three deluded causes are ignorance, craving, and grasping; and the seven uncontrolled results arise from them. This is how life in samsara continues.

Our consciousness is like a basket of billions and billions of imprints, potentials, and seeds of all kinds. These cause us to take all kinds of samsaric rebirths, some of them strange, such as bodies we may have never seen in our lives, or very fearful looking bodies that are big or tiny. Incredible numbers of seeds are already in our consciousness. The seeds will gradually manifest into results according to the intricacies of karma, with, for instance, the heaviest karmic imprints experienced first, followed by the karma we're habituated to, the karma that was done first, and so on.

Just like planting different seeds, such as corn, rice, and wheat, in a big field, through ignorance and karma in previous lives we have already set in motion the twelve links of an incredible number of samsaric bodies to come. If we fail to discipline the mind away from negative action, if we do not create stronger positive karma right now in this life, the results from the twelve links of each of the billion imprints will manifest, bringing us suffering samsaric lives as animals, hungry ghosts, hell beings, angry demigods, and others.

Right at this moment we have a chance to take the better path. We still have this chance. We do this by creating stronger good karma than the karma that causes us to be reborn in an animal realm, for instance, as a snake or a crocodile. We can create positive karma stronger than the negative karma that will cause an animal rebirth, thus creating the cause for rebirth as a human again.

We are on our way to finishing the seven results of the twelve links of this present human body. The cause for these was created in a previous life, so now we are finishing the results. Yet to be finished is death.

However, even if we can stop the result of a lower rebirth as an animal and instead be born as a human, this does not mean the twelve links of that animal rebirth have ceased. Until the karmic seed for an animal rebirth is completely uprooted, the potential for us to experience the twelve links of an animal remains. Thus our only chance to be reborn as a human being is to prevent the craving, grasping, and becoming of an animal by the end of this life.

Therefore, as we have been born as a human being, we need to think carefully about strengthening our resolve to practice the path that breaks the chain of samsara and destroys ignorance, which stops karma and all negative karmic seeds. If we do not do this, an infinite number of troublesome, samsaric rebirths await.

We now have an idea of how deeply ensnared we are by samsara. We are like a person heavily squeezed by a massive red-hot iron. Unable to move we experience pressure and intense painful heat. Feeling tight and hot is the nature of samsara. The twelve links finish in either two lives or in the third life. But eons can occur between the karmic formation, the craving and grasping, becoming, and the seven results.

To see why and how karmic seeds ripen in subsequent lives, it is useful to see how the links operate in groups. Ignorance motivates karma, giving rise to compositional activity or karmic imprints, which are like seeds left on the consciousness. At this time the consciousness is called the consciousness at the time of the cause, as it carries the imprint from an action freshly done. These three links (links 1, 2, 3) of ignorance, karmic imprints, and consciousness at the time of the cause are called the throwing or projecting limb, as in throwing into a future rebirth. Craving and grasping (links 8 and 9) then nourish the karmic imprint into producing a result, the becoming (link 10).

Craving arises by clinging to the three types of feeling—pleasant, unpleasant, and neutral—which increase in intensity, leading to grasping. The combined effect of craving and grasping brings the imprint closer to fruition or actualization into a result. These three links of craving, grasping, and becoming are called the establishing limb. If the karma is to ripen in two lifetimes, these six links will occur in the first life.

The projected limb consists of consciousness at the time of the result, namely, the ripened aggregates represented by name and form, the six senses, contact, and feeling (links 4, 5, 6, 7). After the consciousness, name and form, and six senses make contact with an object, feelings of pleasant, unpleasant, or neutral arise. The result or established limb is the "birth link" (link 11), which results in aging and death (link 12).

From the moment of birth, aging and decay begin. Aging is not only about wrinkles and white hair. Death can happen before what people ordinarily call old age. Death can happen at any time. Many die in the womb.

At death the consciousness, which is still under the control of karma and delusions, separates from the body. The body ceases but consciousness continues, carrying whatever imprints are planted in it into the future life. Those imprints then cause us to again commit thoughts and actions habituated by delusions, dooming us to again experience the resultant sufferings. These twelve links explain the process of samsara.

Without question it is very useful to meditate on the twelve links and how we have already started numberless sets of twelve links from the past until this minute. Only when we fully understand the cyclic suffering of samsara will we grow weary of it and become willing to renounce it. When we generate renunciation of samsara there is no place for the corrosive eight worldly concerns or attachment to samsaric pleasure.

Sometimes we tell ourselves, "I know samsara." But if there is no change in our minds and our actions we will not have fully renounced samsara but will have achieved only a halfhearted, partial renunciation.

As Lama Tsongkhapa said, "When there is the intuitive desire day and night to seek liberation, at that time the renounced mind of the samsara is attained." Just as a being trapped on a red-hot, burning iron ground constantly seeks release, so should we seek to be freed from samsara.

The twelve links illustrate how the suffering of samsara comes about, and at the same time they also explain the true cessation of suffering. The seven results arose through the force of delusion and karma. Stopping the suffering of death, old age, and birth depends on stopping the stage of becoming. This depends on stopping craving and grasping, which in turn depends on stopping the karmic formation (otherwise called compositional activity), which in turn depends on ceasing ignorance.

This is a very important point to understand. Removing ignorance is the key to avoiding experiencing all these sufferings. Every single problem in the whole of samsara arises from ignorance.

What is the method to destroy ignorance? It is to realize how all things dependently arise and are thus empty of inherent existence. Through this path we can be released from samsara and from all suffering.

A consciousness imprinted with ignorance commits actions tainted with ignorance and with the host of other delusions. This in turn leaves more such imprints on that consciousness. During life and at the time of death craving and grasping arise easily, rendering the imprints ready to be manifested as another samsaric body in rebirth. As our aggregates are caused by delusions and karma, they cause us to experience the suffering of rebirth, old age, death, sickness, and problems.

We endure the suffering of suffering, which are pain and troubles. We experience the temporariness of samsaric pleasures, which shows the suffering of change. These two sufferings occur due to the foundation of pervasive compounding suffering, which is our aggregates tainted by karma and delusion.

Whatever appearances we perceive, whatever views we possess, whatever we have surrounding us, all came from our consciousness. These phenomena include nice people, negative people, whatever is beautiful or ugly, dirty or clean, bad-tasting food or good-tasting food, bad sounds, interesting sounds, criticisms, praise, the whole world around us, what each of the senses perceives, the whole thing. Phenomena arising from our consciousness include whether something is a living being or a non-living thing, hot or cold weather, whatever appearance we have, whether the environment is a desert or not, the entire appearance around us.

I previously talked about mental labeling and how depending on that our lives are happy, unhappy, or neutral. Where did all of this come from? Why do we label people and experiences the way we do? It all came from the twelve interdependent links we generated from karmic seeds, from negative, positive, and neutral imprints left on our consciousness. It is therefore very beneficial to practice mindfulness about how we see and experience things, knowing it all came from our minds.

With this understanding, if somebody gets upset with us or some problem arises when we are working or walking, we won't be bothered because we will know the problem came from our own consciousness, our own karma, our own ignorance. When we fail to think this way it becomes easy to get angry or to blame somebody else, to blame external things and end up creating more negative karma or even doing harm to others.

The Buddha said we create our own happiness and suffering. It is up to us, it is up to our minds. Right now we have the freedom and free choice. By changing our attitude we can produce future happiness instead of suffering.

Using the Truth of Suffering to Gain Happiness

Studying suffering equips us to tackle the cause of suffering—our delusions and karma—and to apply the antidotes and get closer to real happiness and a meaningful life!

The most effective and practical method to combat laziness in apply-ing the antidotes and practicing Dharma, to enable us to extract the most out of our lives, is thinking "I may die today." What betrays us, cheats us, and enslaves us to attachment and anger is the thought "I am not going to die today."

Most of us presumptuously feel "I am not going to die today. I am going to live." This is our assumption. This is how we think when we wake up each day.

If the opposing thought that death can come at any time arises strongly enough, there is no question of our being able to let go of petty, worldly concerns and being inspired to take concrete steps to overcome the delusions that have tortured us. We will awaken to the fact that delusions bring no happiness and thus have no worth. For our daily actions to gain greater meaning, we need to continuously hold on to this thought that death can come at any time. This is what is missing from our daily routine.

If we check carefully, we can see how potently remembering imper-manence and death can wake us up, like a hammer that smashes the stones of complacency into pieces. Meditation on impermanence and death has incredible power over all delusions.

By studying, reflecting, and meditating on the second noble truth of how suffering is caused by delusions and karma, and how our daily lives are filled by these two, we become wiser. We begin to recognize delusions when they appear, we see how every single unhappiness we experience arises from them, and we come closer to understanding what we need to abandon and what we need to practice.

We begin to understand what liberation means. We start to realize what we need to achieve, what we must do, and what is missing in our lives right now. We become more determined to control the mind and guide it toward happiness. By renouncing the clinging and grasp-ing mind, the door to lasting peace and happiness is finally opened. Through familiarity with the methods of overcoming delusions, we sever the root of all suffering.

Whether we are eating food, drinking tea, going for a walk, listening to music, feeling warm, feeling cold, whatever we do we need awareness of how delusions deeply influence our thoughts, speech, and action. Only then will we be able to vanquish the inner enemy of delusions.

Our day-to-day life and its environment—bad appearances, good appearances, happy experiences, and unhappy experiences—all depend on our own mind. Due to the ignorance that believes in the inherent existence of "I" and the ignorance about how karma operates, we remain karmic slaves, unliberated. However, although we have not yet achieved liberation, practicing awareness of how ignorance deceives us, how desire breeds dissatisfaction, and how anger ruins peace for everyone places us in a better and much happier condition than someone who does not possess this awareness.

Look at the person who has no understanding of the cause of suffering and has no awareness of dependent arising, who totally believes in the hallucination of an inherently existing "I." Such a person's life is one of agitation and ups and downs, with very few happy moments and many disturbing thoughts. In addition the lack of understanding interferes with the person's ability to benefit others. This is such a great pity.

Happiness! By conquering the delusions happiness comes, good karma is generated, and negative karma is abandoned. As we stop creating the cause of samsara we get closer to achieving liberation, we approach full enlightenment more quickly. Even while we are in samsara, we will go from happiness to greater happiness. Think over how worthwhile it is to overcome delusions.

A story involving Shariputra, one of Guru Shakyamuni Buddha's disciples possessed with clairvoyance, illustrates how the shortcomings of samsara produce terrible and tragic consequences.

One day Shariputra passed a family house while he went about for alms in a village. As he looked into the courtyard of the house he saw a man eating a fish while his newborn baby was resting on his lap, and nearby the pet dog was eating the fish bones, causing the man to beat the dog.

Through Shariputra's clairvoyance he could see the past-life relationships between these beings: The fish being consumed was the man's late father, who used to fish from the pond behind the house and was now reborn as a fish in that same pond. The dog was the man's mother, who had been so attached to the family that after she died she was reborn as its pet dog. The baby was in fact a person the man had killed for raping his wife.

Due to that rapist's strong desire for the man's wife, he had been reborn as a child of the wife. The man caught his father (now a fish) and while he ate its meat, his late mother (now a dog) ate the fish bones (of her former husband), causing the man to beat the dog. The baby (the rapist) was now the man's beloved baby and sitting on the man's knee. Seeing this, Shariputra lamented:

> He eats his father's flesh and hits his mother.
> The enemy he killed sits on his knee.
> A wife gnaws at her husband's bones.
> Samsara is such a tragic farce!

This shows how nothing in samsara is as it appears. The problem is that we cannot recognize past relationships. Therefore when we meet other sentient beings there is a feeling of distance between ourselves and the others. There is no feeling of closeness. We feel we have nothing to do with them and they have nothing to do with us. But nothing is as it seems. Few things are how they appear.

How can we escape the challenges of our life as long as we remain ignorant of the nature of mind? How mind is the creator. Our troubles will continue as long as we point toward external things as the cause of our happiness or unhappiness. As long as we believe happiness is created not by ourselves but by somebody else or some external circumstance, our troubles will continue.

Through frequent contemplation on the first noble truth of suffering and the second noble truth of the cause of suffering—how delusions and karma drum up all the unbelievable suffering sentient beings endure—we cannot help but awaken some level of compassion in our hearts. It is highly meaningful to meditate on the suffering of sentient beings and its cause. Like a fire that is started with only a small spark, this understanding can grow into something that offers warmth and comfort to so many.

I was born into a Sherpa family in the Himalayas, very far from Kathmandu. It takes many days of hiking to get to my first home, crossing nine mountains by going up and down the steep mountain passes. *Sher* in Tibetan means "east" and *pa* means "person." So Sherpa means "a person who lives in the east."

The Sherpas originally came from the lower part of Tibet, the region call Kham. They came with their animals, mainly the goats and sheep that provided the meat the Sherpas ate. But the rocky Himalayas can be harsh, so after some time there were no more animals to feed on. The Sherpas then had to scout for food growing on the mountains, which they found according to their karma. They came across potatoes and learned how to plant them in small fields, so potatoes became their staple. It was very cold up there on the mountains.

I remember when I was very small my siblings and I would huddle together and sleep under my father's *chuba* (a Tibetan-style long coat with long sleeves). This chuba was made from animal skin and protected us from the cold. My mother worked very hard. She had to go into the forest, high up in the mountains, to get firewood. She spent many, many hours in the forest. We did not have matches, so we used primitive ways to light fires. A few sparks were all we needed to start a fire, and once ignited those sparks would blossom into a big, warm blaze. That is how it was growing up.

In the same way, we can kindle the fire of compassion within our heart. As we contemplate on the first two noble truths day after day— on how all living beings suffer but do not understand the causes of their suffering, on how they yearn for happiness but do not know how to create the causes for it—we will become more and more kindhearted. This year will find us kinder and better than the previous year, with less and less ego, less and less self-cherishing.

After two or three years we will notice there is still less ego, less selfishness, more compassion. Therefore like making a fire, first we need to generate the spark of understanding. Once that is alight, the warmth of kindness comes. With persistent effort the fire of compassion becomes bigger and bigger. When great compassion is combined with wisdom understanding reality, infinite happiness becomes possible for us and then we can be of real benefit to all living beings.

ANECDOTES FROM THE LIFE OF KYABJE LAMA ZOPA RINPOCHE

Wandering in a dream

We stopped for dinner at a food court on the drive to Kaohsiung, Taiwan. It was around midnight and not easy to find a vegetarian stall open. So we settled for the only thing available for midnight vegetarians—tea and sandwiches made of delicious white bread. Rinpoche was sitting at the table contemplating as he watched the crowd moving around the shops that were still open.

Rinpoche then shook his head and said with a mixture of sadness and compassion, "When people don't think of the next life . . . they wander as in a dream, believing 100 percent that the dream is real. This is like an illusion or mirage . . . believing it's all real. Imagine walking around like this, having no idea of your next life and the fact that the next life will not be according to your choice but will be up to the karma we have created. Most likely it will be the life of an insect, a jellyfish . . . what suffering."

So knowing the Dharma is a huge benefit! We are so very fortunate having met the Dharma. Knowing the Dharma is a huge opening of the eyes; the need for money in this life becomes like nothing.

Blessing the worms

Rinpoche finished self-initiation at the California center about 4:30 a.m. Rinpoche asked to stop the car at the foot of the road leading to the house because it was raining. Rinpoche was concerned there would be many worms out on the road due to the downpour. It is now 5:00 a.m. Rinpoche and Sangha got out of the car in the rain and started to carefully and delicately remove the worms from the road, placing them in a bucket to be blessed with mantras, circumambulated around relics, and then put carefully back in the garden.

We know it is very hard not to drive over worms, squashing them to death. Rinpoche mentioned that even though we don't have the intention to kill the worms when we drive, they do in fact get killed and there is still karmic result flowing from that. So Rinpoche is making ten stupas, each about ten inches high, for the worms accidentally killed during this rainy season.

Giving for the long term

Rinpoche says the suffering of disease, poverty, and despair in poor countries comes from nonvirtuous actions from the past, so helping people avoid such negative action is the most effective way to end their suffering.

"If one has the capacity one should help the poor by giving them material things, but that alone will not change their minds and make them turn to virtue, understand attachment, the good heart and so forth," he said. "Yet if they don't change their mindset and don't stop negative actions, they will continually create the cause for poverty. Stopping the causes of suffering depends on the teachings, and the existence of the teachings depends on the existence of Sangha and holy objects such as statues, scriptures, and stupas. Whenever we help others for the short term by giving medicine and shelter, the long-term goal of liberation from all suffering also needs to be facilitated."

3 : THE TRUTH OF CESSATION

The noble truth of the cessation of suffering is this: It is the complete cessation of that very craving, which means giving it up, renouncing it, emancipating oneself from it, detaching oneself from it.

—DHAMMACAKKAPPAVATTANA SUTTA

Is Suffering Forever?

WE MIGHT WONDER, "If mind is beginningless and thus the unenlightened mind has always been ignorant, is there any possibility of removing suffering by removing ignorance?"

This is definitely possible. Removing the delusion of ignorance will remove all other delusions that hinder our liberation and enlightenment. How is this possible? The answer is that the mind itself, the nature of the mind itself, is not in oneness with ignorance. The nature of mind is not merged with ignorance. The mind is only temporarily obscured by ignorance.

It is therefore wrong to believe we are stuck in samsara forever, that there is no freedom from suffering and no means of attaining liberation or release from cyclic existence. We are *not* stuck in samsara forever.

Although a piece of white cloth covered with dirt looks dark and dirty, the whiteness is merely temporarily obscured by the dirt. With proper cleaning the stain can be removed. Likewise, the nature of the mind is clear and its deluded states of ignorance, attachment, and anger are not fused with it. Study, meditation, and living one's daily life in accordance with ethics and with the Dharma all work toward lifting the stains of delusions from our minds.

Some think that achieving liberation, attaining everlasting happiness, means their mind ceases. This is a completely wrong idea. It is impossible to stop the mind, to cease the mind. Mind is a continuum, which means that mind has no beginning, it has no end, and there is no period in which mind is not. Nirvana and enlightenment are mental states, but they are not zero. Mind does not end, but suffering can.

By applying meditation to understand the nature of mind better, our minds become much more powerful and better equipped. There is more wisdom to quickly destroy the delusions and wrong conceptions that make us see things in a distorted, wrong way. As we go through the levels of meditation, in particular the meditation that realizes the true nature of the "I" and of reality, the dangers posed by the delusions weaken and eventually are eradicated.

When Guru Shakyamuni Buddha gave his first teachings on the four noble truths, or what is often described as "the first turning of the Dharma wheel," to his followers in Sarnath, he began with the true nature of suffering, followed by the true cause of suffering, before he showed the actual path to cessation or nirvana. Why? He did this because we first need to understand the suffering that appears in many forms so we can then have a clear idea of the causes of suffering, namely, delusion and karma.

Once we recognize delusion and karma as the sources of suffering, our minds are capable of uprooting the causes of suffering and accomplishing the cessation of suffering. Here we are not talking about just temporary relief from health problems, money woes, relationship difficulties, or even death. We are speaking of attaining everlasting peace and happiness. However, as long as we allow the true causes of suffering to endure within our minds, there is no way to achieve the ultimate happiness of real peace.

So what is real peace? The true cessation of suffering or nirvana is real peace and can only arise when we end the torture of delusions and karma. Nirvana is the absolute nature of our minds when purified of delusions. Only then is there total freedom, only then is there liberation from suffering. Achieving true cessation of suffering becomes the reason to seek the path. The path through which we cease delusions is the fully realized wisdom that realizes the nature of reality.

Severing the Root of Suffering

The greatest discovery of life begins when we realize the root of all our problems is the ignorance apprehending the "I" and all things as truly and inherently existent. When we realize this, the poisonous root of ignorance can be severed once and for all.

The oceans of suffering and sorrow have come from this deep-rooted view of inherent existence, fueling all the other delusions. To be free of samsara one has to gain the wisdom realizing emptiness, which pierces the hallucination of inherent existence and is the direct antidote to ignorance.

Even though loving-kindness and compassion are important virtues needed in daily life, practicing them alone will not remove the delusion of ignorance. Only wisdom realizing emptiness can directly eliminate ignorance. Understanding emptiness and meditating on it until one directly experiences it is imperative if one is to secure freedom from ignorance.

Just doing breathing meditation for a lifetime will get us nowhere. Meditating just to gain some rest for the mind, some relaxation and inner quiet, does not bring inner peace because it does not work on overcoming the delusions. Meditating only for personal peace of mind and nothing else becomes another form of worldly concern centered on relief in this life. It does not become a cause of long-lasting happiness, neither for us nor for others.

Therefore we need to find the courage to examine our motivation for meditation. If we discover we're meditating just for worldly reasons, we are underutilizing and wasting that effort. It would be far more meaningful to use meditation to examine the shortcomings of samsara and delusions and to develop the unshakeable determination to gain liberation.

Concentration meditation or calm-abiding meditation is where we develop stable focus on the object of meditation, which should be vivid, clear, energetic, and undistracted. If the water in a pond is dirty, we will not be able to see what is underneath. For us to see through the water it must first be clean, and then it has to be calm. In the same manner for us to clearly see and realize the nature of mind, the absolute nature of ourselves, we need a concentrated, undistracted mind we can control to steer away from agitation, sluggishness, and other mental hindrances.

Accomplishing concentration depends on controlling mental scattering and mental dullness. Succeeding in this establishes control over the mind. The mind can then be calm, clear, and focused. Then we should apply analytical meditation on the topics of the noble truths because without it we will be unable to recognize factors, including impermanence and samsara.

Without analytical meditation we won't recognize the impact of ignorance in our minds, which has created wrong conceptions about the self and everything around us. As long as we're unaware of these mistaken conceptions, we can't dispel or stop them. If we don't dispel the wrong conception of "I," we cannot realize the absolute nature of ourselves. To attain liberation from samsara and find everlasting happiness we must realize emptiness, the absolute nature of all things.

With the calm-abiding mind established, we can easily realize emptiness. The underlying factors for this attainment are to keep our body, speech, and mind clean, and of these primarily the mind. We achieve this cleanliness by guarding against negative actions of speech, body, and mind. Failure to discipline our mind is like churning water, which creates barriers to clarity and realizing the nature of mind.

The great yogi Milarepa said in his verses, "I was scared of death and escaped to the mountain. I have since realized the nature of the mind, which is emptiness. Now even when death comes, I have no upset, no worry."

However, even if we achieve liberation, this alone is not sufficient. We cannot be satisfied with just our own liberation because that would simply be securing happiness for ourselves, which is nothing special.

After all, even animals down to the tiniest insects seek happiness for themselves. There is nothing special about that attitude.

Our precious human rebirth is capable of much more than just attaining self-happiness. We should look more broadly, reflecting on how everything valuable we possess has come from the kindness of others. This includes the kindness of numberless hell beings, hungry ghosts, animals, human beings, demigods, god-realm beings, intermediate-stage beings, and everyone else. We fail to realize this because we cannot see these beings with our bare eyes, so we cannot remember their kindness.

Do we think it right to seek happiness for only ourselves? Even difficult people, those we dislike or who dislike us, who hate us, who provoke and abuse us, who disrespect and treat us badly, have been kind to us in that we have learned much from them. We learn of our mistakes, we discover our strengths. Whether such people intended to help us or not, they have contributed toward our deeper understanding of ourselves. This helps us attain insight into the delusions and develop more empathy, more compassion, more patience, and more wisdom, and it enables us to practice virtue and gather merit, the source of happiness to come.

By thinking about these possibilities for growth and generating a positive mind, we can achieve much temporary happiness while in samsara, let alone in future lives. In addition, when we practice the good heart and consistently meditate on emptiness and why there is little sense in grasping at the "I," enlightenment comes within reach.

Our enlightenment becomes possible through sentient beings. Yes, *through* sentient beings, especially the difficult, hurtful beings. Whether sentient beings intend to benefit us or not, their "troublesome" ways present us with opportunities to confront our delusions and to put the teachings into practice. They offer us the means to secure the ultimate prize, our enlightenment. This is why sentient beings are most precious, most kind, and most special, and why is it befitting that we constantly strive to benefit them.

The end of all samsaric suffering is called cessation because we are no longer shackled by delusion and karma, the causes of circling in misery. Eliminating the causes of suffering will be an extraordinary, amazing event, a completely new experience for us.

Until now all our worldly successes and excitements have offered nothing new. We have experienced them numberless times in samsara. We have gained them and lost them over and over during the course of beginningless rebirths. The rewards of ordinary life are stale. By clinging to worldly enjoyments, we have kept our ignorance, attachment, and anger fresh and active; we have created the causes to repeatedly return to samsara, to suffer, die, and repeat the cycle. Yet we look to the sky in despair and wonder why this is our lot.

When we conquer delusions we halt the cause of suffering. This is like wielding a giant knife that cuts off the vast expanse of suffering. This cessation is the most worthwhile, joyous thing to do, so that delusions, including their seeds, will not arise again.

Imagine never suffering again. When delusions and their seeds are uprooted, on what basis would suffering germinate and bear fruit? Because of this, eliminating delusions is one-time work. Striving toward liberation is a one-time task. Don't you wish to start right now?

This task begins with fully understanding the first noble truth of suffering, which is recognizing that samsaric existence is like being in the center of a raging fire. It is like dwelling in a thick nest of poisonous snakes. We should find no attraction within samsara, not even for one second. Just as someone trapped in rising flames or a pit full of vipers tries all ways to escape from those dangers, we need to generate a firm determination to break free of samsara. Having recognized the second noble truth of the cause of suffering as the delusions and karma, we then persevere, day and night, to achieve liberation.

If we do not analyze carefully, we might not realize that attaining perfect peace or nirvana requires the total cessation of delusions and karma. If we don't realize this, we will have no interest in working toward it. Yet if we don't apply effort, we will never gain perfect peace and will be back at the starting point of suffering and complaining about problems! Sentient beings remain in samsara because they see little value in ceasing delusions. Guru Shakyamuni Buddha taught suffering first to get us to investigate its cause so we could turn to ceasing the cause. Ceasing the cause of suffering will bring about the end of suffering, therefore bringing complete, everlasting happiness.

After Buddha taught the nature of suffering, followed by the true cause of suffering, he then revealed the third noble truth of the cessation of true suffering. This is nirvana or liberation, true freedom and ultimate happiness. Nirvana is the mind that is purified of delusions and that has attained the wisdom that fully realizes the absolute nature of mind.

Maitreya Buddha, in his teaching *Uttaratantra*, used the analogy of suffering as an illness. He said we need to understand the illness, we need to avoid the cause of the illness, we need to fully understand the cure, and we need to know the medicine, which we can rely on to achieve the cure. This is how the Buddha guides us. When we recognize we are sick we see a doctor for help. The doctor will prescribe medicine, but if the patient does not take the medicine there will be no recovery.

Likewise, we suffer in samsara and delusions and karma are the cause. The Buddha is like a doctor who prescribes the Dharma path as medicine to remedy the sickness of delusions. However, if we don't utilize the Dharma that we learn, our afflicted minds will not be healed and our suffering will continue. Only when we recover from the true causes of suffering will we gain the cessation of suffering.

Guru Shakyamuni Buddha taught the third noble truth of cessation to explain nirvana, the state of freedom from suffering, the state of perfect peace. He did this to provide the reason for following the path. If our minds and bodies are tied down by delusion and karma, the mind has no freedom, no peace, and is beyond our control. That is pure suffering. We have long believed that gaining some worldly pleasures will make us content and happy. Yet we have seen how these pleasures are not only temporary but in fact generate more dissatisfaction.

When people turn to temporal, worldly methods to remove suffering, such as changing homes, changing partners, getting new jobs, and buying more things, the relief does not last and suffering arises again.

This is because worldly methods leave untouched the root causes of the problems, delusion and karma. The Dharma method permanently removes suffering because it targets every delusion with direct antidotes. If this were not so, Dharma practice would be meaningless, there would be no enlightened beings, and any expounding of the teachings by enlightened beings would be nonsensical.

A child who starts life with very little knowledge changes while studying at school, developing knowledge and wisdom. Similarly, through Dharma practice and mental purification we can achieve all knowledge with nothing missing, full omniscience. We can definitely achieve the enlightened mind that can clearly see every sentient being, know every tiny karma ever created by each sentient being, know each second of each day of each being's life, and be able to provide the precise remedy needed to solve each sentient being's problems.

Right now we do not possess this ability. We can think of only one thing at a time, so that when we listen attentively to someone we can't clearly hear what anyone else is saying. When our minds are preoccupied we can't read a book thoroughly and recall all its details. At this moment our minds have many limitations.

The omniscient mind has no such hindrances. It stretches our understanding to even try to comprehend the enlightened mind, which sees all past, present, and future existence. Consider the number of sentient beings just on planet Earth. The number of humans is nothing, there are numberless sentient beings, including animals and insects, everywhere—in trees, in houses, underground, in oceans, in the stomach, some visible, some invisible. Yet the omniscient mind is completely aware of each and every one of them in each split second and is simultaneously aware of each atom of nonliving matter.

We should never discourage ourselves and think enlightenment is beyond our reach. If we were unable to enlighten the ignorant mind, we would be unable to educate a child. The ignorant mind is not eternal. After all, the mind of the person who invented the rocket did not always possess that knowledge. He learned the basics, how to design and construct it, and gradually eliminated his ignorance of that subject matter.

In exactly the same way, we can achieve the cessation of ignorance, including the ignorance of enlightenment. We have the means to directly experience enlightenment through Dharma study, virtuous deeds, purification practice, reflection, meditation, and gaining realizations, just as we experience our ordinary education.

Leaving ignorance alone is dangerous because ignorance causes more ignorance. However, once ignorance is lifted suffering cannot return, as there is no cause for it. The cessation of ignorance cannot give rise to new ignorance. Instead, eradicating ignorance removes all suffering, bringing the perfect peace of nirvana.

OBSCURATION TO LIBERATION AND OBSCURATION TO OMNISCIENCE

What blocks our attainment of liberation and enlightenment? It is the mind afflicted by gross and subtle delusions or obscurations. The obstacles posed by the afflicted mind have two aspects. The first is the obscuration to liberation (Tib. *nyöndrip*, where the word *nyön* refers to delusions and *drip* means "obscuration"). The second is the obscuration to omniscience (Tib. *shedrip*, where the word *she* refers to existence), which is the subtle imprints left behind by delusion grasping at true existence, which in turn hinder realizing omniscience or full buddhahood. Together these delusions hinder us from attaining liberation from samsara.

These subtle imprints are so refined they are said to be mere inclinations or tendencies toward believing in inherent existence. The dualistic view is the subtle defilement that obscures omniscience. When this is finally removed, the mind becomes fully enlightened.

The obscuration to liberation arises when delusions such as the three poisons of ignorance, attachment, and anger arise, particularly the ignorance that grasps at the "I" and things as inherently and truly existent. This ignorance leaves a heavy imprint on the mind. We had earlier discussed how the "I" that seems to exist is not truly existent but is instead merely labeled on the base of aggregates. In other words, the

"I" exists dependently and not inherently. Yet due to wrong concepts and negative imprints left on the mental continuum, ignorance projects the hallucinated appearance of a truly existent or inherently existing "I." This mistaken appearance causes us to completely believe in true existence.

From that moment flow all other deluded attachments to this seemingly truly existing "I," including anger, pride, and jealousy. How? Let us recollect the evolution of wrong view. When we believe an inherently existing "I" exists right here, the desire to satisfy the needs and wants of this "I" arises. From this, attachment arises, followed by anger if our attachments are not fulfilled, pride at the importance of the "I," and jealousy toward others who possess what the "I" seeks.

All these deluded, disturbing thoughts began with the mistaken concept of an independently and truly existing "I." We forget the "I" is merely imputed by the mind to the aggregates; it is a mere mental construct. The mind has been obscured from seeing the reality of all things, which is the lack of inherent existence, the emptiness of all things.

Ignorance and the other delusions bind us to samsara. When we fail to apply the antidotes, we cannot rid ourselves of the delusions, we cannot lift ourselves out of samsara to gain nirvana, which is why the delusions, particularly ignorance, are called obscurations to liberation. The primary interference comes from the imprint left by ignorance grasping at the idea of inherent existence. Without eradicating ignorance grasping at inherent existence, we cannot attain nirvana or liberation.

Even if this first level of obscuration is removed, subtle imprints continue to stain the mind in the form of dualistic view. They cause us to see objects and beings as existing on their own without any involvement with our minds. As long as these imprints remain, the misconception of self-existence or true existence continues.

Therefore the next level of obscuration is the obscuration to omniscience, or full knowledge of all existence. This is a subtle part of the imprint left by ignorance grasping at the idea of inherent existence, which produces the appearance of inherent existence. The appearing object is merely labeled by our minds and is not inherently there, but we believe it is inherently and truly there, existing from its own side. Like the movie projector that produces images on a screen, the imprint of ignorance causes us to see any sense object as truly existent.

Let us take the example of ice cream. When we are offered an ice cream cone, we tend to see the ice cream as self-existent. However, if we analyze more closely, how did the notion of "ice cream" arise? The base material first appeared to us, and only after that did we affix the label "ice cream." The base and the label did not arise at the same time. Mental involvement intervened.

As another example, we see someone who looks like an old friend walking on the street. First we notice a person. Then we observe the person's appearance, voice, shape, and size, and slowly our memory prompts us to think, "Oh it is my old friend!" Here again we see the base (the person's form) first, and then once we recognize familiar features on this base, we label it as our old friend. The base becomes the reason that persuades the mind to craft the label of "old friend."

As with the case of the ice cream, the base and label did not arise together at the same time. But when we do not analyze, it looks as if the base and label come into existence at the same time. We believe the label and the base are the same, inseparable, and then we react to the object.

Therefore right now all the things we see around us—people, floor, carpet, room, all phenomena—these appearances are labels our mind imputed and then believed in. Our entire world is dependent on causes and conditions and the mental labels our minds put on different bases.

Everything is a dependent arising. Since all phenomena exist in the manner of mental labels, there is nothing inherently existing within them. We have total freedom, we can change. We can remove the causes of suffering that are imprinted in our minds and be free from suffering.

In short, we have the capacity to actualize the path and achieve liberation and enlightenment. When that understanding comes right into our heart—that the projections of our ignorant mind have tricked us into believing in true or inherent existence—we will see how we have clung to the biggest superstition, the king of delusions, namely, the belief in inherent existence that has been left on our mental continuum over countless lives.

If you wear a pair of red glasses you see everything as reddish. Even the color white will appear as red. Just like that the subtle imprint of the ignorance that believes in inherent existence influences our entire perception. Therefore in order to cut off this ignorance we need to cultivate the wisdom that realizes emptiness, realizing that everything exists in mere name, is merely imputed by mind, and is therefore totally empty of existing from its own side.

When I say that all truly existent appearances are false, this includes the truly existent "I." The "I" that does exist is the one that arises dependently on, and not independently of, the mind placing the label "I" on the base of aggregates: form, feeling, consciousness, discrimination, and karmic imprints.

As is the case with everything else, all these are merely labeled. So why do things always appear to us as inherently existent, even though in reality they do not exist that way? Why is it that from the first second that consciousness takes place on the fertilized egg in the mother's womb, that being perceives "I" as truly existent and grasps on to the perception with ignorance?

After birth, when the six senses begin to function, why does our body and everything else appear as truly existent? The Buddha explained that everything is merely labeled but never appears to us in this way. Things appear concrete-like, independently and truly existing. Why?

The answer is that we have been trapped in the iron cage of the ignorant belief in true existence over beginningless rebirths. The imprints left by ignorance on consciousness were not uprooted life after life. They leave us firmly stuck in this hallucination, so we are overwhelmed by the ignorance that believes in inherent existence. This ignorance works like a drug, so that how we see things is the opposite of the truth.

That part of the imprint left by ignorance that causes us to see things as truly existent—both the appearance and that imprint—is called "shedrip," or subtle obscuration. This type of obscuration does not interfere with achieving nirvana because it is so subtle that it remains after liberation. Even arhats who have achieved liberation see things as truly existent. Therefore unless shedrip is completely removed, this subtle obscuration will interfere with achieving omniscience.

Arhats, as well as eighth- and ninth-level bodhisattvas who are not in the state of meditative equipoise on emptiness, possess this type of subtle obscuration. It hinders the final achievement of omniscience or enlightenment. That is why it is called the obscuration to omniscience. It is very good to remember this.

Therefore the synonyms of cessation, nirvana, or liberation from samsara all refer to the end of suffering and its causes. What all sentient beings yearn for, the freedom from suffering and the attainment of happiness, is within our reach if we successfully cultivate the methods to eliminate delusion and karma, which are the causes of suffering.

Two Nirvanas: Liberation and Enlightenment

In the mind of every sentient being dwells the wish to be free from suffering and to achieve the highest and longest-lasting happiness. For this to happen, we need to eliminate suffering. However, until now we have had a limited understanding of what suffering means. We think of suffering only in terms of poverty, disease, relationship problems, or not having a job. We tend to understand only a part of samsaric suffering but not its entirety.

As a result, the cessation of suffering most beings seek is very limited. What we seek is to remove what troubles us now and perhaps in the near future. We give very little thought to removing suffering for all time, and because of this we make mistakes in our spiritual goals. The liberation many of us seek is incomplete. Consequently, our efforts do not produce ultimate liberation. They do not result in nirvana.

Nirvana is the cessation of the true causes of suffering, which are delusions and karma. By ceasing the causes of suffering—ignorance, attachment, anger, and so forth—we can completely stop all suffering, all problems. How amazing that would be! That is the ultimate happiness or liberation.

In everyday life when we make an effort to lighten and eventually remove the grip these delusions have over us, we will find our mind becoming increasingly peaceful and decreasingly dissatisfied. A major obstacle to achieving liberation is the discontented, dissatisfied mind. By cutting off such a prickly mind, we can persevere and complete the work of attaining ultimate happiness.

The way to achieve happiness in life is from within our minds by transforming the mind imprinted with delusions and karma into the virtue that is the cause of happiness, the cause of success. Dharma practice is about removing the delusions and transforming the mind into the causes of happiness and success.

We can do this! When we achieve liberation, when we achieve full enlightenment, the work is finished. We would no longer rely on temporary samsaric pleasures dependent on external objects; we would instead generate happiness, attainments, and bliss from within.

When we speak of cessation or nirvana in the Mahayana tradition, there are two nirvanas being considered. The first is the lower nirvana, overcoming delusions and attaining liberation from samsara for oneself. The second is great nirvana, which is overcoming delusions, including the subtle obscuration to omniscience, thereby attaining full enlightenment for the sake of all sentient beings.

A short prayer Guru Shakyamuni Buddha taught to arhat meditators contains the line "Avoid dust and avoid smell." Merely looking at these words does not offer much insight. However, they contain a profound meaning on the Buddha's methods, the path.

"Avoid dust" refers to removing ignorance, attachment, anger, and the other delusions, which prevent attainment of the lower nirvana, liberation from samsara for oneself. Without the practice and realization of emptiness we're unable to cut the root of samsara, namely, ignorance.

"Avoid smell" refers to removing the subtle delusion that is the hurdle or obscuration to attaining full enlightenment. What is this subtle delusion? It is the dualistic mind that grasps at inherent existence. This defilement is so refined and so subtle that it is described as the mere tendency of the mind to see inherent existence. We could say it is the tendency of the mind to hold on to the "smell" of seemingly true existence. This mistaken view blocks our attainment of omniscience, the enlightened mind.

The cessation of delusions, and therefore freedom from samsara for ourselves by following the Hinayana or Small Vehicle path, can be termed as the "lower nirvana" or "lower cessation." Reciting prayers sincerely can become the cause for ourselves to receive lower nirvana, to attain our own perfect peace. However, without the mind of bodhicitta, which is the altruistic mind that has the welfare of all living beings at heart, our actions do not become the cause of our achieving the higher cessation or great nirvana of enlightenment. Therefore removing the subtle delusion requires the added element of bodhicitta.

After a practitioner attains the lower nirvana, the mind is absorbed into that blissful state. It is like a musician who spends the whole day playing beautiful music, listening to it with wholehearted attention, paying no attention to anything else, the mind completely focused on the music.

Similarly, the arhat dwells in that meditative blissful state for many eons. After a very great length of time, the Buddha persuades the arhat's mind, through light energy or something similar to that, to follow the Mahayana path in order to benefit other sentient beings. Therefore it is worthwhile to aspire beyond merely gaining for ourselves the blissful state of peace or lower nirvana. The important thing is to benefit not only ourselves; we must benefit all sentient beings who suffer so much in samsara. Therefore we should strive for the great nirvana, for full enlightenment, in order to benefit all other sentient beings. This is the motivation of the Great Vehicle or Mahayana path, the bodhisattva's path.

In summary, the lower cessation or lower nirvana refers to liberation, as it frees us from delusions that obscure us from liberation. The higher cessation or the great nirvana refers to great liberation or full enlightenment, as it removes the two obscurations, namely, the obscuration to liberation (the delusions) and the obscuration to omniscience (subtle dual view). When these two obscurations are eliminated, the pure, sublime, blissful state of full enlightenment is accomplished.

Enlightenment means we have purified all obscurations, both gross and subtle. While we cultivate the path, we work on purifying different levels of obscurations, which become more and more subtle as we progress.

We first purify the most gross obscuration of delusion. When we clean a greasy pot, we first wash the gross parts of oil and dirt and then later clean even the stains of dirt that might have remained in the pot. In the same way, we have to purify the various levels of inner obscurations gradually. We will finally arrive at a stage where not a single aspect of knowledge is missing, where we have perfected all knowledge and purified all hindrances and obscurations, even subtle ones, to attain omniscience.

Our minds are like mirrors in which we can see the whole world and everything in it, except that they are obscured by dust. Our minds are temporarily obscured by mental impurities brought about by delusions. But the mirrors, our minds, are not actually fundamentally changed by the dust, but only temporarily obscured by the dust. If the mirror itself were merged with the dust, there would be no way to clean the mirror. When all the mental dust and obscurations are purified, this mind becomes an omniscient mind. When the mind reaches that stage, it is called enlightenment.

Why is full enlightenment everlasting? This is because once the obscurations are removed, the delusions, their seeds, and the subtle imprints that are the cause of all suffering are completely eliminated. It then becomes impossible for suffering to return, impossible for happiness to degenerate. It is impossible because there is no longer a basis for the cause of suffering to reemerge and interfere with happiness. For example, today our minds are controlled by disturbing thoughts of ignorance, anger, and attachment. Our minds are presently obscured by these afflictions because they are the continuation of the mental afflictions that existed yesterday. We did not remove yesterday's disturbing thoughts, so they continue today.

It is the same with the life before this one. If we had completely removed the delusions by actualizing the remedy of the path within our mind in past lives, it would be impossible for us to be born with such mental afflictions in this life. There would be no disturbing thoughts if the continuation of those delusions had been stopped, so there would be no unhappiness or problems in this life. The logic is plain: if a cloth covered with dirt was completely cleaned yesterday it would be clean today, as there would be no "continuing dirt" from yesterday. Similarly, once the delusions and obscurations are completely removed, there will be no continuing delusions and obscurations to trouble us.

I wish to say again that even if we are able to achieve the cessation of delusions and thereby attain liberation for ourselves, it is not sufficient. That is not the real purpose of life; it is not why we have taken this precious human body. The real meaning of life, the real goal, the real purpose of having this precious human body is to bring all sentient beings to the everlasting peerless happiness of full enlightenment by liberating them from delusions and the mental stains of obscurations. How wonderful! This is how to repay the kindness of sentient beings.

Achieving Nirvana

The path to achieve nirvana and the path to attain full enlightenment are elaborated in the chapter on the truth of the path, but here is a brief outline of each.

Due to ignorance, the wrong conception of the "I" as truly existent arises, and from there ignorance of karma arises. As this ignorance of seemingly true existence has no beginning, the ignorance of karma also has no beginning. As ignorance has prevailed in our mindstreams, we have circled in the six realms of samsara during beginningless lifetimes, experiencing sorrow and fear again and again until now. Having accumulated so much karma through ignorance, we are repeatedly born in the suffering realms. Can you now see how crucial it is to break free of ignorance of inherent existence and of ignorance of karma?

Liberation begins with a genuine, heartfelt renunciation of samsara. Through observation and analysis, we become convinced of all of samsara's shortcomings and of the terrible suffering delusions bring to our lives. If we are halfhearted in our efforts, sometimes renouncing samsara but sometimes seeking out samsara, our progress toward liberation will be slow and difficult. Our determination will always be in danger of growing weak.

We see the value of cultivating the noble eightfold path—right speech, right action, right livelihood, right effort, right mindfulness, right concentration, right view, and right thought—and we put effort into it. The eightfold path can in turn be grouped into the three higher trainings of morality, concentration, and wisdom. The training in moral conduct forms the basis for actualizing the other two trainings—concentration and wisdom.

There is a reason for describing morality, concentration, and wisdom as higher trainings. Other religions include their own moral standards, such as avoiding killing humans, and may also teach some practices to develop concentration of mind. However, in Buddhism morality covers a wide range of conduct. It includes avoiding the ten nonvirtues we discussed earlier, namely, abstaining from harming any living being, killing, stealing, engaging in sexual misconduct, lying, harsh speech, divisive speech and idle gossip, covetousness, ill will, and wrong view. Buddhist morality also includes holding precepts and vows, such as lay vows and ordination vows, which are to be guarded even at the cost of one's life.

In Tibet we have an animal called a yak, a big and strong animal that looks something like an ox. These yaks are very protective of their tails. If while walking in the forest their tails get caught in the bushes, they will not pull themselves free in a hurried manner. Even if a hunter is about to shoot them, they will not run off quickly because they do not want to damage their tails by dragging them through the bushes. Losing a few strands of hair for the sake of freedom seems too much for these yaks!

This is the same way holy Lama Atisha upheld his vows, from the minor vows to the major ones. He protected his vows the way a yak protects its precious tail, caring more about his vows than his life. Morality is premised on refuge in the Three Jewels of Buddha, Dharma, and

Sangha. So the three higher trainings mean practicing morality with refuge, cultivating meditative concentration with refuge to analyze the Buddha's teachings, and practicing wisdom or penetrative insight with refuge to gain direct realization of emptiness and nonduality.

Achieving Full Enlightenment

We should well understand that realizing the absolute nature of self as lacking inherent existence does not mean we automatically cut off self-cherishing. The antidote to ignorance is undisputedly wisdom realizing the emptiness of all things, but self-cherishing can only be dispelled by bodhicitta. As long as the self-cherishing thought is not destroyed, even the full realization of emptiness will enable us to merely remain in individual nirvana for a very long time but not work for sentient beings.

Therefore the practitioner who aspires to do more, who abandons mere self-liberation and seeks full realization to benefit all beings, as bodhisattvas do, first must develop unshakeable renunciation of samsara. This person then needs to practice the six paramitas, or six perfections, of generosity, morality, patience, perseverance, concentration, and wisdom that form the bodhisattva's conduct, followed by the practice of tantra, which will be elaborated on in the next chapter.

The Differing Qualities of Nirvana and Enlightenment

I mentioned before that nirvana can be categorized into the lower nirvana or liberation and the great nirvana or full enlightenment. These two states differ, which means the qualities of the attainments differ.

Nirvana, or liberation, is the cessation of all conceivable forms of suffering. In this state, we are no longer subject to the suffering of suffering, the suffering of change, and pervasive compounding suffering. We gain release from samsara and we experience everlasting happiness for ourselves and can remain in that solitary, blissful state for eons.

Enlightenment or the great nirvana is likewise the cessation of all forms of suffering and, beyond that, is the completion of all realizations, including the eradication of subtle grasping at inherent existence. It is the state of peerless happiness where the perfect qualities of an enlightened one's holy body, holy speech, and holy mind, motivated by the welfare of all beings, is now able to benefit and guide all sentient beings without the slightest mistake.

Upon attaining enlightenment, a being becomes a fully awakened one, a buddha, whose holy mind of transcendental wisdom is called the *dharmakaya* and whose holy body is called the *rupakaya*.

THE FOUR KAYAS

When we attain enlightenment, the mind becomes the dharmakaya, the omniscient mind. The nature of this mind is that of the nature truth body, the *svabhavikaya*, which is free of all stains. In other words, the enlightened mind is fully knowing, and its absolute nature is completely pure of all the gross delusions and subtle delusions. Thus the enlightened mind is not like an empty sky but instead is all-knowing and totally pure.

The holy mind of dharmakaya is completely purified of the subtle dual view, free from the appearance of true existence and the obscurations to omniscience. It abides in equipoise meditation on emptiness forever, directly seeing the emptiness of all existence without the duality of subject and object. The omniscient mind's realization of emptiness is like pouring water into water.

The durability of the omniscient mind's realization of emptiness is distinct from that of the practitioner who may have realized emptiness directly, one who, during the time of equipoise meditation directly concentrated on emptiness, subdues the subtle dual view. Despite being subdued, the stain of that subtle dual view remains as an obscuration to omniscience. Thus such a practitioner cannot meditate in equipoise on emptiness forever, like the omniscient mind can. Such a person's realization of emptiness is not like pouring water into water without needing to arise from that meditation. During the break from that meditation, the suppressed dual view arises again and once more sees the apparition of inherent existence.

By comparison, the holy mind of dharmakaya is completely free from this and all stains, even the subtle dual view.

However, we cannot guide sentient beings simply by abiding in dharmakaya, in a mental state. The omniscient mind must be manifested in a form that can be perceived by beings. Sentient beings have different levels of mind, so to guide each of them, omniscient beings must manifest in different forms: as a king, a leader, a worker, a beggar, a virtuous teacher, a butcher, a prostitute, a judge, and so forth.

Therefore the form aspect of the Buddha that living beings can perceive is called the rupakaya and includes two aspects, the *samboghakaya* and the *nirmanakaya*. The samboghakaya form is visible only to arya bodhisattvas, those realized ones who have perceived emptiness directly. The nirmanakaya form is visible to ordinary sentient beings and is the form Guru Shakyamuni Buddha took when he turned the wheel of Dharma and revealed the path.

The enlightened state of Guru Shakyamuni Buddha's holy body, holy speech, and holy mind have infinite good qualities.

Sentient beings derive many benefits from looking at the Buddha's holy body. A being contemplating the Buddha's appearance, with its thirty-two major marks and eighty minor marks, feels an immediate peace within the mind and experiences a subdued calm. Merely looking at the Buddha purifies vast amounts of obscurations and negative karma. In addition by making devoted offerings to the Buddha, while keeping in mind his qualities, such as knowledge, wisdom, and compassion, we create positive connection and karma. This helps us in our ordinary lives and sets us on the path to actualize our fullest potential of buddhahood.

The Buddha's holy speech is so vast that just one line of advice is heard by countless sentient beings in their own languages and contains advice suited to each sentient being's needs and karma. The Buddha's holy speech also guides us through words in books, teachings, and chronicled conversations.

While there are many methods to reveal Dharma to sentient beings, those beings can't realize the teachings until their minds have reached the karmic level or condition to receive them. Otherwise teachings will benefit little, as the mind is not able to digest what is being revealed. For instance, god-realm beings lack strong karma to receive teachings from a Buddha manifestation. Very few god-realm beings have affinity to the Dharma and hear those teachings only on special days like full moon days, and only in the form of Dharma drum beats from a god-realm drum not made by ordinary beings.

The Buddha's holy mind is infinite and precise in its knowledge. For instance, if we cut up many different plants from different countries into tiny pieces and then pour these particles into the ocean for one hundred years, the Buddha's omniscient mind will be able to perfectly identify the plant type of each particle and where it came from. This illustrates the incredible psychic power, clairvoyance, and perfect knowledge of the Buddha's mind.

The Buddha's omniscient mind sees all existence. The Buddha's holy mind is everywhere. Omniscience means the Buddha's mind knows every situation, every single sentient being's mind, every being's karma, and every being's characteristics, strengths, weaknesses, and wishes in complete detail. This also means Buddha's mind knows the guidance that is exactly suited to each sentient being, according to their level of mind and karmic condition, to help each sentient being's mind become purer and more developed. The Buddha's holy mind knows every method shown to each sentient being to guide that being to enlightenment.

In my own experience, there have been many times when I sought to clarify a Dharma point and somehow always easily found the text or passage that gave me the explanation I needed. This would happen even when I was unaware the answer would be in the text. I used to get the feeling something was directing me to the Dharma source I was looking for. This is what the action of the Buddha's holy mind is like. Just as falling rain enables crops to grow, the omniscient mind nourishes the field of sentient beings' minds and helps them grow in virtue, thus leading sentient beings away from suffering and toward enlightenment.

THE FIVE PATHS

In science, we learn how things come about, how they function, how to solve problems through remedial methods, and how atoms, upon meeting each other, produce power and so forth. In the same way, Dharma explores how samsara functions, what its causes and consequences are, and the remedies. Dharma examines the potency of the mind that meets the Dharma and the subsequent results of liberation and full enlightenment. Therefore we progress spiritually by removing layers of obscurations and gaining more profound realizations toward the goal of the cessation of suffering.

The five paths are the stages at which different types of obscurations are removed and realizations gained. The five paths enable the practitioner to better understand the entire process toward liberation and enlightenment.

First, here is a general idea of the five paths. The first two paths relate to the gathering of virtue and preparation for the direct realization of emptiness. This realization occurs in the third path, also called the path of seeing, where the obscuration to realizing emptiness is removed. The practitioner then continuously develops the wisdom seeing the absolute nature of things and reaches the next level, where the subtler obscurations are overcome. This gradual progress continues until all the gross and subtle obscurations are removed.

Therefore, it is not the case that a practitioner sits in meditation and suddenly all obscurations are removed. It is not like this. Instead, obscurations are removed in layers, through following a gradual path of cultivation and meditation.

At present our minds are temporarily obscured and impure because they are obstructed by delusions and the negative actions and thoughts produced by delusions. By purifying such pollution through doing virtue, undertaking purification practices, and meditating on the absolute nature of things, the mind can be restored to its completely pure state.

When a piece of white cloth is stained, this does not mean the white color below the dirt has vanished. The whiteness continues but is temporarily obscured by the dirt. Similarly, the essence of every sentient being is the clear, light, pure nature of mind, but that is temporarily overshadowed by delusions. This pure nature of mind is exactly why we can attain enlightenment, simply because our minds are not permanently tainted by ignorance and delusions. Remember this.

The five paths are:

> The path of accumulation (or merit)
> The path of preparation
> The path of seeing (or path of right seeing)
> The path of meditation
> The path of no more learning

Both the Hinayana Vehicle and the Mahayana or Bodhisattva Vehicle use the term "five paths," although they differ in how obscurations are removed and in the realizations involved.

According to the Hinayana Vehicle, we must proceed on the five paths to attain nirvana, which is the release from samsara. As the Hinayana practitioner's goal is personal liberation or the lower nirvana, such a person enters the Hinayana five paths by generating the stable and pure renunciation of samsara.

A person seeking full enlightenment on the Mahayana or Bodhisattva Vehicle also pursues five paths with the same names. But as the goal of the Mahayana Vehicle is the welfare of beings, a person enters the Mahayana five paths by renouncing samsara and generating bodhicitta, the altruistic intention to attain enlightenment for the sake of all sentient beings.

Hinayana five paths

When a practitioner strives day and night to be free from samsara and finally actualizes this renunciation, he or she enters the Small Vehicle or Hinayana five paths. The first stage is called the path of collection or accumulation, where the practitioner collects merit through engaging in virtues. Then through virtuous conduct and meditation the person enters the path of conjunction, also called the path of preparation, gaining profound understanding of the true nature of things and preparing the mind to achieve freedom from delusions, the source of samsara.

This is followed by a life of virtue and more meditative efforts leading to the path of right seeing, where the person attains direct realization into selflessness.

Within this path of seeing there are two stages: the stage without hindrance and the stage of release. When the stage without hindrance is completed the stage of release is simultaneously achieved, removing 112 delusions. Next the practitioner enters the path of meditation, where the remaining gross and subtle delusions are removed. When this is complete the practitioner achieves the path of no more learning, attains nirvana, and becomes an arhat.

The Hinayana Vehicle path speaks of two levels of practitioners: The hearer (Skt. *Shravaka*) receives teachings from the guru and then explains the teaching to others. The solitary realizer (Skt. *Pratyekabuddha*), after receiving these teachings, enters a state of solitude to meditate until realizations are attained.

The Hinayana five paths lead to liberation, which is the cessation of samsaric suffering and its cause. Ignorance, the root cause of suffering, is eliminated by realizing the ultimate, empty nature of the "I." By developing this wisdom, all the other delusions are eradicated, so that actions produced by delusions cease and even the seed of ignorance left on the consciousness is completely removed. When even the seed is completely removed, one becomes free from samsara as well as all forms of problems, including ordinary death and rebirth into samsara.

By completing these five paths, the practitioner stops delusions in his or her mental continuum, attaining what is called nirvana or liberation, the sorrowless state of peace.

However, it is not sufficient that an individual gains complete freedom from suffering and its causes. Because numberless sentient beings remain locked in great suffering, practitioners need to enter the Mahayana path, the Great Vehicle path that seeks to liberate all sentient beings from suffering and bring them to the bliss of enlightenment.

Mahayana five paths

When we have explored the nature and extent of the sufferings of samsara and see how that strikes ourselves and numberless beings, we come closer to establishing the firm renunciation of samsara. From that basis of renunciation, we then generate bodhicitta, the altruistic intention to benefit all living beings, in order to enter the five paths of the Great Vehicle or Mahayana. These are the Mahayana paths of accumulation, conjunction/preparation, seeing, meditation, and no more learning. By completing these while also engaging in the bodhisattva's deeds of the six perfections or paramitas, we achieve full enlightenment. It is only then that we are able to perfectly benefit all beings.

The first stage, the Mahayana path of accumulation or merit, is divided into small, middle, and great. The first step is the realization of bodhicitta, the constantly arising altruistic intention to lead beings to enlightenment, which is the door of the Mahayana path. Generating bodhicitta brings us into the Mahayana path of accumulation, where we collect merit through listening to Dharma teachings—we reflect, contemplate, and meditate, and we act virtuously and live life in accord with the Dharma. As we deepen our practice at each level, gross delusions are gradually removed.

The minute our minds reach this great path of accumulation, we see enlightened beings in the nirmanakaya form wherever we are, whether it be outside in the open or inside doing chores. Before that our minds were far from purified, so we did not see buddhas in this way. Instead we saw a buddha as an ordinary human in a totally ordinary form. This is simply because our minds are impure and not free of obscurations.

Buddha appears according to the level of mind. Because we're habituated to believe in "reality" just as it appears to our senses, and because we limit our understanding of people according to what we see, we wouldn't see the Buddha as the Buddha even if he were sitting next to us! This old habit of believing in ordinary appearances blocks realization on many levels, from guru devotion up to recognizing a buddha as a buddha. But when we achieve the great path of accumulation or merit, the mind is much more purified, so we see numberless buddhas right there in the nirmanakaya aspect, the form that is visible to sentient beings.

The bodhicitta motivation enables a person on the Mahayana path of accumulation to create more merit than would be created by a person following the Small Vehicle path of accumulation, because the Mahayana motivation goes beyond liberating only oneself and extends to liberating all living beings.

We next move to the Mahayana path of preparation. Here through continued practice, virtues, and meditations we gain realization into the four noble truths and the absolute nature of reality. We continue to remove more layers of delusion and obscuration, preparing us to attain the third stage, the right-seeing path. This Mahayana path of seeing removes 112 obscurations.

At this level, we gain the wisdom of *directly* perceiving emptiness, moving beyond a merely profound understanding of emptiness. We now directly experience emptiness. Once direct perception is attained, all gross delusions in our mindstreams are destroyed, the obscurations to liberation are purified, and we are released from all of samsara.

Right there we become an arya being, a holy being who has seen emptiness directly and who is free from suffering, sickness, death, and uncontrolled rebirth. At this stage, the mind is so much more purified that we see all buddhas in their sambhogakaya aspect, the aspect visible only to arya beings.

Once the gross delusions have been eliminated at the path of seeing, there remain only the subtle defilements. The subtle defilement that obscures omniscience, this subtle stain of the mind, is the subtle negative imprint in the mental continuum caused by past misapprehending of "I" and all phenomena as inherently and truly existent. This subtle defilement obstructs full awakening or omniscience.

After we enter the third Mahayana path of seeing, we start cultivating the ten grounds or ten stages. In Sanskrit these are called the ten *bhumis*, referring to ground or base. The Small Vehicle path does not have these ten bhumis or ten levels of realizations. There are more realizations in the Mahayana path. When we enter the Mahayana path of seeing, we begin to cultivate the first bhumi, followed by the next bhumi and so on. By the time we attain the eighth bhumi, all the gross delusions have been removed. The uninterrupted path is completed here and the path of release achieved.

While we are cultivating the first to the seventh bhumis, delusions remain in our minds. But after we attain the eighth bhumi, all gross delusions are removed and cease completely.

When this occurs, we are no longer in samsara. This is why the eighth and subsequent ninth and tenth bhumi stages are called the three pure stages—gross delusions are gone. The earlier seven stages are called the impure stages because delusions remain in the mind of the practitioner. The function of these three later stages is solely to remove the remaining subtle obscurations of the dualistic mind.

In addition to its mighty motivation to benefit all sentient beings, the Mahayana path is called the Great Vehicle path because it generates more realizations, it has more functions, and it purifies and removes more obscurations. Each of the Mahayana paths generates more knowledge, realizations, and skills than the corresponding paths of the Small Vehicle.

The ten bhumis continue into the fourth stage, called the Mahayana path of meditation, where through continued equipoise meditation without interruption, realization of the absolute nature of reality is continuously developed and refined. There remain only the subtle obscurations.

Again, there are two stages: the uninterrupted path and the path of release. The uninterrupted path becomes the remedy to our subtle obscurations in relation to the emptiness of the "I" and phenomena. The completion of the uninterrupted path coincides with the attainment of the path of release, where these remaining subtle obscurations are finally uprooted.

After this completion, no blockages remain within our mental continuum. The remaining 108 subtle obscurations are removed. The obscuration to omniscience is completely eliminated. At that time, we enter the final path of no more learning and become a fully enlightened buddha, at one with all buddhas.

Try to remember the function of each of the five paths of the Small Vehicle and the five Mahayana paths as well as the ability of the right-seeing path and the path of meditation to remove delusions and subtle obscurations. It is very, very helpful to do self-checking and analytical meditation on our Dharma practice to remember the significance of each path and its function for removing specific types of delusions and obscurations.

As we actualize each path, various levels of delusions, obscurations, and wrong conceptions get removed. That is how the Dharma releases us from the grip of samsara all the way to the subtle obscurations. It is now easy to understand.

We receive guidance and help from the Buddha because of the Dharma. If Guru Shakyamuni Buddha had not trodden this path he would not have achieved enlightenment and he would not be able to help or guide us sentient beings. His benefiting us illustrates the ability of the Dharma, how it enables us to leave all suffering behind.

There are two ways to analyze the Dharma. We can check how Dharma knowledge and advice offered by realized beings guides all living beings out of suffering. We can also check how the Dharma we have actualized within our own minds guides us out of suffering in the short term and in the long term. Both analyses encourage us to practice and persevere.

Guru Shakyamuni Buddha completed the collection of merit and the collection of wisdom and thus achieved all the kayas. He then revealed all the teachings to us sentient beings to enable us to accomplish the cessation of suffering and taught the methods in a very detailed way.

On altars at Tibetan monasteries are placed volumes of the Tengyur and the Kangyur, which contain these teachings of the Buddha as well as commentaries from the great Buddhist masters. All these teachings were left in this world for us to study, contemplate, and meditate on— and to live our lives accordingly.

So when we enter a gompa and see these scriptures, let us take the time to remember that the Buddha taught the Dharma to guide sentient beings to the great cessation, to enlightenment.

ANECDOTES FROM THE LIFE OF KYABJE LAMA ZOPA RINPOCHE

Offering to the mosquitoes

While at Deer Park Center in Madison, Wisconsin, Rinpoche had been going for daily walks in the evening as the sun set. We walked for an hour along a narrow country road with corn fields on either side. Rinpoche walks while reciting a scriptural text out loud. Each day Rinpoche recites by heart a different text.

However, the area attracts lots of mosquitoes and other kinds of sharp-biting insects! The bites really sting. Suggestions to Rinpoche about using something for protection falls on deaf ears. Rinpoche isn't interested in any protection for his body because he thinks that even if they bite and feed on his blood and flesh, it is just a small offering to these little guys.

Blessings and missed flights

It's time to leave the small Indian hotel for the airport. Everything is packed and ready and we are making good time. Suddenly a hotel staff person has fallen seriously ill, a plea is made to Rinpoche for a puja to be done . . . Rinpoche says he will do it now!

We all anxiously wait. Of course it's important the puja is done, but it's just that something always happens when we desperately need to be somewhere on time—like being at the airport to catch a flight. The puja begins . . .

Fifteen minutes later Rinpoche's puja continues. In these situations, Rinpoche seems to have no concern about the time. He carefully explains to the person what the puja is about and what to think, how to motivate, what to understand. What can the rest of us do but wait? It's getting late . . .

Half an hour later we're still at the hotel. We're trying to leave, but another man from the hotel staff wants Rinpoche to write something so that he can frame it in his house as a blessing. Rinpoche writes a verse about bodhicitta. It's getting terribly late, so I think I will have to rush ahead first to check in the luggage and hope that Rinpoche can come soon after.

Four hours later we finally arrive at the airport, but other people have as well, still asking for things to be signed. Rinpoche is taking time and care to not only sign but to also write something meaningful. We rush through check-in, but when we get to immigration they say that because we didn't register at the Foreign Registration Office on entering India we cannot fly today! Rinpoche never gets upset or distressed over such things—it is time to relax and have a cup of tea and a nice samosa!

Coca-Cola and bodhicitta

A man who had started a meditation center in a Malaysia port town had come to seek advice from Rinpoche. He told Rinpoche that he felt that he had some kind of special sensory perception and wanted to develop that into clairvoyance so as to be able to help more people and even heal them. He went into detail about his abilities and asked what practice he should do to develop clairvoyance.

Rinpoche listened intently, remained silent for a while, and then looked at the man and said, "Drink more Coca-Cola!" The man was startled by this unorthodox advice. Rinpoche burst into laughter and patted him on the shoulder, saying, "Just joking!" and then said in a more serious tone, "Clairvoyance itself is a low-level attainment. It is better to aim for bodhicitta. Put your effort into developing that because when the realization of bodhicitta comes, clairvoyance also comes, and then one can really help others."

4 : THE TRUTH OF THE PATH

SUFFERING IS the subject to be known, the true cause of suffering is to be abandoned, the cessation of suffering is to be actualized, and the true path is to be relied on to accomplish the end of suffering. This is the advice of the Buddha in revealing the four noble truths.

In the fourth noble truth of the path, the Buddha revealed the skillful methods to achieve the cessation of suffering and release from samsara. It is the path of virtue, the path of happiness for this life and all future lives.

Pivotal to the Buddha's methods is not harming other sentient beings. This is illustrated by the Buddha's four-line prayer:

> Do not commit any unwholesome action.
> Commit only wholesome actions.
> Subdue your mind.
> This is the teaching of the Buddha.

The only complete way to end all our suffering is to destroy ignorance, the source of all delusions imprinted deep in our consciousnesses. No outer method can reach ignorance to expunge it. Only the inner method of the Dharma equips us to uproot ignorance and its tricky delusions. However, gaining mastery over our minds is not easy, it's not like microwaving popcorn. It does not speedily pop up just because we wish it. Mastery of the mind requires training and perseverance in applying antidotes to neutralize delusions.

Think about the great lengths we go to in order protect ourselves from dangers like thugs and wild animals, yet these are not as perilous as the negative, deluded mind. A thug or a wild animal may destroy our present lives, but the negative mind will destroy our present lives as well as many future lives to come, not to mention harming others. In this way, a mind controlled by delusions is far more dangerous than anything we can imagine.

When we are ill and are prescribed medicine, merely keeping the medicine in its bottle will not cure us. We need to consume and digest the medicine. Similarly, merely admiring the insight and logic in Dharma teachings is insufficient. We need to integrate Dharma methods into our daily lives to solve problems and experience firsthand their effect. There is no point in reading Dharma books without utilizing the advice. That would be as futile as a sick person reading the prescription on a medicine bottle without consuming the medicine! Dharma methods have little to do with mere physical actions and outer appearances. They are all about training one's mind.

As earlier mentioned, the mind can be like a dusty mirror. As dust doesn't merge with the mirror it obscures, we can feel encouraged that the mind is not merged with the delusions or with the obscurations to liberation and enlightenment. The unsubdued mind is neither eternal nor arising all the time. To suit the mentalities and inclinations of sentient beings, Buddha taught a multitude of methods to overcome delusions, the cause of all suffering. These methods are the path.

Suffering arises dependently; it does not exist on its own. It depends on the causes and conditions that underlie all our daily life problems. To stop the problems we need to change the causes and conditions. This is entirely within our control. Instead of planting causes for misery, sow seeds for happiness. Blaming others, the government, our parents, God in heaven, even the stars is not only useless but also wholly mistaken. We determine whether our lives will be happy or miserable. Since suffering is caused, it can be altered and eliminated by eradicating the cause. Everlasting happiness and perfect wisdom can be attained.

Study and analyze the Buddha's teachings, not just one or two topics but the complete teachings. Apply the methods and examine their effects. We can end our samsaric entrapments by removing delusions and pacifying our unsubdued minds, thereby generating the path in our minds. By completing the path, we attain nirvana, the stage of the arhat.

However, achieving liberation for ourselves alone is not sufficient. How tragic if only a few beings gain release from suffering while countless sentient beings continue to drown in oceans of sorrow! Therefore we should not settle for liberation for ourselves only, but rather aim for full enlightenment in order to offer perfect service to all sentient beings.

What Is Dharma?

Dharma means to hold the mind, to keep the mind in virtue, thereby saving ourselves from falling into the lower realms of indescribable suffering. Dharma is any action of body, speech, or mind that acts as an antidote to delusions. In relation to this definition, I wish to address people who do not believe in reincarnation, karma, or similar Buddhist principles but who seek the happiness of this life. Such people also need the Dharma because it contains remedies to delusions that interfere with happiness in the short term and long term.

Dharma is not about external action or religious dogma. It is about training the mind to be healthy, joyful, wise, compassionate, and courageous in helping others. It is not Dharma to merely chant mantras, recite sutras, meditate, or even do charity work with a worldly intention that seeks this-life happiness, such as recognition, wealth, or power. The test is whether our actions are chipping away at delusions or strengthening them.

His Holiness the Dalai Lama often says Dharma is what mends the mind, makes the mind better. We utilize Dharma methods to transform the angry, impatient mind into one that is more tolerant, more useful, more relaxed, wiser, and stronger. We change a mind that is self-centered and egotistical into one that cares about the well-being of others. We transform the craving mind into one that is more satisfied, more content. This is called mending the mind and this is the Buddhadharma.

In short the Dharma protects our minds from negativities. When we protect our minds we shield ourselves from suffering. How is this?

When we practice the Dharma our minds are devoted to the guru, the Three Jewels. We live an ethical life that strives toward bodhicitta and wisdom rather than immersion in delusions and negative thoughts. We are less likely to harm ourselves and others. When we do not cling to the concerns and happiness of just this life, we instantly feel as if a giant load has been lifted off us, and there is an immediate sense of freedom, lightness, and joy.

Does renouncing samsara mean giving up happiness? Oh, no! Not at all! Buddhism and the Dharma path are about how to achieve the *best* form of happiness, happiness that lasts! We enjoy so much more when we are not choked by delusions. If we do nothing to overcome the delusions, we will be like alcoholics who are unable to abandon their addiction to illusory, temporary pleasure and who end up increasing their suffering. Life then becomes filled with problems.

Indulging in delusions creates myriad forms of addiction and regaining control over our minds becomes extremely difficult. On TV and in newspapers we often see stories of millionaires and billionaires who are so unhappy in their hearts, in their inner lives. Some end up like terrified, caged creatures hiding away from others; some even take their own lives.

The tsunami in Indonesia and the hurricane in Louisiana overwhelmed many lives. Allowing our lives to be flooded by the delusions of anger and attachment creates a tsunami in our minds, a tsunami of attachment, an overpowering overflow of the dissatisfied, crazed mind. This tsunami is much more destructive than a physical one because it harms us now and from life to life. It becomes the cause of samsara from life to life.

Delusions destroy our happiness and bring endless problems to ourselves, our family, and the world. They inflict harm through leaving negative imprints, causing us to repeat negative actions and to mislead others to do the same, bringing nightmarish hardship. Our daily lives may appear orderly, but in truth we are living under the tsunami of delusions.

The outer tsunamis, dangers from water, fire, wind, and earthquakes, are not the creation of a god but the creation of delusions. Beings are impacted by these terrible disasters because of underlying causes—the delusions, the negative actions, and unrighteous actions committed in this and past lives. When karmic seeds ripen, the fruits manifest in ways far greater than the seed itself.

Therefore delusions should never be underestimated. Even if we are practicing very high tantric meditation, if we fail to cultivate the foundational attitudes of renunciation, bodhicitta, and right view, our so-called practice will be like eating poisoned food and will bring harmful effects, and then we shall face death empty-handed.

The pleasures we now experience, such as living in peaceful places, seeing beautiful gardens, having friends, a healthy body, and all forms of enjoyment, are manifestations of the virtuous mind that engaged in positive actions in the past. These are byproducts of actions done by a mind that avoided ignorance, anger, and attachment, and that carried out actions with a good heart, unstained by self-cherishing thought. This means that the joys of life we now enjoy came from our own minds that resisted the delusions.

RECOGNIZING TRUE ACTS OF DHARMA

Picture this: Four people are saying prayers in a gompa or temple. Outwardly all four people appear to be engaging in holy action, spiritual action, seemingly practicing the Dharma.

Now let us look at their motivations for praying. Let us say the first person is raising his prayers without concern for himself, wishing only to benefit others. His motivation is to achieve enlightenment to free sentient beings from suffering and to lead them to enlightenment. The second person is reciting prayers with the motivation of achieving the blissful state of nirvana for himself. The third person is offering prayers for a better future life. The fourth person is reciting prayers with the thought "May I have a long life, good health, and wealth." The last person is not thinking about enlightenment, nirvana, or even a better rebirth. His prayers are aimed solely at the concerns of this present life. His attitude is one of clinging to the happiness of just these few years of life.

Of the four people reciting prayers, only the actions of the first three persons qualify as Dharma action. The fourth person's action is not Dharma action but merely worldly concern, the pursuit of gain in this life only. Even though outwardly he recites prayers and appears to engage in Dharma practice, his action contains no Dharma at all. His action is called worldly dharma because it is limited to this life and seeks nothing beyond this life.

Even praying for the ones we care about is limited because "I" also refers to "mine." So although prayers to benefit loved ones is a start, our intention needs to be expanded to encompass all sentient beings. Offering help to some sentient beings but excluding others is not pure Dharma action.

Thus the fourth person, whose prayers centered around the needs of this life, is not engaging in Dharma at all. But the praying of the first person becomes a cause of enlightenment because his attitude is the wish to benefit all beings. The second person's praying becomes a cause of self-liberation but not full enlightenment because he focused on freeing only himself from his own suffering. The third person's praying for a better future life does not become a cause to achieving nirvana, let alone enlightenment, yet still qualifies as Dharma action because his attitude yearns for the happiness of future lives with the understanding that good deeds are required to obtain that.

Therefore renounce the concerns of this life. Instead train the mind in the compassionate thought that seeks to benefit others. When disciples of the great Lama Atisha asked him what scriptural texts to read or what holy pilgrimage places to visit to nourish their Dharma practice, master Atisha would respond, "Give up this life!" Here he meant giving up clinging to the concerns of only this life. This precious human rebirth is meant for more than just the short-term goals of this life.

It is good to regularly check whether our spiritual actions are Dharma. Ask yourself, "What is my motivation for doing this?" Answer honestly. If our motivation relates to better future lives, gaining liberation, or best of all, attaining enlightenment for the sake of others, then it is likely to be Dharma action. However, if our motivation relates only to the concerns of this life, it is not Dharma at all, no light has entered the prison of samsara.

How many of the actions we take from morning to night will be a cause for achieving enlightenment? How many will help us achieve nirvana or a better rebirth? How many are for this life only? Examine where your mind is and check your motivation.

THREE LEVELS OF CAPABILITY

Nalanda Monastic University in India was for centuries the mighty seat of Buddhism, supporting a large community of Sangha scholars and masters. Lama Atisha was one of the brightest jewels of Nalanda. By the eleventh century, Buddhism in Tibet had degenerated, centuries after it had been established by the Nalanda pandit Shantarakshita, later assisted by Padmasambhava. As a response, the Tibetan king Yeshe Oe wanted to revive pure Buddhism in Tibet, and so embarked on a journey to invite Lama Atisha to Tibet to help.

On his way, the king was captured by a local warlord who held him for ransom. The king's nephew Jangchup Oe pleaded for his uncle's life, but the warlord refused, saying he would release the king only if he was paid the king's weight in gold, and otherwise would execute him.

Unable to raise sufficient gold, Jangchup Oe was desperate. But the old king saw a better use for the money.

"Take the gold and go to India to invite Lama Atisha," said King Yeshe Oe. "Tell him that I have given up my life to this irreligious lord for the sake of reviving the Buddhadharma in Tibet. Ask him to please guide me with his compassion in all my future lives."

At that time, the passage from Tibet to India was extremely difficult. There were no roads and the terrain was mountainous, harsh, and filled with fierce, wild animals. The translator Naktso Lotsawa was chosen for the perilous journey. Without any thought for his life, his only concern the Buddhadharma and the happiness of sentient beings, Naktso Lotsawa successfully completed the journey.

Upon meeting him, Lama Atisha was deeply moved but did not respond right away. He returned the gold and said he would first check whether his going to Tibet would benefit sentient beings there. After making prayers to Avalokiteshvara, the great compassionate one, and to Tara, the female aspect of the Buddha, Lama Atisha received the advice that going to Tibet would greatly benefit the teachings and sentient beings but would shorten his life substantially.

Despite the danger, Lama Atisha journeyed to Tibet. During his time there, he wrote *Lamp for the Path to Enlightenment*, the forerunner of all texts on the graduated path to enlightenment, which contained the essence of the entire Buddhadharma. That is how Lama Atisha revived the pure, stainless Buddhadharma in Tibet.

The omniscient mind sees all beings and has a perfect understanding of the mental qualities of each sentient being. Therefore the Buddha gave teachings suited to sentient beings who could be categorized under three mental levels—lower capability, middle capability, and great capability.

The person seeking only the happiness of future lives is regarded as a lower-capability being, and teachings suited to such a person are termed "small" or "initial-scope" teachings. Such a person shuns lower rebirth and seeks a better future rebirth. To accomplish this, the person trains the mind in devotion to the spiritual teacher—on impermanence and death, on the law of karma, and on refuge in the Buddha, Dharma, and Sangha. The person aspires to avoid the sufferings of the three lower realms of animal, preta, and hell states and understands the need to act virtuously to secure a better future life.

The person who seeks the blissful state of peace or nirvana has turned his back on the temporary happiness of samsara and seeks to cut off cyclic existence in its entirety. The Buddha offered such people, regarded as middle-capability beings, methods to accomplish this goal through the noble eightfold path, the fundamental path to achieve liberation or nirvana. The noble eightfold path of the Lower Vehicle, as taught by Guru Shakyamuni Buddha, consists of right speech, right action, right livelihood, right effort, right mindfulness, right concentration, right view, and right thought. The eightfold path corresponds to the three higher trainings of moral conduct, concentration, and wisdom or higher seeing. This person renounces samsara by meditating on how samsara and its apparent happiness are in the nature of suffering. The person meditates on the true cause of suffering, on the delusions, the antidotes, the evolution of samsara, the twelve interdependent links, the cessation of delusion and karma, and the attainment of liberation.

The person who seeks enlightenment abandons self-cherishing and aims for buddhahood in order to benefit all sentient beings. This person is regarded as a great-capability being. He or she trains the mind in the renunciation of samsara and cultivates the altruistic mind of bodhicitta and the wisdom realizing emptiness. This person seeks to be free from the dualistic mind with its subtle misconceptions and engages in the six perfections of the bodhisattva. Such a person is motivated by the aspiration and courage to attain full enlightenment in order to release all sentient beings from suffering and to guide them to enlightenment.

It is important to understand that the great-capability being's ability to practice this path depends on foundations. In this case, the immediate foundation is the graduated path of the middle capability, which is in turn based on the graduated path of the lower-capability being. Each level of teachings and practices is built on the prior level.

The path or methods we engage in depend on what kind of happiness we want to achieve, on our spiritual goals. All three approaches are premised on taking refuge in the Three Jewels: the Buddha, Dharma, and Sangha.

REFUGE AS THE FOUNDATION

Presently we have neither the power nor the capability to free ourselves from all suffering. We cannot even save ourselves from the ordinary problems of daily life, so forget about closing the door to rebirth in the lower realms!

As we seek relief from life's hardships we take refuge in our friends, our family, our wealth, our reputation, and in external objects. We do this all the time. However, because our motivation for taking refuge is based on short-term goals, and because our common objects of refuge are not true sources of happiness, lasting happiness eludes us.

Reason therefore dictates that we need guidance from one who has freed himself from samsara, who has perfect compassion and enlightened knowledge, and whose successful methods are time tested. We should be careful not to make mistakes when choosing the object of refuge. Buddhists take refuge in the Three Jewels of the Buddha, Dharma, and Sangha, but one needs clear understanding on why these are worthy objects of refuge.

A person who wishes to become a doctor must attend university to learn the subjects needed for a medical degree. He or she needs to understand subjects related to sickness, causes of sickness, and healing. Such a person cannot accomplish this without the help of others, including teachers and doctors who went through medical training themselves, as well as from patients whose conditions allow trainee doctors to understand diseases better.

In the same way, we cannot on our own become the future Buddha jewel and actualize the Dharma jewel by becoming the Sangha jewel. We also rely on the help of others. For this reason, refuge in the Buddha, Dharma, and Sangha is the basis for actualizing the path.

To be a Buddhist means to be an inner being who relies on the guidance of the Triple Jewel. People who pay homage at temples, recite prayers, use religious items, or meditate at Buddhist places are usually called Buddhists. However, these are mere outward appearances. They do not mean such persons are actually inner beings. Whether a person is an inner being or not can only be determined by the state of that person's mind.

Blind faith is unreliable. Proper refuge means understanding what refuge means and abiding by what it entails. For this it is useful to examine the causes of refuge, the objects of refuge and why they are worthy, and the manner of taking refuge.

The causes of refuge

To develop true refuge in the Three Jewels we need two causes: an intelligent fear of samsara and faith that the Three Jewels can guide us out of samsara.

Fear of samsara is a kind of positive rational fear because it will cause us to protect ourselves from harm. Sometimes we persuade ourselves into thinking we have no fear. We may use euphemisms like "I have a healthy respect for the fragility of life," when in truth this is just fear of death talking. We know very well our fears about illnesses, death, hunger, extreme hot or cold, being criticized and maligned by others, being thought of as ugly or badly dressed, becoming bankrupt or losing possessions, and so on.

Our entire lives are driven by dread and fear, yet we run to take refuge in people, possessions, and things that are still stuck in samsara! That is taking refuge in the wrong object. To free ourselves from samsara, we need to be averse to all forms of suffering in samsara.

The second cause for taking refuge is having faith or confidence in the Buddha, Dharma, and Sangha to guide us out of the snake pit of samsara. Buddha has attained liberation and enlightenment. His guidance is therefore relevant to our quest for happiness.

We feel sorry for moths that keep flying into hot light bulbs because no matter the obvious danger, their ignorance and foolishness keep drawing them into the heat, causing their painful deaths. We are not that different from those moths. We are unafraid of the fire of samsara and view it as an attractive source of enjoyment. We rush toward it and get burned every time.

Let us say there is a man who somehow fell onto a rocky ledge just above a volcanic fiery pit. The ledge is crumbling away, so he cries out, "Help, help! Get me out! I don't want to be burned in the fire!" Another man arrives above the ledge and sees what is going on. He throws down a thick rope, but the endangered man does not see the rope even though it is dangling right in front of his face. If the endangered man does not take hold of the rope, he will not be rescued, no matter how great his fear is, no matter how strong the rope is. How quickly he gets out depends on his grasping on to the rope without letting go, having faith in the helper and the rope. Otherwise the flames will catch up with him.

In exactly the same way, we need to have firm conviction in the ability of the Buddha, Dharma, and Sangha to free us from the fire of samsara. Fear alone will not help. Stable reliance on the Three Jewels is vital in the pursuit of liberation.

Why the objects of refuge are worthy

A patient suffering from a serious illness needs a doctor, medicine, and a nurse to help during treatment. The Buddha is like the doctor who explains the cause of samsaric suffering and reveals the remedy, Dharma is the medicine to remove the delusions as the cause of suffering, and the Sangha is like the doctor's assistants who support the patient in the healing process.

The Buddha is a worthy object of refuge because he has freed himself from samsara, and beyond that he has attained omniscience. Owing to his omniscience, he understands all forms of existence, fully comprehends the mental inclinations and karmic conditions of every sentient being, and knows the remedies to help each one. He has impartial compassion for all sentient beings and infinite skillful means to guide them. He works unconditionally for all sentient beings.

The Buddha has both relative and absolute aspects. The relative aspect of the Buddha is the form that is visible to sentient beings according to their karmic levels. The absolute aspect of the Buddha is the dharmakaya, the omniscient mind possessed of realizations—a mind we have the potential to actualize.

The Dharma is a worthy object of refuge because it gives protection from the suffering of samsara—death, rebirth, old age, sickness, and hardships of all kinds. The Dharma also provides antidotes to the delusions of ignorance, anger, and attachment that drive us to generate negative karma and result in misery. The Dharma urges us to renounce samsara, it provides complete training in compassion toward all living beings, and it helps us develop the right view of the ultimate nature of reality—the absence of inherent existence. Dharma is the actual refuge.

The Dharma has relative and absolute aspects. The relative aspect of the Dharma is in the form of the teachings, scriptures, and texts. The absolute Dharma refers to the realizations of the path, born from cultivating the Dharma and from living one's life in virtue.

Sangha members are worthy objects of refuge because they help practitioners on the spiritual path and assist in their development of realizations. The Sangha jewels are the arya beings who have directly perceived emptiness and live in vows purely. The Sangha also has relative and absolute aspects. The relative aspect of the Sangha is that of the ordinary ordained monks and nuns, who may or may not have attained the cessation of obscurations. Nevertheless, relative Sangha members live in vows and inspire others to live in morality and cultivate the path, and thus they deserve respect. The absolute Sangha is the actual arya Sangha jewels.

In Tibetan communities, whenever medicine prescribed for illness does not help, the patient or the patient's family go to their lama for advice on Dharma practices of purification to facilitate recovery. This has proven successful on many occasions, which is why the lama's advice on many areas of a person's life is sought in Tibetan culture.

Whenever you experience fear or fear your life is in danger, the most important thing is to take refuge in the Buddha, Dharma, and Sangha. Even if you have a bad dream at night, even if you see a hungry ghost, single-pointedly take refuge in the Three Jewels.

There is a Tibetan story about a man who was attacked by a tiger and who earnestly thought of Avalokiteshvara, the Buddha of compassion, while he was in the tiger's mouth. Right at that moment the tiger's mouth fell open, enabling the man to escape. There also are many stories where people in great danger were saved through their remembrance of the Three Jewels. This illustrates the potency of taking refuge in the jewels.

The manner of taking refuge

Depending on the mentality of the person, there are three levels of thinking when taking refuge. The most basic intent for taking refuge is simply to gain a better future life. The simple-minded person interested only in great wealth in the future life must also take refuge to avoid the lower realms and to create good karma through virtues.

The next level of motivation for taking refuge is to be entirely freed of rebirth into samsara, that is, to attain nirvana or liberation.

The person with the highest mental ability recognizes that none of us is alone in suffering and that all sentient beings are in the same sinking boat. This person takes refuge with the noble thought of wishing to attain enlightenment to help all beings out of samsara. In this way, the Buddhadharma is described as the perfect refuge because it has methods to suit persons of different inclinations.

REFUGE COMMITMENTS AND ADVICE

A person makes two principal commitments after taking refuge in the Buddha. The first is to strive to engage in virtue and avoid nonvirtue, as advised by the Buddha, rather than get drawn to other beliefs and practices. When doctors prescribe medicine to patients, they often also advise the patient to avoid certain lifestyles to prevent relapse. A patient who consumes the medicine but ignores this additional advice will not fully recover. For example, the Buddha advised us to overcome anger. But if we ignore this advice and instead get waylaid by other beliefs, which, for instance, encourage outbursts of anger, there's danger we will develop mistaken understanding about how to subdue the angry mind to gain peace and happiness.

There is the very real danger of being misled. Once wrong understanding sets in, it's very difficult for right understanding to take root. All actions flowing from wrong understanding are flawed and create the cause of suffering.

The other commitment requires us to always be respectful toward any image of the Buddha, as a remembrance of his immeasurable kindness in revealing the path. Any statues or images of the Buddha should be respected as the Buddha himself. Even if we think the artwork poorly done, we should avoid criticizing or treating the Buddha image as inferior, to be thrown away like garbage.

The mind of respect is very important. All Buddha images should be placed in a clean, high place and not on the floor. When we see a Buddha image, we should think that we are really seeing the living Guru Shakyamuni Buddha right there.

Taking refuge in the Dharma requires us to undertake two main commitments. The first of these is that we should avoid harming sentient beings, and if we cannot help them we should at least not harm them. This is the fundamental principle.

The second is that all Dharma books, pages, and bits of paper with Dharma words or even a single-syllable mantra must be treated with respect. We should never place such items lower than our bodies, such as on the floor, under our beds, on a sitting cushion, or in unclean places. Dharma words explain the path that leads to enlightenment.

We should place any Dharma words on a high, clean shelf. If we have no choice but to burn them, we should first meditate on emptiness, then visualize all the words in the Dharma papers to be burned entering into the syllable *AH* (symbol of the Buddha's holy speech), and the *AH* then entering into our heart. If we come across a scrap of paper or cloth with Dharma words on it, we should pick it up and place it up high like on a tree branch. Only Dharma texts should be placed on our altar. It is better to keep Dharma books and ordinary books separate, as this contributes to the mind remaining clear and uncomplicated.

Taking refuge in the Sangha requires us to keep two things in mind. First is that whenever we see monks or nuns who make up an ordinary Sangha, we should think each Sangha member represents the absolute, arya Sangha. We should do this regardless of whether we think that Sangha member has realizations or not, no matter their actual level of mind.

Thinking this way helps keep us from judging, often wrongly! Refraining from judgment is important because most of us cannot know the realization of another person. If we think negatively of another person and it turns out that person is more realized than us, we commit heavy negative karma.

Generally a person living in vows is karmically higher than a layperson, so criticizing a monastic generates negative karma. Furthermore, a fully ordained monk, *bhikshu*, or *gelong* lives by 253 vows, more than most ordinary people can manage. Therefore if we see a piece of red or yellow cloth on the road, we should realize these are the colors of monastic robes; out of respect for monastics we should pick the piece up and place it on a tree branch. Lift it off the ground. This is not a silly, petty act. It will help train the mind in many ways.

Also, once we take refuge in the Sangha we should avoid contact with distracting people who discourage us from engaging in Dharma. Blindly following such people risks weakening our efforts to overcome delusions and harms right understanding. While we may not be able to avoid such people, we must guard the mind against distraction and negativity. Wrong conceptions that promote delusions can slip in easily and without notice.

Once we have taken refuge in the Buddha, Dharma, and Sangha, we should offer prostrations of respect to the Triple Jewel three times each morning and three times at night. Before we eat or drink anything always remember to offer it to the Triple Jewel first, with respect and devotion. These simple practices strengthen our mind of refuge.

Benefits of taking refuge

Taking refuge is the foundation of all vows, including the five lay vows, the eight precepts, ordination vows, bodhisattva vows, and tantric vows. It helps us generate merit and purifies negative karma collected from countless lifetimes, which would have brought us untold suffering. It is said that a handful of water may be counted by its drops, but the benefits of refuge can never be measured. The person whose mind continuously lives in pure refuge cannot experience harm from other human beings, nonhuman beings, and beings in other planes.

Laypeople in Tibet often do retreat on refuge practice. This includes meditations on what refuge means followed by recitations of the refuge prayer. The latter is a very powerful purification practice. Most of us are unaware how much negative karma we have committed, especially in relation to the Three Jewels and ordinary beings. Because of this it's especially effective to purify negative karmas through meditation on refuge.

Once a group of monks were journeying through the forest near a river outside the northern Indian town of Kalimpong. One monk separated from the group and rested on a huge rock, when suddenly a huge snake appeared and very quickly coiled itself around him. The other monks were terrified and had no idea how to help the stricken monk.

Soon the snake had lifted its head above the monk's head. Terrible fear swept through the monk's mind. No matter how much he struggled he could not escape from the snake's tight grip.

Suddenly the monk remembered Tara, a female manifestation of the Buddha. Despite his great fear, the monk did his best to strongly focus on Tara and take refuge in her. As he did so the snake loosened its grip and simply slid away.

After that episode, the monk praised Tara because he realized that taking refuge in her had saved his life. Later he found a small golden statue of Tara and brought it to His Eminence Song Rinpoche, seeking blessings. When they met, Rinpoche was struck by the fact that the monk was from the Theravada tradition, because these monks normally only have Guru Shakyamuni Buddha statues and not statues of other emanations of the Buddha. But when Song Rinpoche asked the monk to explain the Tara statue, he explained how he had been nearly killed by the snake, and how taking refuge had saved him.

Refuge is particularly effective at stopping fearful dreams. Some people feel something formless pressing down on them when they lie down to sleep, and they cannot move or scream for help. Reciting the refuge prayer helps in such a situation. Taking refuge with proper understanding brings protection and all forms of success. The prayer's ability to remove negative karma, accumulate merit, and provide life guidance brings success to whatever we do. It is worthwhile to reflect on the benefits of taking refuge.

When we say Guru Shakyamuni Buddha revealed the path, you may wonder why we use the word "guru" when referring to the Buddha. Why do we need a guru at all?

Guru as the Root

Shakyamuni Buddha made several predictions about future learned ones who would clearly explain his teachings. For instance, the Buddha prophesied that Lama Tsongkhapa would be born in Tibet and would explain the path to enlightenment clearly while performing the deeds of a Buddha.

Lama Tsongkhapa fulfilled the prophesy. He became a great scholar, a great practitioner, and founded the Gelug tradition. Lama Tsongkhapa wrote many scriptural texts, including the *Great Treatise on the Stages of the Path to Enlightenment*. He also wrote concise texts such as the *Foundation of All Good Qualities*, which says:

> The kind and venerable guru is the foundation of all good
> qualities.
> Seeing that reliance on him is the root of the path,
> please bless me to have respect and continuous effort.

This raises the question, "Why is the guru the 'root' of the path?" Whatever we wish to become—a doctor, teacher, scientist, cook, or any person with good skills— we depend on a teacher to explain and clarify learning points. Likewise, without a guru we cannot achieve liberation from samsara even if we possess intellectual knowledge of the Dharma. Just as a boat needs a helmsman and cannot reach the other shore on its own, without a guru we cannot cross the ocean of cyclic existence let alone achieve enlightenment.

Some Dharma students generate wrong views when they hear the word "guru" or the phrase "guru devotion" because they do not understand the philosophical points behind this practice. Students think negatively about gurus, believing gurus praise themselves, inflate their own importance, and ask disciples to look at them as buddhas and make offerings to them.

It looks like Dharma politics! It looks like spiritual abuse. It looks to these students that the spiritual teacher or guru is trying to take advantage of them. It looks as if the guru is seeking more followers and more offerings. But it is not like that.

Some people regard guru devotion as some kind of Tibetan lama "trip," something Tibetan lamas created for their own benefit. Guru Shakyamuni Buddha often taught on the subject of guru devotion, including in the *Laying Out of the Stalks Sutra* and the *Essence of the Earth Sutra*. In these sutra teachings, Guru Shakyamuni Buddha explains the value and importance of a guru for our spiritual path. He offers clear instructions on this practice.

The guru is very important in the Hinayana tradition, whose fundamental path for achieving liberation is living by the Vinaya, the moral conduct of the ordained ones. In this tradition, a person can't receive the lineage of ordination without a teacher.

In the Mahayana tradition, the guru is the virtuous friend who gives teachings, clarifies the points of the path, and guides the disciple on his or her journey to realizations and enlightenment.

In tantra, we can't achieve enlightenment without a perfectly qualified vajra guru planting the seeds of the four kayas in our minds, through granting the four complete initiations of highest yoga tantra. We will gain no realizations if we try to practice highest yoga tantra without a guru, let alone achieve enlightenment itself.

We might think, "There are books on achieving liberation and enlightenment. I can read them and practice. Why do I need a guru?" In fact we need a guru's commentaries and explanations to fully understand Dharma teachings, especially the subtler meanings. There is a big difference between gaining insight through studying under a teacher and just gathering information.

Listening to a teacher greatly affects the mind, whereas parroting words from books does not equal correct understanding. Our goal is not to gain a dry, textbook understanding of the path to enlightenment. It is instead to taste the actual experience of it, to attain realizations of the Dharma. If we don't directly experience the path, our understanding will be neither clear nor complete.

Gaining such realizations depends on receiving guidance from the guru and blessings of the guru within our own mental continuum. Blessings of the guru refers to how the points of the path deeply benefit our minds. This starts from a clear, strong feeling in our hearts of the nature of suffering, followed by suffering's causes, its cessation, and the remedies to accomplish cessation.

This is why mere academic knowledge is insufficient! If we want only intellectual understanding of the Dharma in order to write a book or get a college degree, we do not need guru yoga practice. However, it is quite different if our aim is to subdue our delusions and accomplish realizations on the path to liberation and enlightenment. This is a specific, special aim.

The point to understand is that we need a guru to focus our minds on the path, pure and simple. We can make many mistakes if we miss the point of having a guru. Just as we can run off the road if we do not concentrate when driving a car, we can run into many problems if we do not understand the aim of having a guru. In America and some other Western countries, some meditation teachers have actually met to discuss whether guru devotion is really necessary on the path to enlightenment. Some think that while guru devotion might have been practiced in olden times, it is not needed nowadays when information is highly accessible.

I think this discussion has come about because of problems relating to some so-called gurus in the West in recent years. People who assert this have missed the usefulness of this practice, its infinite benefit in our spiritual evolution. These people think guru devotion is antiquated and merely cultural, that we can effectively meditate on the path without guru devotion practice. It is not so.

We need a teacher to gain knowledge about ordinary life activities, for example, we need someone to teach us the alphabet, mend a bicycle, or bake a cake. We even need to learn from somebody how to clean a room professionally. In the same way, we need a guide when traveling to a remote place we have not visited before. So without question we need a guide on our journey to enlightenment.

Why is guru devotion the root of the path? Visualize a wonderful fruit-laden tree. Enlightenment is like the ripe fruit at the top of the tree, the path to enlightenment is like the trunk of the tree, and guru devotion is the root. Development of the tree's branches, leaves, buds, and fruits depends on the strength of its root. Similarly, our ability to attain the fruit of enlightenment depends on the strength of our guru devotion.

Think of guru devotion as the fuel in a car or a plane, without which neither can take us where we want to go. Our devotion enables us to train our minds, cease all the faults of mind, complete all realizations, and achieve enlightenment. This then enables us to work perfectly for numberless sentient beings, liberating them from the oceans of samsaric suffering and bringing them to enlightenment. This is fantastic.

It is a common experience that when we have strong guru devotion in the heart, we easily feel the preciousness of optimum human rebirth during meditation. Guru devotion also helps us effortlessly experience the transitory nature of life when meditating on impermanence and death and deepens our understanding of compassion, emptiness, or any other Dharma topic. While in a state of strong devotion, our mind is pacified, focused, and clear. Delusions cannot surface freely and are thus easy to control.

On the other hand, when our guru devotion degenerates or disappears altogether, our focus on virtue can scatter. Our delusions bubble to the surface easily and are far more resistant to being controlled. We can check this out for ourselves.

We should regard our guru in terms of the guru's good qualities and not in terms of his or her faults, regardless of whatever the guru may think of himself or herself. It does not matter whether the guru is actually a buddha. For us the practice is to see the guru's good qualities as inseparable from that of a buddha. Practicing guru devotion is not about external gestures of devotion but about humility and heartfelt devotion.

Receiving blessings from the guru depends on how much devotion we hold in our minds toward the guru, not on our physical proximity. Even if we are physically distant from our guru, if we have great devotion we will be mentally close to the guru and will receive many blessings.

Lama Tsongkhapa once asked Manjushri, the bodhisattva of wisdom, "How can we quickly achieve realizations of the whole path to enlightenment?"

Manjushri responded that to grow crops we need to plant seeds in the earth, then provide essential conditions of water and minerals. A seed cannot grow on its own. If the seed is burned by fire, eaten by insects, or taken away by birds, it also cannot grow.

Manjushri continued that in a similar way our realizations cannot grow without the essential conditions of purification of negativities and the accumulation of merit. These two are topped off by single-pointedly requesting the guru, who is inseparable from a buddha, to bring blessings within our hearts. If we strongly practice requesting these blessings every day, realizations will come without any difficulty. The guru is the supreme merit field. This was Manjushri's profound advice.

Anger or loss of devotion can arise when our guru does something we dislike (which is usually something that goes against our self-cherishing) or instructs us to do something in which we have no interest. Allowing devotion to diminish even for a moment is very dangerous because the guru is the most karmically powerful presence in our lives.

If we develop doubts about what the guru is asking of us, we can seek clarification. But we must be respectful in our thoughts and in the way we ask the guru for clarification. Generating negative assumptions and dark thoughts toward our guru is a serious matter, a heavy imprint, which can create obstacles to developing our minds on the path.

QUALITIES OF A GURU AND HOW TO PRACTICE GURU DEVOTION CORRECTLY

Before devoting ourselves to a guru we should properly check. I don't mean we should check for faults, but rather we should look for qualities in the person. The texts speak of ten qualities a guru must possess. They include possessing morality; realizing calm abiding, or better yet, emptiness; being subdued in manner; having greater knowledge than the disciple; and striving to guide the disciple to virtue.

Even if the guru does not possess high realizations or vast knowledge, he or she should be able to explain the nature of samsara, the danger of the grasping at the "I," and the need to be free from delusions. The guru should emphasize the need to always care for sentient beings more than for oneself. At the bare minimum, a guru should stress the importance of the future life over the present life because that will encourage the disciple to pursue methods that will create a happy future life.

Guru devotion practice consists of devoting oneself to the guru in thought and in action.

Devotion in thought

Devotion in thought includes the two limbs of remembering the kindness of the guru and seeing the guru as a buddha. This is illustrated by scriptural sources, reason, and our personal experiences of the guru.

Remembering the kindness of the guru. The guru's principal kindness is in showing the entire path to enlightenment, not only during this life but over beginningless lifetimes. Our guru is like a guide who unexpectedly appears and leads us to safety when we are lost in a dark and dangerous place while surrounded by savage beasts.

Perhaps we did not have the karma to receive teachings directly from Guru Shakyamuni Buddha or from the great Indian and Tibetan pandits. But our present guru continues the Buddha's work by teaching us the Dharma, and in this is infinitely kind. The kindness of a doctor who cures us of cancer is nothing compared to the kindness of the guru, who helps us remove stains from our mental continuum and who steers us toward enlightenment. This kindness is as limitless as space.

Seeing the guru as a buddha. In several sutras, the Buddha promised to repeatedly appear in the future as a guru. Gurus are manifestations of the dharmakaya who appear to us in an ordinary form that accords with our karma so we can relate to them. This ordinary form is the conventional guru. Even if we do not fully realize the nature of this manifestation now, cultivating this awareness helps us listen to the guru's teachings. Awareness of the dharmakaya nature of the guru will connect us more strongly with the teachings and will help us feel closer to all the buddhas.

Devotion in action

In the Hinayana tradition, devotion to the guru through action includes offering massage or perfume to the guru's holy body, making the guru's bed, offering robes, and similar actions. This is service to the guru in relation to the body.

Devotion to the guru through speech includes using an honorific when mentioning the holy name of the guru. This is why Theravadan monks to this day put their palms together and say "venerable so-and-so" when speaking about or to their abbot. Similarly, in a gelong (bhikshu) ordination, the presiding senior monk (*sangdön lopön*) gives monks advice about how to address the abbot and teachers.

Other types of guru devotion through action are carrying out the guru's advice, living life in accordance with the Dharma, offering service to the guru, and making offerings to the guru.

The main practice and best offering to the guru is using our body, speech, and mind to live according to the Dharma advice the guru gave us. As the great yogi Milarepa said, "I have no material offerings. My offering to my father-guru is my practice. The striving and hardships I bear in my practice is an offering to please my father-guru. I repay my father-guru's kindness with my practice."

Offering service includes all the respectful behavior described in *Fifty Verses of Guru Devotion* by Ashvagosha, such as standing when the guru enters the room, prostrating, cleaning, cooking, and offering other services.

We know from our own experience that following the guru's advice is easier when our devotion is strong. When our devotion is weak even a small task seems like a big burden. By offering help to a Dharma center we provide many people conditions to meet the teachings and to practice the infallible path to enlightenment. If we frequently think this way whenever we do tasks, our minds will be very happy.

As for material offerings, we should sincerely offer what we can. Although the guru does not seek material offerings, disciples should still make the best offerings they can manage in order to accumulate merit. The guru is pleased by our Dharma practice, not by our material offerings. However, if we see the guru acting happy at receiving material offerings, it would be an error to think the guru is acting wrongly by being pleased.

To make a disciple happy, high lamas often act pleased when they receive material offerings. Pari Dorje Chang, a high lama of Sera monastery in Tibet, was once offered a leg of mutton by someone who earned his living printing Dharma texts. While the person was in front of him, Rinpoche acted very pleased and said, "Oh, how thoughtful! Now I can make *momos* (dumplings)."

But right after the person left, Rinpoche threw the whole leg of mutton into the toilet pit because it was bought with money obtained by selling Dharma scriptures solely for personal gain. Eating food bought with money earned by selling statues or Dharma scriptures for personal gain is regarded as heavy negative karma. Pari Dorje Chang did not give the meat to other people because they would be tainted with spiritual pollution if they had consumed it. But he showed pleasure at receiving the offering because it was his skillful way of enabling the disciple to accumulate merit by making the offering.

When we don't do analytical meditation on guru devotion, the feeling of devotion quickly disappears. But if we frequently apply ourselves to this meditation, the experience of devotion becomes more stable. Some feeling in our heart that our guru is a buddha, even if it lasts just a short time, is a sign of receiving blessings. It is vital to know how to devote correctly to the guru and how to not mix it with mere external appearances and hollow words.

The four general benefits of guru devotion

Just as rain showers enable flowers and crops to grow, the rain of the guru's blessings moistens the field of our minds for Dharma realizations to blossom. These blessings also shield our minds from delusions and from negative thoughts. As we stop the arising of negative thoughts toward the guru, we avoid destroying our many eons of merit. The fourth benefit is that guru devotion protects us from doing things that delay our realizations.

When we board an aircraft, the cabin crew always gives instructions on safety features. This starts with how to adjust the seatbelt and continues with the location of the emergency exits, the life jackets, and so on. This is all for our safety in case something dangerous happens.

In exactly the same way, the path to enlightenment is filled with many dangers, and guru devotion is the lifejacket for our practice. Guru devotion acts like all the safety devices combined and protects our fragile spiritual efforts. Whether and how quickly we achieve realizations of the path all depend on the stability of our guru devotion.

THE THREE PRINCIPAL ASPECTS OF THE MAHAYANA PATH

We have previously discussed the three types of aspirations or goals that would qualify as Dharma action, namely, the goal of a better future life, the goal of nirvana or liberation from samsara, and finally the goal of enlightenment for the sake of all sentient beings. The path to attain the goal of enlightenment has a common basis with the other paths in terms of taking refuge in the Three Jewels and guru devotion, with the additional altruism called bodhicitta. This path is that of the Great Vehicle, also called the Mahayana Vehicle.

The Mahayana path consists of cultivating these three principal aspects: renunciation of samsara, bodhicitta that renounces self-cherishing and cherishes others, and wisdom realizing emptiness, which is gaining right view.

Our motivation always determines whether our actions are virtuous or nonvirtuous. If an action is done with renunciation and right view, it is virtuous and the cause to achieve nirvana or liberation from samsara. If an action is done with renunciation of samsara, right view, and bodhicitta, it is virtuous and becomes the cause to achieve full enlightenment. Almost any action done without at least one of these three motivations—renunciation, bodhicitta, or wisdom realizing emptiness—becomes worldly action, just another cause of samsara.

There are a few exceptional actions that bring benefits even if done with a nonvirtuous thought like anger, ignorance, or attachment in clinging to this life. These include circumambulating holy objects or making offerings or prostrations to a holy object like a Buddha statue or a stupa. The virtue comes about not from the side of the doer's motivation but from the power of the holy object.

But apart from these exceptions, actions done without at least one of these three principals of renunciation, bodhicitta, or wisdom sets the wheel in motion for future tormented lives in samsara.

Practicing these three principal aspects of the path is indispensable. Practicing tantra without integrating these three principals will not bring you to enlightenment. In fact without at least a firm renunciation of samsara, we will continue to commit negative actions that create the cause of rebirth in the hell, preta, and animal realms.

There was once a meditator who spent his whole life doing retreat in a hermitage, meditating on the tantric deity Yamantaka. After he died he was reborn as a spirit who took on an image very similar to Yamantaka, with many arms, heads, and legs. One night while a retreater living in the same hermitage was doing sur offering, the practice of burning barley flour as a smoke offering of generosity to spirits, he saw this terrifying spirit. He nervously asked the spirit, "Who are you?" The spirit explained, "I am your friend. I was the retreater who was also doing retreat and recently passed away."

How could a meditator and practitioner of Yamantaka become a spirit after passing away? The answer is that although he meditated on Yamantaka he did not cultivate the mind of renunciation, bodhicitta, and right view, and therefore was not practicing tantra properly.

Without these three principles, even tantric retreat becomes ordinary worldly action. This meditator was reborn as a spirit because although he did Yamantaka practice for many years, he did so without the fundamental mind of renunciation, which meant all his actions became nonvirtuous.

From this story comes a lesson for reflection. If we do not study and practice the Dharma properly, if we are not mindful of what is going on in our minds while engaging in Dharma practice and in daily life, we can end up wasting our whole lives. We might get deceived by the mere appearances of doing Dharma practice.

Chanting mantras is easy, visualizing deities is easy, reading Dharma scriptures is easy. But properly practicing Dharma is something else, requiring us to internalize the teachings to subdue our minds and tame the delusions. It is not just about what we do externally.

Practicing Dharma requires us to internally tackle the wild and unsubdued mind, separate it from delusions, and direct it toward benefiting others and gaining nondual wisdom. The Kadampa masters would say that when our actions of body, speech, and mind are able to combat our delusions, when our actions become antidotes to our delusions, only then are we truly practicing Dharma.

RENUNCIATION

Owning material possessions is not the problem. The main problem is the mind that clings to them. For one who has not abandoned the clinging mind, possessions can lead to distraction and harm. Many great practitioners and bodhisattvas have been kings with families and incredible material wealth, but this wealth did not hinder their evolution into higher beings because they understood impermanence. They renounced the grasping mindset, they renounced samsara. Have we done so?

The previous Thirteenth Dalai Lama was required to wear new robes on the Tibetan new year and on other special days. An abundance of treasures and material possessions belonging to the Dalai Lama were at his disposal, and yet on special days His Holiness would ask permission from his servants and administrators. "May I wear the new robes tomorrow?" he would say. "Would you kindly lend me these robes?" It was entirely up to him how to use the Dalai Lama's possessions. He did not have to ask anyone for permission. But by doing so, His Holiness showed that in his mind none of those possessions were really his.

This is the opposite of how we constantly think of our possessions as our own. "This camera is mine," or "This meditation seat is mine!" We are totally possessed by the self-grasping "I." By comparison, the Thirteenth Dalai Lama acted as he did because he had rejected clinging to possessions, renounced the matters of this life, and abandoned self-cherishing.

Common sense dictates that if we want lasting happiness, we should give up suffering and its causes. All our unhappiness comes from our minds that obediently follow the delusions of attachment, anger, and delusion. By seeing how problems begin with the desire for sense objects, leading to dissatisfaction when these objects do not last, we recognize the traps set by the delusions that keep bringing us disappointment and misery.

If a burning piece of charcoal fell on our foot during a barbeque party, wouldn't we immediately kick it off? So why not cast out the delusions that have burned us during beginningless lives? When we stop clutching the smoldering ember of attachment the burning stops and right there the pain ends. There is peace right there. When we finally achieve freedom from delusions, there is lasting happiness right there.

Clinging to people and things that will naturally come to an end causes our happiness to be temporary. On top of that the sticky nature of attachment leaves an imprint on the mind that becomes a habit. As such imprints gain strength they will agitate us whenever things come to an end, and our resultant negative thoughts will throw us into future lives in samsara, with its heavy baggage of troubles. All this is caused by desire. Check it out! Reflect on the failings of samsara and decisively renounce it.

How do we generate renunciation?

First we need to renounce our own samsara before we can help other sentient beings to do so. This necessitates opening our eyes to how our ordinary samsaric lives, including all temporary delights such as our possessions, holidays, and excitements, are totally in the nature of suffering because they will end. Disappointment is endemic to samsara. As attractive as samsara appears, it is like an endless floor of thorns that pierce deeply into the flesh wherever we step.

For countless lives, we have chosen imprisonment in samsara. We have dwelt first on the mistaken view of the self as truly existing, followed by the mistaken view of samsara as a wonderful park, both views causing our minds to become attached to the sights and sounds of samsara. We do not realize this wonderful park has disguised its nature of suffering. When some form of temporary happiness arises in samsara, our attachment rises quickly and we latch on to that temporary happiness, which causes us discontent when the happiness finishes. This drives us to chase after more temporary highs, creating more causes for sorrow. That is the problem. To get out we need to generate renunciation of samsara.

The first step is to renounce this life, but I am not talking about ending one's own life! Suicide is caused by confusion, by not knowing Dharma and by not understanding how delusions drive people crazy. "Giving up this life" refers to rejecting the grasping mind, expelling the deception of delusions through discovering their true nature. Without this mind of renunciation, whatever we do, whether we walk, talk, eat, sleep, do our jobs, go on vacation—even when we pray and meditate— merely becomes a cause of more samsara.

Dromtonpa, the heart disciple of the great master Lama Atisha, lived at Reting, Tibet, back then many days' journey out of Lhasa. One day Dromtonpa saw an old man circumambulating the temple. Dromtonpa asked the old man what he was doing and the old man responded, "I am circumambulating this temple," thinking he was practicing the Dharma by doing that.

Dromtonpa advised him, "It is good that you are doing this but it would be better to practice the Dharma."

The old man then thought, "Oh, perhaps what the master meant was that I should be reading scriptures instead," so he started to read only scriptures.

Then later Dromtonpa came along, saw this old man reading a big pile of scriptural texts, and again asked, "What are you doing?"

"I am reading scriptures," responded the old man.

Dromtonpa then said, "It is good that you are doing this, but wouldn't it better to practice the holy Dharma?"

The old man then thought, "Oh, perhaps he meant I should be meditating," so he stopped reading scriptures and began to sit in meditation.

Then Dromtonpa came along again, saw the old man meditating, and asked, "What are you doing?"

The old man said, "I am meditating," but Dromtonpa responded, "It is good that you are meditating, but wouldn't it be better to practice the holy Dharma?"

By now the old man was frustrated and confused. He had tried circumambulating, reading scriptures, and meditating, yet he kept getting the same words from Dromtonpa. He finally asked, "What do you mean by practicing holy Dharma?"

Dromtonpa answered, "Renounce this life."

Liberation is not something a god or some great being gives us. Our minds create the causes for liberation. In Buddhism, we secure our own liberation.

Whether a person is practicing the Dharma or not cannot be judged from the outside. As practitioners, we must refrain from thinking we are engaging in the Dharma just because we spend long hours in meditation, recite prayers extensively, or go to the temple very often. Our motivation and mental state accompanying our actions is the true measure. The mind of renunciation, the mind that seeks freedom from delusions and clinging to this life, is what determines whether one is engaging in Dharma practice. It is very important to be aware of the difference. Otherwise we will not know how to practice the Dharma.

BODHICITTA

Complaints and more complaints. When we experience one small discomfort, one tiny suffering, one incident of dissatisfaction, we get upset and complain. We complain to our family, to our friends, to anyone who will listen. We yearn for only our own happiness. Day and night we seek only comfort and pleasure. This is exactly the same with all sentient beings—your neighbor, your friend, your enemy, the garbage collector, the insects in the garden, the dogs on the street, the fish in the river—all sentient beings are precisely like us in wanting happiness and not wanting unhappiness.

While we are fundamentally equal in this way, we fail to equalize ourselves with others. Instead we tend to think, "I am important. My happiness is more important. The happiness of other beings has nothing to do with me."

When we adopt this self-cherishing thought we ignore the hardship of others. As we pursue our own happiness we are not mindful about harming other living beings. The field of sentient beings becomes something for us to use and discard rather than to cherish. We do not particularly care for others, especially those whom we feel do not benefit us. We kill this bug, slander that person, and ruin others, all in the name of obtaining happiness for ourselves. This self-cherishing thought has prevented us from making any real progress on the path.

To put just one small bowl of rice on our dinner table, numberless sentient beings living underground and above ground have suffered. Think about it. Starting with the plowing of the field, through the planting, harvesting, and milling, countless beings die and suffer for our one bowl of rice. And this bowl of rice came from previous grains of rice, so the number of sentient beings who have suffered for this bowl of rice doubles, triples, and is multiplied a hundredfold.

I am not saying this to make you feel bad. Instead I ask you to remember the sacrifice and kindness of sentient beings. If we cultivate this attitude, we will not dare to eat a single grain of rice or corn without some thought of repaying the kindness of sentient beings, of doing something beneficial for them.

Our mindset becomes bodhicitta when we feel the suffering of sentient beings like an arrow piercing our heart and are unable to bear the thought of their unending sorrow for one minute. Bodhicitta arises when we have no other thought except striving for enlightenment to liberate beings from their suffering and to achieve their happiness. Bodhicitta is the great compassionate thought, the great altruistic intention to attain enlightenment to benefit all sentient beings. Bodhicitta renounces self-cherishing completely and cherishes others single-mindedly, taking responsibility for the happiness of all sentient beings. There is no casual dismissal that the happiness of sentient beings has nothing to do with us.

Without great compassion, there remains only our ego, breeding the emotional minds of anger, attachment, and the whole range of disturbing thoughts that harm us and so many others. Numberless sentient beings have received harm from us, directly and indirectly, intentionally and unintentionally, from life to life. By cultivating bodhicitta, we cease harming them and instead offer only help to them. How much peace and happiness there would then be.

A buddha arises from a bodhisattva and a bodhisattva arises from bodhicitta. All worldly and transcendental happiness, including enlightenment, arises from the great-hearted and vast bodhicitta mind of altruism. However, bodhicitta cannot be attained suddenly. It does not fall like rain from the sky but requires long training, so we need to start training from this very moment.

Abandon the self-cherishing thought that places our own happiness first. The Mahayana motivation requires us to undertake any hardship to lead beings to the highest bliss of enlightenment. We have to achieve enlightenment ourselves to bring other beings there because only the Buddha's qualities enable us to benefit numberless living beings.

Until we transform our minds into the path, external enemies will harm us. Even arming countries so that they possess enough sophisticated weapons to fill the whole sky is futile. These would only bring harm instead of protection. Resources should be put into the positive development of the mind and the good heart rather than into military development. Then we would be in no danger of being invaded by another country. If every person in a country dedicated their energy to developing the good heart, the danger of conflict would subside.

These days safety and security loom large in people's minds. Some houses have all sorts of locks, gates, and alarms. But better than kung fu and burglar alarms is generating bodhicitta. The attitude of great compassion, altruism, and taking responsibility for the happiness of all beings offers better protection than spending millions of dollars for thousands of years to shield ourselves with bodyguards and gadgets. Devices and guards can't help us destroy the delusions that bring us problems or the delusions of any other person. In comparison, one realization of bodhicitta confers incomparable benefit.

The power of a million atomic bombs is insignificant compared to the power of one good heart. If bodhicitta was in the minds of all the people in this world, we could say goodbye to guns, bombs, and conflicts. Lama Yeshe used to say, "A good heart a day keeps the enemy away."

THE PRELIMINARY PRACTICE TO CULTIVATING BODHICITTA: EQUANIMITY

Releasing just ourselves from the dangers of samsara isn't good enough because freeing just one person from suffering is not satisfying. Numberless sentient beings suffer extremely and are in utmost need. These beings may be trapped in the quicksand of samsara because they lack a guide on the path, do not know what is right and wrong, or how karma works for and against them.

As ordinary beings, we lack the ability to help extensively. Therefore we should aspire to the realization that "I must achieve enlightenment to bring all beings to happiness and enlightenment. To do so requires me to train in disciplining my body, speech, and mind." Quickly actualizing bodhicitta is the key if we are to accomplish enlightenment to deliver early help to sentient beings.

To effectively train in bodhicitta, we first need a fundamental realization of equanimity. Think how it is when we enter a room of many people. We might feel uncomfortable with some people and even recognize them as our enemies, while on the other hand we're attracted to other people or they may already be our friends. We are simply indifferent to the rest of the people and have no particular feeling about them. This is how we intuitively categorize people into "enemies," "friends," and "strangers."

If we carefully and honestly check our minds about why we label people "enemies," "friends," and "strangers," we will discover the true reasons. We label as "friend" anyone who has benefited us or praised us, and we label as "enemy" any person who has criticized us or interfered with what we want. We save the label "stranger" for those whom we know nothing about and thus are indifferent to.

Don't you think that human relationships take up a great deal of our energy and time? When relationship problems arise and the friend becomes the enemy, pain bruises the heart.

Let us analyze this situation, which begins with our ignorant misconception of a truly existent "I." Attachment to the "I" triggers the mental labels of "my friendship," "my body," "my possessions." This misconception does not stop there. The wrong conception also perceives people and objects as truly existent, so that when a person we labeled a "friend" frustrates our expectations, we immediately conclude that a truly existent troublemaker is in front of us and anger is sparked. At that very moment, the label "enemy" arises in our mind, and right there the friend vanishes and an enemy appears in its place. The emotional state of disappointment, distress, and rage then overwhelms our entire being.

Therefore the object of anger we call "enemy," the object of attachment we term "friend," and the object of indifference we dismiss as "stranger" do not truly exist anywhere. They are all labels created by our minds, depending on which delusion is active at that moment. Like a magician who unveils a convincing illusion, through mental labeling our minds conjure a persuasive appearance of friend, enemy, and stranger.

Whose mental labeling? Our own mental labeling, of course. Just as a defective eye sees a distant shrub as a person or a coil of rope as a snake, our completely mistaken minds create something that does not exist anywhere.

In this dangerous way, the ignorant and negative mind, which sees I, friend, enemy, and stranger as truly existent, is a completely wrong and false mind. Yet our days and nights and emotional states revolve around these false appearances, making life exhausting and very messy indeed.

We can check on whether an enemy created by our mind is a true enemy or not, whether a friend is a truly existing friend, or whether a stranger is a self-existing stranger. A true enemy should be an enemy all the time, as with a friend or stranger.

However, our own experience shows this is not true; the status of these people can and does change. We label a person "enemy" who said or did something we disliked. But if two minutes later the person sincerely apologizes, praises us, or does us a big favor, the idea of the person as "enemy" will immediately change. Suddenly he does not appear that bad, and we might even regard him as a reasonable person. Within a few minutes, depending on what the person does for us, the label "enemy" can change dramatically. The enemy of yesterday can become the friend of today, or the friend of this morning can become the enemy of the evening. We may be attached to a person and label him a "friend," but if he unexpectedly does something that disappoints us the label "enemy" will soon replace "friend." It is the same thing with the stranger.

These labels are always shifting and changing as long as we are in samsara. Labels are created and re-created by our minds, changes happen in our minds, all under the influence of delusions. These labels are just the way our minds look at a person, object, or circumstance. There are no inherently existing friends, enemies, strangers, problems, or enjoyments. These are all mental labels. Yet we suffer so much on account of these labels.

Depending on which delusion is dominant at any point in time, ignorance fuels our mental labeling of people as "friend," "enemy," and "stranger." After feeling anger toward a person, we develop aversion;

after attachment, we cling; and after ignorant indifference, we withhold our care and concern. We do not recognize our minds churning out these labels and thus fail to see this particular relentless mental activity as a problem. Worse still we wholeheartedly believe the labels are true and permanent. We assume relationships based on emotional love will last forever, so that if such relationships falter we are shocked and horrified. But in fact those whom we discern as friend, loved one, or enemy do not exist from their own side. They are mere labels of our minds.

Because our labels continuously fluctuate, we cannot trust them. There's no reason to grasp on to them and it's pointless for the negative minds of attachment, anger, or indifference to arise. Why is there no reason to be attached to the friend? Because this friend has also been our enemy numberless times over countless lives. Conversely, the person we call enemy has in numberless lifetimes sheltered us, fed us, protected us from harm, given us everything. As the present-day friend appears to have helped us enormously, likewise the enemy has helped us extensively numberless times in the past. It is the same with the stranger. In this way, all beings are exactly equal.

Whenever we sense our minds affixing labels on to living beings, right there at that very moment we must seize the opportunity to equalize them in our minds. They wish for happiness just like we do. They wish to avoid suffering just like we do. Think that in samsara we have all been mother, father, friend, enemy, and stranger to all sentient beings, and they to us. The enemy has helped and supported you countless times in the past and in past lives. The stranger has sacrificed for you and been kind to you numberless times in the past and in past lives. We simply cannot recall these times.

When we think this way, we equalize the enemy and stranger with the friend. When we can do this, our minds become more relaxed and even-natured. The resentful mind toward the enemy loosens. There is less tightness in the mind. There is less anger toward the enemy, less grasping toward the friend, and more warmth toward the stranger. The negative mind subsides. Equalizing all sentient beings in our minds prepares us to cultivate great compassion toward all.

Every sentient being has equally been a stranger, enemy, and friend to us. There is no new enemy, friend, or stranger to discover. By checking with logic and analyzing how the mind incorrectly discriminates between sentient beings, we come to realize how all sentient beings are equal. Owing to ignorance and delusions, we have committed much negative karma in relation to the friend, enemy, and stranger. Consequently, we experience recurring suffering in samsara.

All other sentient beings have done the same and are thus suffering too. But they may not have encountered the Dharma, and so can't use it to analyze life and its hardships. Since we have developed an understanding of delusions and how they manipulate us, don't you think sentient beings deserve your compassion? We can find in the depths of our hearts the resolve: "I must release all sentient beings from their suffering and lead them to enlightenment. To do this I must achieve enlightenment."

ACTUAL CULTIVATION OF BODHICITTA

To accomplish the realization of bodhicitta, we must steadily train the mind in the teachings from the very beginning. These teachings include guru devotion, not wasting the precious human rebirth, impermanence and death, the suffering of samsara, the workings of delusions and karma, the antidotes, refuge, destroying the crippling belief in a truly existent I, equanimity, and cultivating the altruistic attitude to free all sentient beings from suffering. Attaining enlightenment is uncertain unless we apply ourselves in these ways.

Systematically meditating on the entire path is helpful. If we just meditate on anything we like—sometimes spending time on one topic of meditation and sometimes another, and sometimes missing topics altogether—we may gain some benefit but will be less likely to realize our full potential of enlightenment.

For full enlightenment, it is absolutely essential to gain the realization of bodhicitta. While direct realization of emptiness is vital in attaining liberation and also integral to the path to enlightenment, there is no way to complete the path and achieve enlightenment without bodhicitta. There is no way.

My mother did not have any schooling or the opportunity to receive many Dharma teachings. She did not talk much about bodhicitta, nor did she understand many of the teachings about it. However, she had a deep feeling for bodhicitta and her mind was rich in compassion. She did not read scripture, but she practiced the Dharma with her whole heart. I do not practice it, but she truly practiced.

She was always concerned about anybody who helped her, anyone who did not, anybody whom she saw working hard, and even those who worked very little. She always had kindness in her heart and always noticed the difficulties of others. She always talked about how hard others worked for her, how kind they were, and how unworthy she was to receive help from others.

My mother would say, "My stomach is empty," which was not referring to a stomach empty of food. She meant that her mind was empty of realizations and thus unworthy to be served by anyone, whether by monks bringing tea or by anyone at all. In her daily life, she would express how kind sentient beings were. Every day she circumambulated the stupa, saying, "I must do something. My mind is empty of realizations, yet I received so much help. I cannot sit like this doing so little. I should do something."

She would recite prayers, circumambulate the stupa, and do purification practices to accumulate merit, always keeping in mind the kindness of others.

Once she came to Dharamsala and stayed at the Tushita retreat house. Every day she would go down to circumambulate His Holiness the Dalai Lama's residence. She would save half of her simple breakfast and put it in her pocket to offer to the beggars there. I remember when we went on pilgrimage when I was young, many families would stop along the roadside to make their own food. My mother would do the same but then would give her food to even poorer families, so quite often we ended up not having much food ourselves. I am just recalling how my mother lived her life.

If we are resolute in wanting to generate bodhicitta, the teachings offer explicit guidance on how to accomplish this. Two methods are described. The method of six causes and one effect was passed from Maitreya to lineage masters such as Asanga and Atisha. The method of exchanging self for others was passed from Manjushri to lineage masters such as Shantideva.

Six Causes and One Effect

Asanga was a pandit, a scholar of Nalanda University. He did retreat in a cave hermitage for twelve years trying to achieve the realizations of Maitreya Buddha and also gain a vision of Maitreya. After several years of retreat, Asanga had received no vision and left the hermitage. But he then saw markings on a nearby rock and realized they were made by the wings of a bird brushing against the rock as it flew in and out of its nest.

This inspired Asanga, and he thought, "If even soft feathers can wear down a rock, why can't I persevere and gain a vision of Maitreya Buddha?"

So he returned to the hermitage for another three years of retreat, but still no vision came to him. Asanga again left his hermitage, but this time he saw someone trimming down an iron rod by polishing it with a silk cloth. Seeing this, Asanga thought, "If even silk can wear down iron, why can't I achieve Maitreya Buddha?"

So he returned to the hermitage and did another three years of retreat. No vision of Maitreya came. Feeling discouraged, Asanga again left the hermitage, but then noticed how a small trickle of water dripping onto a rock had made a hole in it. Asanga thought, "If even drops of water can make a hole, why can't I achieve Maitreya Buddha?"

So he returned for another three years of retreat. Now twelve years had passed with no vision of Maitreya Buddha. Asanga then decided he would definitely leave the hermitage.

When he came down out of his cave, he saw a wounded dog. An open wound on the dog's lower body was filled with maggots. Asanga felt immense compassion for the dog and wanted to help it without harming the maggots. So Asanga cut a bit of flesh from his own leg and spread it out on the ground so he could place the maggots there. Asanga then closed his eyes and lowered himself to lift the maggots from the dog's infected wound with the tip of his tongue. As he did so he found that he could feel neither the maggots nor the dog.

When Asanga opened his eyes the dog had disappeared and he saw Maitreya Buddha before him.

Asanga exclaimed, "I have been meditating for a long time, why did you not appear to me earlier?" Maitreya Buddha replied, "I was there in the hermitage with you but you didn't see me." Maitreya Buddha went on to explain that karmic obstacles had blocked Asanga's ability to see him, until the day when his unconditional compassion and sacrifice for the dog and the maggots purified all his obstacles to seeing Maitreya Buddha directly.

Maitreya Buddha explained to him that the bird, the man polishing the iron rod, and the drops of water were all emanations of Maitreya Buddha, which had manifested to encourage Asanga to persevere in his practice.

The method of six causes and one effect is sometimes also called the sevenfold cause-and-effect method of developing bodhicitta. The underlying premise is that from birth our mother, father, or someone took care of us, provided for us, sheltered us, and sacrificed much so we could survive. Even if our relationship with our mother was not always a happy one, she was still especially kind in bearing the hardship of carrying us in the womb for so many months, in not aborting us, and in caring for us.

The main point is that all sentient beings have been our mother numberless times and have been infinitely kind over countless lives. Even until this very moment they are unbelievably kind. Therefore we have to do something meaningful for them. Even the enemy who is now harming us has also been our kind mother in the past. There is no way for us to ignore others and be concerned only about ourselves. We have no choice but to cherish sentient beings and strive to benefit them. The six causes of attaining bodhicitta by this method are as follows.

1. *Seeing all sentient beings as our mother.* Based on equanimity and the equality of all sentient beings, reflect on how sentient beings have been our kind mother in countless lives. If your father brought you up instead of your mother, then reflect on your mother's kindness in carrying you in her womb, then your father's kindness in caring for you, and how all sentient beings have been your mother and father in countless lives. Every sentient being has been kind to you over beginningless rebirths.

2. *Remembering the kindness of our mother.* The reason the mother is referred to in the texts is because from the time your consciousness arrived in the fertilized egg in your mother's womb, she took care of you. For nine months she carried you in the womb despite personal hardships. That itself is unbelievable kindness, even if that is the only thing she did for you, so remember that. If she had aborted you or did not take care of you in her womb, you would have no life now. You would not have this precious human body and no human pleasures, but most important, you would have no opportunity to meet the Dharma and practice it to attain the complete path. You would have no opportunity to liberate yourself from samsara and to bring numberless sentient beings to enlightenment!

All these infinite benefits have been made possible because of your mother. You might think, "Oh, my mother abandoned me. My mother is terrible. My mother was totally useless and bad. Somebody else took care of me."

You may remember the kindness of the person who cared for you, but if you do only that you ignore the kindness of the mother who cared for you in her womb. Remembering only the kindness of those who cared for you, while forgetting the one who carried and gave birth to you, is reflecting in an incomplete way.

3. *Repaying the kindness of our mother.* This reflection will help you generate the wish to repay the kindness of your mother or the person who cared for you, and is very worthwhile.

There are four ways of meditating on your mother's kindness: First is the kindness that produced this human body with the opportunity to actualize enlightenment. Second is that your mother protected your life from hundreds of dangers each day from the time you were born. Third, your mother taught you how to navigate ordinary life, including how to feed yourself and how to clean yourself. Fourth, she bore great hardships for you in this life and over countless lives.

Watching how mothers care for their children reminds us of this. It is a very demanding responsibility. Over many years parents give up so much for their child's sake.

In Himalayan villages mothers suck snot or phlegm out of their babies' noses with their mouths. Sometimes they feed their babies with food they chewed in their mouths to soften the food, exactly as mother birds do. Mothers feed their babies with their own breast milk, which is demanding on the mother's body.

Therefore you should remember all your mother's hardships. Think how your mother, father, or the person who cared for you got exhausted, worried, fearful, and labored at a job to earn a living for your shelter, food, and clothing. Your mother gave you medicine when you were sick, food when you were hungry, and drink when you were thirsty. Hundreds of your needs had to be attended to each day, and she attended to them as best she could. The best way to repay this kindness is by practicing the Dharma so you can bring all beings to the ultimate happiness. To be of real help, you need to study the Dharma and apply its methods in your own daily life before you can liberate other sentient beings from samsara. You also can achieve realizations by taking ordination or by taking laymen's vows, all of which protect karma. These are the best ways to repay the kindness of your mother.

Therefore when someone becomes angry toward you or mistreats or harms you, whether for a day or ten years, understand how delusions and karma control sentient beings, cause them to commit negative actions, and guarantee their suffering and rebirth in the lower realms. Thinking this way allows us to keep practicing patience when faced with difficult people.

Practicing patience even just one time makes our lives worthwhile. Patience saves others from being harmed by us, and thus spares us from the suffering results of karma. Patience also makes our parents' lives worthwhile, knowing their sacrifices have produced something meaningful, like our good quality of patience and our Dharma efforts.

4. *Generating loving-kindness.* Recall the love and care you received from your mother, your father, or your beloved care person. Reflect on how they felt toward you, their beloved child. Our parents cherished their children deep in their hearts, so in a similar way we can generate the same feeling toward every single sentient being without discrimination. This is what is called loving-kindness.

The Tibetan term is *yi-ong kyi jampa,* the feeling of great affection in our hearts. It is similar to saying "dear" or "most dear" in English. We should generate warm affection toward every single sentient being, even the person who abused us whom we call "enemy." Think it through. Based on the above logic, we can generate loving-kindness even to that person by remembering how kind that person has been to us in the past.

Meditating in this way may not be easy, but whenever we generate loving-kindness with a sincere heart it makes our life joyful and filled with a sense of thanksgiving. All sentient beings seek happiness but do not know what the causes of happiness are. They think the causes of happiness are actions done in this life influenced by attachment, anger, ignorance, and in particular by clinging to this life. They mistakenly think these actions will bring happiness, but instead they bring only suffering. Beings weep in sorrow, never understanding why they have to suffer.

In light of such pitiful circumstances, don't you think they need your compassion?

5. *Generating great compassion.* Nagarjuna said, "Actions born from anger, ignorance, and attachment are nonvirtue. From that all the suffering of transmigratory beings arise."

Look around. Everyone suffers, it is only a matter of how. From this we generate the strong, intense thought of how wonderful it would be if all sentient beings could be released from suffering and gain every happiness, including the peerless happiness of full enlightenment.

6. *Generating altruism.* When a mother sees her child deathly ill, she rushes about seeking a cure. When a child falls down into a fire pit, nothing exists in the mother's heart apart from saving that child. In the same way, try to generate the compassionate heart that finds the suffering of all sentient beings totally unbearable.

Imagine if a mother sentient being that has been so kind to us were in danger of being attacked by a ferocious tiger. As the child of this mother, we would not merely stand on the roof singing songs! Instead we would spring into action to try to rescue the mother.

Reflect, "While my kind mother sentient beings are suffering so much, it would be selfish, shameless, and cruel to ignore them. It is my turn to help them. I have all the opportunities, so I am able to take the responsibility to help them." When we set up such a determination to take responsibility for the happiness of all sentient beings, we give rise to altruistic intention.

ATTAINING BODHICITTA

At the start, we generated equanimity that equalized all sentient beings. Then we saw them as our kind mother and resolved to repay their kindness. Next, we generated loving-kindness followed by great compassion. Now we resolve, "I will free all sentient beings from suffering and lead them to enlightenment by myself alone."

Remember that extra word "alone." It is not arrogance but the courageous heart of altruism that inspires us to make that resolution. At the moment we cannot guide even one sentient being to enlightenment. But who can do perfect work toward sentient beings? This is the Buddha, the omniscient one who knows every single being's mind, their individual karmas, and the most appropriate method to bring them from happiness to happiness up to enlightenment.

So think, "I must therefore achieve buddhahood in order to lead all sentient beings to that state." This special thought, this special mind, is bodhicitta. When we have actualized bodhicitta, we feel uncomfortable every time we see a living being in difficulty.

When Lama Yeshe would see a cow tied with ropes to a stake he would refer to the cow as "mother." He would speak of the cow with a genuine heavy heart, saying, "Mother is suffering."

Realizing all sentient beings have been our mother is the first cause for generating bodhicitta. When we spontaneously feel a strong aversion to the sufferings of sentient beings every moment of every day and we resolve to help them by attaining enlightenment, when this wish is constantly felt deep in our hearts and remains stable over a long period of time, this is the bodhicitta realization.

When we gain that unshakeable determination to liberate all beings and lead them to happiness, we have entered the door of the Mahayana path. We then become a bodhisattva, the heart son of all the buddhas. The heart son of all the buddhas has nothing to do with gender. It is about the mind that is imbued with bodhicitta and that seeks enlightenment for all beings.

Exchanging Self for Others

Shantideva was a monk at the famed Nalanda University. Outwardly Shantideva showed no signs of being a great master. In fact the monks living in the monastery gave him the name Busuku, which means the one who only does three things: eat, sleep, and make ka-ka. They never saw him reading texts or engaging in religious activity. They felt he was just wasting monk community resources that had been offered with devotion by benefactors. When monks do not practice the Dharma or keep the precepts well but just use things offered by benefactors, they create much negative karma.

Therefore many felt Shantideva should be driven out of the monastery. They saw him as useless. A group of monks contrived a plan to drive him out by ridiculing him. They based their plan on a practice whereby monks have to memorize many sutra texts and then recite them before an assembly of monks. The group thought that Shantideva would be unable to do this, which would be a reason to expel him.

The invitation was made to Shantideva and he accepted. In a mocking way, the monks created a very high teaching throne for Shantideva to sit on, expecting he wouldn't be able to do even that.

But when the time came, Shantideva ascended the throne without any difficulty. He then asked the audience, "Should I recite a sutra text that you all know, or one that has not yet been heard?" The audience replied, "Please give a teaching on a text that has not been heard."

Shantideva then delivered what has become the renowned *Guide to the Bodhisattva's Way of Life* (Skt. *Bodhicaryavatara*), which contains the 84,000 teachings of the Buddha in a simple and easy-to-understand way. The ten chapters of the text include a chapter on the cultivation of wisdom, shunyata. While Shantideva was teaching this chapter, he levitated higher and higher until he was no longer visible to the audience, although his voice was still clearly audible. The recitation showed not only Shantideva's profound knowledge of the Buddha's teachings but also his great supernormal powers. After this public incident, all of Nalanda realized the great being they had in their midst.

The essential way to practice exchanging self for others is to regard the suffering of others exactly as our own suffering and to help others as if they were ourselves. We need to completely change our old motives and selfish actions! Abandoning self-cherishing and cherishing only others is the bodhicitta method. Nurture the mind that cares only about alleviating the suffering of others with a sincere, generous, and uncrooked attitude. This is how the bodhisattva acts, renouncing himself and focusing only on the well-being of others.

We are nowhere near approximating this state of mind. Every time we encounter any living being in hardship, we should feel as if that other being's body and mind are our own. We need to cultivate this attitude to the point where we experience whatever is happening to that other being's body and mind as also happening to us. If we do not equalize others with ourselves, many realizations will not come.

We can mentally picture a bodily injury like a toothache and feel the pain from that, so why not do the same about the pain of others? We can train our minds to feel another's bodily sensations or mental anguish as our own. Originally our body was linked to our father's and mother's bodies, but the mind learned to regard it as our own, thinking, "This is me." Why does such a concept arise so early and so strongly? Why do we take such good care of this body?

The answer is that we have become habituated to thoughts like "This is me" and "This is my body" since beginningless lives. We have excelled in training the mind to grasp at the "I." We take better care of this body than we do our parents' bodies, even though ours began from theirs. Exchanging oneself for others is an essential bodhisattva practice to achieve ultimate happiness for ourselves and others.

We may be surprised to hear how the Buddha first generated compassion in the hell realm. In one of his past lives the Buddha was born in a hell realm, pulling a carriage alongside another hell being, like two buffaloes pulling a heavy cart. Yama, the lord of death, sat in the carriage. When the other hell being became too weak to pull the carriage, Yama punished him by piercing him in the chest with a trident, causing him great agony, so he screamed.

The Buddha-to-be felt great compassion for this other hell being and pleaded with Yama, "Please let this sentient being go. Put his ropes over my head and I will pull your carriage myself." Yama was enraged and also pierced Buddha with the trident, killing him. By virtue of the Buddha-to-be's great act of compassion, his consciousness was transferred and he reincarnated in a god realm.

Think about it. It is no more logical to think "I am more important than this person" than it is to think "I'm more important than this insect." Such a view has not one single logical reason to support it but is merely dictatorial and egotistical reasoning. An ant's life may be of little consequence to us, but to the ant it is everything.

The self-cherishing view makes us tight with pride and willing to harm others who don't obey our ego-based commands. How dangerous that is! Expel this self-important and self-cherishing mind that seeks happiness for ourselves above others. This mind has brought you all forms of dissatisfaction and denied you the happiness of this life, let alone liberation and enlightenment!

As ordinary people, we often complain about others abusing us, disrespecting us, and harming us. But if we practice exchanging self for others—the letting go of self-cherishing thought and cherishing others instead—these troubles simply stop. As we do this practice we will find we no longer receive harm from others and instead experience much peace, happiness, and success. Practice becomes easier and liberation and enlightenment become that much closer. Every moment of every day becomes one of contentment and happiness. Cherishing others is like a great holiday for the mind, a wonderful vacation from the oppressive self-cherishing thought.

If we do not realize that categories such as "good," "bad," "friend," "enemy," and "stranger" come from our own mental labels, we will see harm coming to us when somebody says words we interpret as unpleasant. In a flash we will see an enemy abusing us. Our suffering will become tangible.

Therefore self-grasping and self-cherishing are the real enemies to be kept out at all costs. As we overcome them, we will be destroying the creator of all problems, the delusions. If we peel back the layers of thought to find out why we repeatedly experience depression, disharmony, anger, attachment, dissatisfaction, jealousy, pride, and ill will, we will see that at the core of all our troubles is the thought "I am the most important; my happiness is paramount." Numerous negative emotional states spring up because the "I" doesn't get its way.

Anyone who successfully shields himself from the self-cherishing thought will find benefit in adverse situations, even the bad treatment and criticism of others. To such a person, these difficulties become meditations or Dharma challenges that are forceful ways to conquer the selfish mind. This kind of practitioner considers people who criticize him and treat him badly as the kindest and best of friends.

Such a person would offer the whole earth filled with diamonds to someone expressing criticism, seeing the situation in this way: "I have long followed the self-cherishing thought that brought endless sufferings of mind and body. I therefore know the painful lesson of being a slave to the self-cherishing thought. This critical sentient being is helping me by reminding me of that lesson. Together we are destroying my self-cherishing thought. How unbelievably kind this person is."

When the practitioner thinks this way and sees the difficult person no longer as a harm-giver but as a helper in his progress, everything changes. Negative becomes positive.

The practice of exchanging self for others (Tib. *tonglen*) is meditating on taking the sufferings of sentient beings on ourselves and giving them every happiness. The elements of loving-kindness, great compassion, and the great will of altruism to carry the responsibility of helping sentient beings are infused into this practice.

As a preliminary to tonglen, first meditate on equanimity, equalizing oneself with others. We do this before starting the actual meditation of exchanging self for others. If we discriminate some sentient beings as close to us and some as distant from us, this causes bias, helping only some and not helping everyone. When we equalize all beings with ourselves, we cherish all beings as much as we cherish ourselves. It then becomes possible to work toward eliminating the sufferings of sentient beings by offering happiness to them equally.

This tonglen practice of exchanging self with others, of taking and giving, is very, very important. During this meditation, we visualize and mentally take on ourselves all the hardships of sentient beings with our in-breath, absorbing these into the self-cherishing, egotistical mind dwelling in our hearts and expunging that self-cherishing attitude. With our out-breath we visualize giving happiness to all sentient beings.

For example, if we are being scolded, instead of retaliating with abusive words we quietly and mentally take on ourselves the anger of the person scolding us, as well as the anger and sufferings of all sentient beings. We think, "May all their delusions and sufferings ripen on me right now and destroy my self-cherishing mind. May they receive wisdom and happiness." In this way, we straightaway turn the anger directed at us on to the path to enlightenment.

Tonglen practice works similarly with situations of attachment, such as worry about our physical body if we are sick. During the practice, we visualize taking the sicknesses of all sentient beings on ourselves and we use that to destroy clinging to the "I." We then send out thoughts of perfect health and joy to all sentient beings. Do this exchanging-of-self-for-others meditation repeatedly. It is only a mental practice, but a profound one.

Our enemy is not outside but in our hearts; it is within us. Our enemy is the selfish mind fueled by delusions that has colored our world black and brought countless lifetimes of suffering. Waste no time in completely destroying the selfish mind. If we do this practice of taking and giving, the real inner enemy has no chance of survival. This practice will allow us to gain the realization of bodhicitta in our hearts. It is unbelievably powerful.

When we take on ourselves the anger and suffering results of numberless sentient beings, hell beings, hungry ghosts, animals, human beings, demigods, and gods, giving them only happiness in return, can you imagine the impact? It is magnificent. How much merit is generated!

It is the same with taking on the attachments of sentient beings and all of the attendant troublesome results. Whatever sufferings they experience, we visualize ourselves taking them on and using that to uproot our selfish mind. We then give away to others all merits and happiness, past, present, and future, including ultimate happiness. This is the main practice of exchanging self and others.

While skies of merit are accumulated through this practice, it also accomplishes a great purification of our negativities. Numberless eons of negative karma from beginningless rebirths get purified through this practice. It is amazing.

Exchanging self for others is the best practice to do when you are dying. When death comes, just do tonglen. Wow. We will have incredible inner peace, happiness, and satisfaction from doing something so meaningful. We will die with bodhicitta. This is what His Holiness the Dalai Lama calls "self-supporting death."

Whenever a doctor says to us, "You have cancer," the mind usually goes blank or sinks into panic. But those who understand and practice tonglen are unafraid and even feel ready for the challenge because they see it as an opportunity to "experience" cancer for others. Such people feel self-empowered, confident, brave, and able to benefit others. They are able to do this because they have a spiritual practice. They know how to do tonglen, the meditation on the exchange of self for others.

Therefore, if ever a doctor says we have cancer or some terrible disease, immediately stop and think how we can rely on the very special practice of exchanging self for others. This will enable us to make the best use of our sicknesses and our lives.

Through this practice, we purify oceans of negative karmas and generate heaps of merit, which helps us in this life, at the time of death, and also in future lives. If we have cancer, then our remaining days can become a special and quick method to achieve enlightenment. The cancer becomes our own unique stick of dynamite, which if used together with tonglen is potent medicine to combat defilements and expedite our passage to enlightenment.

We can see the power of actualizing bodhicitta in the lives of two great Tibetan masters of the twentieth century.

The late Kyabje Khunu Lama Rinpoche, a learned and pure practitioner of bodhicitta, was tutored by the great Buddhist masters in Tibet on philosophy and other types of knowledge. During the early days of Tibetans arriving in India after the Chinese takeover of their country, Khunu Lama Rinpoche lived like a yogi, dwelling with the Hindu sadhus in Varanasi along the Ganges River. One day, clothed like a sadhu—wrapped up in plain cloth and looking unwashed—Rinpoche went to a local Tibetan monastery to ask for a small room. The monks there did not recognize Rinpoche and said no room was available. Rinpoche slept outside on the bare ground, the way the beggars did.

His Holiness the Dalai Lama was visiting that place at the time and knew what was happening, so he went directly to where Khunu Lama Rinpoche was and requested teachings and commentary on the *Bodhicaryavatara*. Word quickly spread that a great bodhisattva was living there, and soon long lines of people gathered seeking advice from Rinpoche.

Kyabje Khunu Lama Rinpoche was able to recite by heart passages from any root text of the Buddha's teachings and any of the commentaries. His mind was so robust and totally clear it was most amazing. His holy mind was like the entire Buddhist library.

I once went alone to Rinpoche to request a commentary on the *Bodhicaryavatara*. Rinpoche declined on that occasion but gave me the complete oral transmission of that text. Rinpoche then told me to translate the *Bodhicaryavatara*, even though he knew others had already translated it. "You translate," Rinpoche said to me, advising me that before translating one must know the language and the subject well. I have not yet done the translation, but hope to do so sometime in the future.

I once attended teachings by Rinpoche that went on for a whole day with no break. Rinpoche then approached the wisdom chapter of the *Bodhicaryavatara*, an unbelievably precious teaching for one who seeks freedom from samsara.

However, the minute Rinpoche started teachings on that chapter, I fell asleep. Until that moment I was wide awake. But when Rinpoche began the commentary, sleep overcame me. Some unbelievably bad and heavy negative karma from my past life must have caused that. Imagine—at the wisdom teaching that will bring liberation, I fell asleep!

After the teaching, Rinpoche gave some *kambu*, which are apricots in a bottle, that I think were from Ladakh. As he gave me the apricots, he said, "Subdue their minds." I think that that was the last advice I received from Rinpoche. "You have the responsibility to subdue their minds."

I have not yet subdued my own mind, so I do not know how to subdue the minds of others. But I try to offer advice when I am asked to give teachings.

Another great ascetic lama, Kari Rinpoche, spent his early days as a monk in a monastery in Sherka, close to the peak of a very high mountain. When I was still quite young and journeying to Tibet with others, we would stop and gaze up high into that isolated mountain monastery, which looked distant and tiny from where we stood. We wondered how we could get up there. Then we discovered a tiny uneven road spiraling around the mountain, constructed from rocks, wood, and patches of grass, that led up to the rocky mountain monastery.

When we arrived at the monastery, a community of about five hundred monks, we found everything very clean and neat. Kari Rinpoche had been asked to be the monastery administrator, which meant collecting barley from the villages and fields associated with that monastery and bartering for barley supplies. Barley was the main form of food for monks.

However, Kari Rinpoche was unskilled in business, so he completely failed in the task. Rinpoche said this failure was a profound lesson to him. By failing in business, he gained insight into samsara, which helped him generate renunciation. From that time, he committed himself to studying and meditating on the Dharma, doing extensive practices.

When traveling in Tibet one can see numerous mountains dotted with caves that were often used as hermitages by meditators who would spend years, sometimes their entire lives, meditating on the Dharma. Kari Rinpoche lived in such a hermitage for many years and never went outside. For sustenance, he relied on the *chu-len* practice of taking the essence of flowers, plants, and even stones, and transforming it into tiny mud pills that served as food. This reduces food preparation time. Just one pill suffices for the day, making the mind clear and enabling one to easily achieve the nine levels of the calm-abiding meditation.

Kari Rinpoche accomplished the renunciation of samsara and gained the realizations of bodhicitta and emptiness, after which he had clairvoyance and could tell the future. If you met this lama you did not have to ask your question. He could tell you what you were about to ask. He would know your intentions and your plans. He would offer you the advice you needed to fulfill your plans. His heart was filled with bodhicitta.

Kari Rinpoche was much sought after by people seeking prayers for help in daily life problems. He also offered prayers for those who had died, to liberate them from the lower realms or to prevent them from being reborn in the lower realms. This ascetic lama lived simply and kept nothing. He used any offerings he received to take care of the monks and nuns and whoever needed it. Due to the power of his bodhicitta, everything about him—his body and even his robes—became holy relics. When the time came for Rinpoche to take on the aspect of illness, he would sometimes vomit blood. His disciples would mix that with *tsampa* (roasted barley flour) and create small medicinal pills with extraordinary healing power.

Whenever we visited him when he seemed to be sick, and brought him news of Dharma teaching or something good happening in the world or for Tibetans, Rinpoche would immediately take on the aspect of recovery. Every part of Rinpoche carried blessings. These are just a few of the many results of actualizing bodhicitta.

WISDOM REALIZING EMPTINESS

We now turn to the third principal aspect of the path, the wisdom realizing emptiness, which can be understood through the logic of dependent arising.

Dependent arising

When we see our mother do we see her first or do we first see the base of mother, the aggregates of form, feeling, consciousness, discrimination, and karmic imprints? Of course we see the base first. Without seeing the base on which we place the label "mother," there would be no way to point to mother. The sequence is: first we see the base and then the mind creates the label "mother."

The designation "mother" therefore came into existence in reliance on the base. Mother does not exist from its own side but arises from the mental label projected on to a base. Therefore "mother" is a *par tak tsam* or *par tak*, meaning "labeled there by thought."

Similarly, a base of aggregates is behind someone we call "enemy." Because our minds associate this base with harm caused us in the past, our minds impute the label "enemy" to that base, just as it does with "friend." All existence is mentally labeled on a base, but we mistakenly believe these designations are self-existing—truly existing out there independent of our minds. We have forgotten that our minds created the labels in the first place!

This process of designation includes the "I." Lama Tsongkhapa said, "The being, the self, is imputed existence, imputed by thought. The self or I is mere name (label)."

Therefore the "I" is not independently existing; it does not exist from its own side. The arising of the "I" is dependent on a mental imputation to a base. The "I" is a dependent arising. Meditating on dependent arising is the best way to realize the infallible right view without falling into the two extremes of nihilism (believing that nothing exists) and eternalism (believing in true, inherent existence).

A clear understanding of dependent arising—how things appear to exist and how the "I" and all things are merely imputed existence—is extremely crucial. By practicing awareness of dependent arising, we begin to realize the "I" is merely labeled on the aggregates. People are merely labeled, as are animals, noises, places, situations, ka-ka, phenomena—all objects of consciousness are merely labeled. Therefore when we are angry with our "difficult" neighbor, we are actually upset with the creation of our own minds!

Remembering dependent arising weakens the false notion of "true existence," of "inherent existence," of "independent existence." Persevere in this analysis and meditation. It will eventually clarify that the concept of a "truly existing I" or "inherently existing I" cannot be supported.

At that moment, it will be evident that the "I," which we for so long believed really existed from its own side, is in fact empty of true existence. So when we talk about the "I" we must discern that what exists is the dependently arising "I," while what does not exist is the inherently existing "I." Is this clear?

One point should be kept in mind. When we hear the words "merely labeled by thought," we may think we can simply label a base in any way we like and it will become so. But obviously it is not like that.

If this were so, if things were created only by mind, then even if we were living in a mud hut, a bamboo house, or a grass hut, we could think, "This is a diamond palace," and it would become so. As another example, we could label a pile of *ka-ka* "gold," and we could take that pile and sell it as gold. But clearly it is not so.

For a base to be valid it needs three qualifications: the base must be able to function as indicated by the mental label (in this example of gold, our pile of substance must be able to function as gold), the valid minds of others would not refute that the base is appropriate as a base for the mental label, and the label likewise is not refuted by absolute wisdom.

From reason and logic, the concept of a "truly existing I" or an "inherently existing I" has no basis. The "I" is merely labeled on the aggregates. Therefore the "I" is empty of true existence.

Emptiness

Language sometimes obstructs correct understanding. When the word "emptiness" is used, most ordinary people think of a mere absence of something, like when saying, "My cup is empty. There is no tea in it." Using the English word "emptiness" to explain the Buddha's teaching on the absence of inherent existence is not ideal. The word tends to give the mistaken idea of nothingness.

The Tibetan word for emptiness is *tongpa nyi*, which is made up of two words. *Nyi* means you are cutting something off. What is being cut is *tongpa*, which is "nothingness" or "emptiness" in the ordinary sense of the word. Thus *tongpa nyi*, or *emptiness* in the Dharma sense, is not nothingness but rather the absence of true existence. This is very specific.

Without explaining what emptiness is in the Dharma sense, one can mix it up with ordinary emptiness. This can create wrong concepts, so a phrase like "The 'I' is empty" can be misinterpreted to mean "There is no 'I.'" That would be nihilistic and a totally mistaken view. What does exist is the dependently arising I; what does not exist is the inherently existing I. Existence is a mental construct and is illusory—it is not an illusion, but it is like an illusion, like a dream.

When cultivating the wisdom realizing emptiness, the first step is to recognize how ignorance perceives the self. We tend to have a feeling of the "I" existing somewhere on or around the aggregates. Sometimes we feel the "I" is in the mind; sometimes we feel it is in both the body and mind. The existence of the "I" is unclear, like a mixture of milk and water.

Further, the "I" appears to us as truly existing, so when we believe in that appearance we conclude there is a solid, "truly existent I" sitting here or standing here. The fact that the appearance is a mental construct fades, which is how ignorance grasps at a self. We do not recognize this process happening because most of the time the "I" does not strongly appear. When there is no danger present or when we are not being criticized or praised, our emotions are not invoked. Thus it is not easy to recognize this imputed "I."

But if someone suddenly shouts "Fire!" or points to us, saying, "You are a liar," then a strong feeling of the "I" who feels threatened by the fire or the slander suddenly emerges.

Look at a flower. Do you see any clear difference between the base, which is the object being perceived, and the label "flower"? As we cast our eye on the flower and see the base of the flower—the petals, their color, the stem and leaves—the label "flower" surfaces in our minds. Right there we see a flower existing in front of us from its own side; we perceive a truly and inherently existing flower.

In designating inherent existence, we have overlooked the fact that "flower" is our mental label on a collection of phenomena (petals, leaves, and so on), and that it arose from interdependence between the base and our mental functioning. We totally forgot the involvement of our minds and how mental labeling quickly produced the appearance of the flower, because upon seeing the flower we think, "Ah, here is a truly existent flower in front of me." We forget the fact we created the mental label.

This is exactly what ignorance does to everyone all the time. This is how the mistaken, ignorant view of the "truly existent I" (and all phenomena) comes about and plants deep, far-reaching roots.

When we do not analyze our perceptions, when we do not meditate on dependent arising and emptiness, we believe that whatever we encounter exists from its own side. We erroneously believe things we encounter truly exist. The imprint left on the mental continuum by ignorance causes us to project true existence on to everything. We convince ourselves of the true existence of things that in fact we have merely imputed.

The result is we believe there are truly existing enemies, friends, strangers, objects, statuses, and experiences. Our misapprehension of these as real in turn stirs up our emotions, causes us to commit negative karma, disturbs our minds, and brings about a myriad of problems. We turn off the light at the end of the tunnel, never gain liberation for ourselves, and never lead other sentient beings to liberation. This is the lethal consequence of believing in true, inherent existence. This is why we need to cultivate the wisdom realizing emptiness.

Emptiness is the nature of the self and all things. Our mental imputations and labels are just like decorations crafted by our consciousness and pinned on to things.

Seeing emptiness directly

It is useful to frequently remind ourselves that whenever things appear to us, they take on the appearance of inherent existence. This is because we still possess the subtle imprint of dual view, the view that there is an ultimate distinction between subject and object because they are inherently existent as they appear. To overcome this dual view, we must forcefully apply the understanding of how mental labels are imputed to a base.

When we are finally able to realize that "I" and all phenomena exist only in a dependent manner and are thus empty of inherent existence, when we gain the realization that dependent arising and emptiness are not merely side-by-side but are unified, then our analysis of emptiness is complete. At that time, we see emptiness directly.

At the moment of seeing emptiness directly, when we see a table we know that while it has the appearance of an inherently existing table, it does not truly exist on its own at all. We know the image of the table is like a mirage. When we are able to see emptiness directly, when we actualize the realization of emptiness, the dual view vanishes. When we see the "I" is empty, there is no differentiation between the subject and object; there is no view that "this is the object of emptiness and this is the 'I' realizing emptiness."

During this time, there is no experience of "this" and "that." There is no appearance of any conventional phenomena, only full awareness of the ultimate nature of all things, which is emptiness. This is a very intense experience.

Here is the most important instruction when meditating on emptiness: It is crucial to remember that when this intense experience of nonduality arises, we must persevere in the meditation. During that experience fear may arise, accompanied by thoughts like "I am falling into nothingness." This kind of fear can become the greatest obstacle to completing our direct realization of emptiness.

Thus we must persist in the meditation. Even though we may experience some sensation of disintegration, in reality there is no way for us to fall into nothingness or lose the "I." This is because consciousness will always continue and will never stop. Since consciousness never stops there is no way for the "I," which is merely imputed on to the consciousness, to stop.

Therefore if, due to this fear of losing ourselves, we were to stop the meditation on emptiness, it would be holding on to a nihilistic view. Stepping back from meditation due to this fear would be such a great waste, a great hindrance to realizing emptiness.

Khunu Lama Tenzin Gyaltsen Rinpoche advised His Holiness the Dalai Lama that a meditator who stops his meditation when faced with this situation is like a child riding on a horse. Such a child may know a little bit about horses but does not know them well, so when an obstacle arises the child rider may become fearful and totally give up.

We should remember that as we approach the realization of emptiness we should persevere despite the fear of losing our habitual sense of being a solid entity. We must continue despite feeling there is nothing to hold on to and nothing to self-cherish, for only by continuing will we see the middle way and realize emptiness directly.

The Two Truths: Conventional and Ultimate

Conventional truth refers to the way we ordinarily see ourselves and the world, which is that we see ourselves and the world as truly and inherently existing. *Ultimate truth* is the actual nature of existence, that is, the absence of inherent existence of the "I" and all phenomena. In other words, we conventionally see everything as truly existing. But this ends when we apply the understanding of emptiness that realizes all these truly existent appearances are false, and that the ultimate truth is that appearances are merely imputed by the mind to bases. This is what is meant by the two truths, namely, conventional truth and ultimate truth.

There is benefit to understanding the two truths. When we see conventional truth, we see the happiness of the conventional "I," the ordinary nature of the "I." Likewise we see the sufferings of the conventional "I." We see the positive results from virtue and the suffering results from nonvirtue, giving us a clear understanding of cause and effect. Conventional truth helps us see how karma functions, which gives us faith in karma. Otherwise we might mistakenly think, "Since there is no inherently existing "I," it does not matter whether I do virtue or nonvirtue," or, "If there is no truly existing "I," what is the point of spiritual practice?"

Conventionally there are consequences to actions. Conventional truth, the ordinary way we see people and things, enables us to understand why suffering exists, why happiness exists, what causes both, and how they are all in the nature of dependent arising.

The benefit of understanding ultimate truth is that attaining direct realization of ultimate truth cuts off ignorance forever. This realization unhooks us from samsara. It brings us to liberation and to enlightenment. The attainment of shunyata, or the direct realization of emptiness, is the actual direct seeing and experiencing of ultimate truth.

Arya beings—those who have gained direct realization of emptiness—have realization into these two truths. However, while they are doing equipoise meditation focusing on emptiness, they cannot perceive conventional truth. The "I" does not appear to them during that time. While their minds are abiding in emptiness, the dual view is absorbed. For them there is no separation between subject and object, no thought that "this is emptiness and this is the mind concentrating on it."

Conversely, when they no longer abide in the equipoise meditation on emptiness, conventional truth reappears to them. Therefore even though arya beings have direct realizations of the two truths, they cannot have those realizations simultaneously.

On the other hand, the enlightened mind not only realizes the two truths but also realizes both simultaneously. When a buddha sees the emptiness of the "I," he also sees the conventionally existing "I" and every form of existence. Only a buddha can simultaneously be in the states of equipoise meditation and postmeditation. While a buddha one-pointedly abides in ultimate truth, he simultaneously sees conventional truth. This is one of the many qualities of a buddha's omniscient mind.

MEDITATION: MINDFULNESS, SHAMATHA, AND VIPASSANA

The purpose of Buddhist meditation

The practice of Buddhist meditation is not just to relax the body or help it recover from a headache. It's not something to try out simply because your friends are into it!

What we want is to destroy the root of suffering, the source of all unhappiness. That poisoned root lies within us and is what we seek to eliminate. Only then will we gain the lasting happiness we seek. This is the main emphasis of the Buddha's teaching and path.

However, if we know only one or two points to meditate on and put little effort into deeper study and meditation, thinking, "Oh, I have read many Dharma books. I have done enough meditation. I know enough," we end up blocking our wisdom. We block the door to ultimate happiness.

As putting sugar into our mouths gives rise to the experience of sweetness, examining the teachings through meditation will allow us to experience the meaning and quality of the Buddha's teachings. To actualize the path, we begin by studying the teachings, contemplating the points of study, and then familiarizing our mind with them through meditation while analyzing the points well. We need to persevere in meditation to attain the state of concentration or calm abiding (Skt. shamatha), for only then is it possible to gain the higher seeing or special insight into emptiness (Skt. *vipassana*).

How do we meditate to gain realization on the path, to attain shamatha and vipassana?

First I would like to highlight a major wrong conception about meditation, which is that we should cut off all thoughts during meditation and that our minds should be kept blank. Keeping our minds blank throughout our meditation is nothing more than spacing out! It may offer some form of relaxation but it does not bring us insights into the Buddha's methods to overcome delusions. In addition, cutting off thought is impossible because the mind has to be conscious of something. Once the mind is conscious of something there is thought. The cognitionless, sleeping mind is not meditation. Otherwise all forms of deep sleep, including the states of animal minds, could be called meditation.

At the start, concentration on the breath is easier than concentration on other objects. The breath is constant, so focusing on that will help draw the mind inward and away from distractions. Concentration is a powerful tool to gain realizations. However, achieving concentration itself is not the purpose of pursuing the path. After all, people in many non-Buddhist traditions also achieve high levels of concentration. In Buddhism, the purpose of training in concentration is to enable us to progress on to analytical meditation, which analyzes the Buddha's teachings in a profound way and relates them to our lives. This then equips us with the means to get out of samsara and on to enlightenment.

A word of advice. Starting to meditate at a time when we are angry, upset, or in the grip of strong attachment is difficult and often unproductive. During such times, the mind is unable to stabilize or analyze anything effectively because the mind is saddled with emotions. It is better to meditate when we're not emotionally overwhelmed. If possible, start meditation practice when the mind is a little quieter and more subdued.

Mindfulness and introspection

Beginners should accomplish single-pointed concentration without the two faults of the sinking thought (mental dullness) and the attachment-scattering thought (excitement). To do this we need to strengthen the two mental qualities of mindfulness and introspection.

Mindfulness is mental awareness, the quality of recognizing the object of meditation. Introspection is the quality of mental alertness or remembrance, which checks on the strength of our mindfulness.

For example, if we meditate on the Buddha's image while our mindfulness is weak, we are unable to maintain a strong, continual hold on the object of meditation, allowing distraction in. Introspection notices our mindfulness is slipping and thus brings our minds back to the object of meditation.

We can always tell when our mindfulness has weakened. It becomes evident when an object other than our meditation object appears; for instance, we start out meditating on the Buddha's image and then pizza appears.

When pizza appears in the place of the Buddha, we can still recognize the mind is distracted even while it is grasped by the excitement. Just there is where we summon the introspection that recollects our awareness of the Buddha, our original object of meditation. Likewise, if we meditate on Guru Shakyamuni Buddha and after a while the Medicine Buddha image takes its place, we have lost our recollection of the original object of meditation. We have lost the connection.

Mindfulness relates to the recollection of the original meditational object, in this case Guru Shakyamuni Buddha's image. Therefore while we're focusing on the object of meditation, introspection checks on the quality of our mindfulness, and we remain attentive to attachment-scattering thoughts or sinking thoughts surfacing. We develop stability in concentration by avoiding the two faults.

When we are placing the mind one-pointedly on the chosen object of meditation, we should examine the quality of our concentration according to our own experience. For instance, our experience may indicate that "if I hold the object of meditation this tightly, the mind easily breaks into distraction and excitement rises. But if I hold the object this loosely, the sinking thought rises." We should be able to recognize our own experiences.

If our concentration is overly tight and intensive, the scattering thought of excitement arises. We can loosen that intensive concentration slightly to the point where, according to our experience, this move toward laxity causes the sinking thought of dullness or fogginess to rise in the mind. Learning from that experience, we then tighten our concentration a little. Balancing our own experiences in this way enables the mind to abide in concentration—two minutes, three minutes, four hours, or however long.

As we manage this balancing act we try to make the concentration last. Keeping the mind away from the attachment-scattering thought and the sinking thought, we try to continue single-pointed concentration on the object of meditation. If we drive a car too fast, there is danger of losing control or getting in trouble with the police; if we drive too slowly, we might be hit by faster cars, and we might be late for work and lose our job. Therefore we drive the car in a manner that keeps us away from both dangers. Take the same balancing approach to meditation. As we train our mindfulness and introspection, they will become stronger and more efficient.

Shamatha

To achieve shamatha, or calm-abiding concentration, we need to remove the five faults of our mental processes through the application of the eight methods or antidotes.

The five faults are laziness, forgetting the object, dullness and excitement, nonapplication of an antidote, and overapplication of an antidote. The eight antidotes overcome the five faults in multiple ways. The four qualities of faith, aspiration, perseverance, and pliancy overcome laziness; practicing recollection opposes forgetfulness of the object of meditation; vigilance overcomes dullness and excitement; applying the antidotes overcomes nonapplication; and equanimity balances overapplication of antidotes.

Laziness is a great shortcoming that prevents one from establishing concentration. Therefore we should start meditation by first setting the motivation of practicing, which is attaining enlightenment for the sake of sentient beings. Then with strong determination we can think, "I will single-pointedly hold this object of meditation without distraction, without the mind moving away from the object." From the wish to accomplish concentration, perseverance arises; and from perseverance the fruit of our effort arises.

Starting meditation with the Buddha's holy body brings great benefit. Meditate in a detailed way from the top of the Buddha's crown down to the lotus seat, analyzing that the Buddha's hand is here and the Buddha's feet are there, and then returning back to the crown. Do this several times, back and forth, to establish clarity.

Beginners may find it very difficult to hold a clear vision of the Buddha's entire body and instead can only hold a partial image. But if we can hold the image of just half of Buddha's overall holy body clearly, we will have established the object of concentration. We should be satisfied with just the half visualization and not at this stage expect it to be clearer. Then we should hold that object of meditation firmly and intensively through remembrance. In this way, the mind will be trained to focus and abide on the object without coming under the control of dullness or excitement.

The image becoming unclear is caused by sinking dullness. When this happens, achieve clarity by reapplying the meditation on the details of the Buddha's form. If the image of the object is very clear but the mind lacks energy to intensively support that clarity, tighten the mind to regain focus on the object.

Sometimes the sinking thought causes discouragement and the thought arises, "I am hopeless. I cannot do this." At this point we should temporarily stop focusing on the object and uplift ourselves by thinking,

"How amazing it is that I have achieved this precious human rebirth complete with all the eight freedoms and ten endowments, which is highly meaningful. I have the freedom to accomplish whatever I wish! And this is the only time to do it. This precious human rebirth will be difficult to find again."

Advice to overcome drowsiness

Since sinking thought or dullness is one of the most common obstacles arising during meditation, here is some advice for quickly cutting off dullness:

1. We can mix our consciousness with the sky by visualizing the mind as a shining white light the size of a pea inside our central channel. From the navel we can shoot up a ray of light like an arrow straight through our crown, while at the same time vigorously uttering the word *phat*! (pronounced "peh"). Mixing the consciousness with the sky dissipates the sinking thought. If the thought does not dissipate that means the sinking thought is heavy and gross. Therefore we may need to stop the session for a while.

2. If we are meditating in a room without much light, we can take a break outside and look at something bright. If we are in the mountains, we can go out and look at a distant mountain peak. These help to refresh the mind.

3. If the sinking thought arises during our analytical meditation, we can return to simple breathing meditation to refocus the mind. This will help a great deal when we resume our analytical meditation.

Conditions needed to accomplish shamatha

When we decide to meditate in a more intensive way, such as in a retreat, we start out by looking for a quiet place free of distractions, a place where we can meet retreat needs like food. While finding such a place is useful, the fundamental cause for success with shamatha is living in pure morality and having few wants. Perfect causes and conditions for attaining shamatha come from within our own minds.

If we delay meditation practice until we find the perfect external conditions, we might never do it! We tend to blame external circumstances for not accomplishing anything. Failure comes from not living according to the teachings, from not mixing our minds with the Buddha's advice. Thus many hindrances seem to crop up. It is very important to know that shamatha, vipassana, and all attainments depend on our minds. The best preparation is to live in accord with the Dharma.

When I was young and journeyed from Solukhumbu to Tibet through the mountains, nearly every mountain was topped with a monastery. Many of the mountains were dotted with holes—some large and some small—like ants' nests. These holes were the meditation caves of practitioners who committed their lives to meditation on the path. Meditators strived to actualize the path in cold, barren caves on these incredibly high mountains. I often wondered how they managed.

Tibetan lama gurus commonly gave experiential teachings to such lifelong retreatants, and then the disciples would go back to their cave hermitages and meditate on Dharma teachings such as precious human rebirth, impermanence, bodhicitta, and wisdom.

After practicing for some time, these retreatants would return to the lama guru to check on their meditations. The lama guru himself would have had direct experience of the steps on the path to enlightenment, and he would know if his disciples had generated realizations on the subjects. If the disciples made a mistake in the meditation the guru would point out the mistake and clarify the disciples' understanding. If the disciples had attained correct realizations on a subject the lama guru would teach the next subject of meditation, and the disciples would return to their hermitages to meditate on that meditation subject. This way of teaching by the lama is called giving commentary from experience.

Analytical or vipassana meditation:
Four-point analysis of the emptiness of the "I"
Analytical meditation examines in depth the Buddha's teachings on impermanence, samsara, and the causes and antidotes. Vipassana refers to special insight into emptiness. As we stabilize the mind through shamatha realization, we use that stable concentration to analyze the nature of the "I." We reveal the emptiness of "I" through the four-point analysis of emptiness:

1. Recognizing the object to be refuted, in this case the illusion of a truly existing "I."
2. If this "I" truly exists, it should exist either in oneness with the aggregates or separate from them.
3. Examining whether the "I" exists as one with the aggregates.
4. Examining whether the "I" exists separate from the aggregates.

That is the general outline. How should we do this analytical reflection? We proceed with one point at a time:

1. *Recognizing the object to be refuted.* The object of investigation here is the "I" that appears to us, which we think of as truly existing. Perhaps the words "true existence" may not be clear enough and may imply something else, such as actual reality. For those who do not understand what I mean by the "I that appears to be truly existing," just think of it as "the seemingly real I." Perhaps those words are better than the philosophical term "true existence." So the object of analysis is the seemingly real "I."

2. *If this "I" truly exists, it should exist either in oneness with the five aggregates or separate from them.* When you reflect and meditate on the seemingly real I, try to make it as vivid as possible. For example, think of the past when you got excited, when this "I" had a great time, when this "I" received a college degree or a wonderful gift. Think of when this "I" did good deeds or received praise. Recall the "I" that got upset, got angry, quarreled with another person, made mistakes, and acknowledge that by thinking "I have done this." Recall past fears when this "I" faced danger, and think about the "I" that experienced criticism and insult.

These help bring up a very clear sense of this seemingly real "I," the object of this investigation. Once a strong mental sense of the "I" is felt, meditate slowly with the thought "If this 'I' really exists, I should be able to find it either as merged with my aggregates or separate from them." Do not rush this meditation.

3. *Examining whether the "I" exists as one with the aggregates.* Picture a vase and ask yourself, "Does the vase exist as one with its aggregates or separately from them? If I break the vase into pieces and I hold up one broken piece, is that piece still a vase?" If not, then "vase" does not inherently exist based on its parts. Similarly, picture a table and ask, "If I dismantle the table into its parts and hold up one table leg, is that a table?" If not, "table" does not inherently exist in the parts of the table.

Now come to the seemingly real "I." Is this "I" one with its aggregates? For instance, is my arm me? Is my leg me? Is the aggregate of my physical form me? Is my consciousness me? If the answer is yes, there would be five "I"s, as there are five aggregates. In this case, we would require five passports and five tickets every time we travel! It makes no sense. Do you see the logic?

Next, if the "I" is one with the aggregates, or put another way, if the "I" is another name for the aggregates, such as one's body and mind, there would be no purpose in giving oneself a name like Harry or Tan. Instead, each one of us would have several names according to the aggregates: leg, thoughts, happy and sad, consciousness, and so on.

Another analysis on whether the "I" is one with the aggregates has to do with how tempting it is to think the "I" is one with consciousness or mind. However, apply the same logic: since there are six types of consciousness—five relating to the physical senses plus mental consciousness—does that mean there are six "I"s?

The great master Nagarjuna said:

> These aggregates, which will take the aggregates of a being's future lives.
> If this is I, then there's no I who possesses these aggregates.

We may think of the aggregates, and for this let us take consciousness, as being something owned or possessed, as when we refer to "*my* mind." Thus if mind is a possession and the "I" is the possessor, this separation of ownership illustrates that "I" is not in oneness with the aggregates, that the "I" is not merged with the aggregates as we earlier thought.

A parallel quandary is that since consciousness is also made up of parts, if each of these is one with the "I," this would lead to each of us having multiple "I"s.

This then leads to the logical conclusion that since the "I" is not in oneness with the aggregates, the "I" will not cease. This is even though the body, the aggregate of form, does end at death.

At death, consciousness separates from the body and continues. One's consciousness continues from here to the next rebirth, and if cultivated correctly and completely, it continues on to the enlightened state. Consciousness always continues. Therefore the "I" that is merely imputed to the aggregates always exists. There is continuation of the "I." There is no cessation of the "I," because the "I" is not one with the aggregates.

4. *Examining whether the "I" exists as separate from the aggregates.* If it were true that "I" exists apart from the aggregates, then it would be possible for "I" to exist and appear even without the aggregates! Actually, the "I" exists by depending on the base of aggregates and mental labeling or imputation. When base and mental labeling meet, the "I" comes into being. Through the interdependence of base and thought, the "I" arises and functions. This means the "I" is what is called "dependently arising."

All objects are forms of dependent arising. To make this clear through an example, the $100 note consists of a particular design and the number 100. On the base of that piece of special paper with the design and number, we designate this $100. Even though the $100 is merely imputed, it exists because the paper and number are valid bases, and on them $100 comes into being and functions as money. Even though it is merely imputed, even though it exists in mere name, the $100 note can function as money.

In like manner, the "I" exists as an imputation to the base of aggregates and is able to carry out functions. However, without the label there is no existence, and without the base there is no existence. The designation of "I" is solely a product of dependent arising. The "I" does not exist separately from the aggregates.

After doing the above four-point analysis, one arrives at the conclusion that the seemingly real "I" is not real in terms of existing on its own. It is not truly existing but exists dependently on the base of aggregates and mental labeling.

So we have just analyzed the emptiness of the "I," which is the non-duality of the person. Once we are able to gain realization of this, seeing how all other phenomena are also empty becomes easy. We simply apply the same reasoning and logical analysis as above to any other object, experience, or phenomena, in the same way we did with the "I." Nagarjuna said that when we gain the realization of the nonduality of the "I," we will realize the nonduality of all phenomena.

While we meditate on emptiness as the absolute nature of reality, the blissfulness of body and mind increases and profound investigation becomes effortless. Through this realization, we achieve the higher penetrative insight, otherwise known as special insight, or vipassana.

Generally, shamatha meditation is concentrated, single-pointed meditation, which, upon being used to deeply analyze emptiness, brings about vipassana, or special insight into emptiness, the absolute nature of reality. There are various schools that explain the term *vipassana* differently, but here the main point is that the goal of meditation is to use shamatha, or calm abiding, to gain special insight into emptiness, which is the direct antidote to ignorance. This realization is essential in attaining liberation and enlightenment.

Central to the Mahayana path and our progress along the Mahayana five paths is engaging in the bodhisattva's deeds of the six perfections or six paramitas.

SIX PERFECTIONS

The six perfections are (1) the perfection of generosity, (2) the perfection of morality, (3) the perfection of moral patience, (4) the perfection of perseverance, (5) the perfection of concentration, and (6) the perfection of wisdom. The first five perfections accumulate the merit of method and the sixth perfection accumulates the merit of wisdom. Both types of merit are necessary for full enlightenment.

The perfection of generosity

Generosity or charity means cultivating the will to give our material possessions, merits, and even our bodies to others, and carrying out all actions of body, speech, and mind with this magnanimous thought. This generosity develops the will to give to others, which erodes miserliness. Through reflecting on the shortcomings of miserliness and greed, we cut off our attachments, seeing them as illusory and dreamlike. By practicing in this way and dedicating our efforts to obtain the greatest peace for sentient beings, we quickly complete an infinite accumulation of merits.

You might wonder about giving up one's body to others. You might have read stories about the Buddha, who in one of his previous lives encountered a starving tigress that was so hungry she was about to kill and feed on her own cubs. The Buddha compassionately offered himself to the tiger family. As beginners on the path, although we offer body, speech, and mind in the service of others, the body does not actually have to be sacrificed in the manner of the Buddha now. On the contrary, to sacrifice the whole body physically before one attains a sufficiently high level of realizations can interrupt our Dharma practice. But once we have gained those realizations and our determination to benefit beings becomes steady and powerful enough, we will be able to do so.

When we practice each of the six perfections, our actions should contain all six perfections. Otherwise the success of our efforts may be limited, just as a soldier who does not protect each part of his body with armor risks incurring a fatal injury.

There are three types of generosity:

1. *The generosity of Dharma.* This includes sharing the Dharma with pure motivation, as well as reciting prayers for others and even teaching subjects like religious painting and mandala construction.
2. *The generosity of fearlessness.* This means saving living beings from dangers caused by humans, animals, or the elements.
3. *The generosity of giving away material possessions.* We should regard all things we have as the possessions of others, which we are merely holding for safekeeping. When we part with those items, we should think we are returning them to their rightful owners.

It is important to check our minds when performing generosity. For instance, we should abandon the erroneous idea that generosity is pointless and has limited results. When we give, it is important to abandon the prideful thinking that we are doing the recipients, such as beggars, a big favor or that we are competing with other givers. Any expectation of getting something in return should be totally avoided, and we should give impartially. While carrying out an act of generosity, never be discouraged by difficulties surrounding it. Never regret being generous, as this only weakens the merit. At a time of generosity, have no worry or fear of becoming poor in the future, have no treacherous thoughts of betraying the recipient of our generosity. If we observe a recipient demonstrating certain faults, it is important not to regret our giving and to give up any ill intent of announcing what we have seen, because the act of giving is purest when it is unconditional.

It is worthwhile to examine ourselves when we give. For instance, we should not give inferior articles while justifying this by reminding the recipient how generous we have been. Acts of giving should not involve forcing others to commit negative actions such as killing, harming, or destroying, and should not force others to undertake very hard work such as that usually done by animals. We should not give as charity anything taken by force. We should not frighten recipients of our generosity with harsh words criticizing them for not helping themselves. In other words, all things given as generosity should have been honorably obtained and given without a miserly, calculative mind seeking reciprocation of some kind.

The perfection of morality

Morality means giving up the thought of harming sentient beings with actions of body, speech, and mind. Three aspects of morality should be considered:

1. *The morality of abstaining from vices.* This means avoiding the ten nonvirtues previously discussed. This abstention is a requisite to the second and third aspects.
2. *The morality of gathering virtue.* This means the morality of cultivating in our minds realization of the perfections, including living the precepts. It also includes effort to create meritorious actions such as rendering service, doing prostrations, making offerings, thinking and meditating on the teachings, and explaining the Dharma.
3. *The morality of working for all other sentient beings.* This means constantly holding the thought of benefiting others in whatever we do.

Our experience shows us that most animals can hear us, so we should offer prayers within earshot of these animals and others. In addition, we can offer prayers to animals unable to hear by blowing our prayer recitations on to water and sprinkling it on to those creatures as a blessing. Thus we can benefit living beings at many levels, according to their situation. Similarly, we can help beings who are dying by reciting powerful mantras, blowing on water or talcum powder, and then sprinkling those substances on the beings' bodies to purify their negative karma so they are not born in the lower realms and so they may be reborn in the Buddha's pure realm.

These prayers and blessings may sound easy, but how well they work depends on how much faith we have in them. In one way, it seems simple to purify karma and influence rebirth, but this only works for those who have the karma to receive such help. This is illustrated by the differing circumstances under which people or animals die. Only a few die in the presence of very high yogis or lamas or very pure practitioners who can help the dying with prayers.

The perfection of patience

Practicing patience means developing a tranquil and compassionate mind even with difficult people and situations. Perfecting patience does not come about because sentient beings no longer bother us. Rather it depends on us fully training our minds to arrest angry reactions when they do. In the *Bodhicaryavatara* Shantideva wrote:

> Bothersome sentient beings are like the infinite sky, but once the angry mind is destroyed, all enemies are destroyed. There can never be enough leather to cover the Earth, but with the amount required to make the sole of a shoe, it is as if the whole Earth were covered. Similarly, while I cannot dispel external phenomena themselves, I can get rid of them by dispelling my own disturbed mind.

How do we cultivate the perfection of patience? The overall method is to be very familiar with the great benefits of patience and the shortcomings of anger. The patient person enjoys a clearer mind, experiences less distress, creates the good karma to have fewer enemies in this and future lifetimes, dies without worry, and is reborn in the upper realms. Patience guides us away from anger, which is our real enemy because it destroys our merits and those of others.

Continuously practicing patience keeps us happy during our lives, closes off lower realms upon death, and also brings us closer to the ultimate goal of enlightenment. Therefore present and future lifetimes are always happy when we practice patience.

An example of how this works is the great pandit Atisha's decision to retain a very bad-tempered assistant. When people asked Guru Atisha to dismiss the man, Atisha declined, saying, "Through this, I have completed the perfection of patience."

Patience has three divisions:

1. *The patience of bearing the harm received and having compassion for the harm giver.* When living and nonliving beings become harmful antagonists, remember the shortcomings of anger, such as getting upset, feeling physically uncomfortable, acting irrationally, and losing the clarity of mind to find a solution, and strive instead to give some mental space to yourself and the harm-giver in order to deescalate the problem. In other words, be patient. Although practicing patience is difficult at first, we can become accustomed to it by training our minds in this way.

There are reasons why we should not get angry with the so-called enemy. For example, if a stick wielded by somebody strikes us on the head, instead of getting angry we should analyze like this: To be angry with the object causing me pain means I should be angry with the stick. But the stick itself is not responsible for this, for it is under the control of the person. Similarly, the person wielding the stick has no control; he is compelled to do so by the delusions influencing his mind. Therefore, as I cannot get angry with the stick, why should I get angry with the person?

Furthermore, being struck by the stick is a cooperative cause, but the principal cause of this suffering result is my past karma, such as harming other beings. It is the fault of such karma that I now have a sore head. Therefore why should I get angry with the result of karma created by myself when it ripens on me? Rather I should try to dispel the other person's delusion without getting angry with him; he has no control and has become crazed with delusion. This is the same thing that a father would do if his son became crazy and started to beat him. Instead of fighting the son with anger, the father would try all means to help his son.

We could also think this way: When fire burns my hand, it is my fault for touching it. I should not get angry with the fire. Just as I should not get angry with the fire, I should not get angry with the person, the outer enemy, because it is my own fault that person is placed in a position to harm me. Just as it is the nature of fire to burn, and thus I do not get angry with fire when it burns me, likewise it is the nature of sentient beings to be afflicted with delusions, so I should not get angry at them. When our bodies and minds suffer from the physical and verbal assaults of others, the best thing to do is to recollect the workings of karma, how we created the causes for our hardships. With this understanding, we keep anger at bay and succeed in practicing patience as the antidote to anger.

2. *The patience of voluntarily bearing suffering.* When difficulties such as sickness and troublesome people arise in our lives, in our Dharma practice, or even in dreams, we should bear these difficulties with the knowledge they can be helpful for Dharma practice. For example, experiencing hardship extinguishes the underlying karmic cause, it reminds us of the workings of cause and effect and how these troubles were authored by our past negative actions, it allows us to cultivate compassion toward others undergoing similar hardship, and it trains us in patience. Patience has the ability to transform suffering into spiritual practice.

Just as someone to be executed is willing to cut off his hand to escape from the gallows, we should view present-moment hardship as removing future suffering, and thereby see the value of cultivating patience in the face of our difficulties.

It is extremely worthwhile to cultivate a feeling of genuine compassion for the enemy, as that being is creating negative karma that will result in certain future problems. Many great beings experienced great hardships when engaging in their Dharma practice, such as Guru Shakyamuni Buddha when he was in the form of a monk, as well as Tibetan yogis such as Milarepa, Lama Tsongkhapa, and Lama Ensapa, who all achieved the rainbow body in their lifetime.

When Lama Tsongkhapa went into solitude with eight disciples to do a purification retreat, they had only eight copper coins between them. They used this as an opportunity to cultivate contentment and reduce desire. Patience to take on the hardship of exhaustion caused by doing virtue equips us to handle trouble when we're leading others away from life dangers.

3. *The patience of abiding by the Dharma.* The patience of abiding by the Dharma includes learning by heart the graduated path to enlightenment and understanding its meanings, developing knowledge of the Three Jewels and the profound and extensive teachings, and cultivating realizations through meditation.

One of my gurus told me a patience-related story about a meditator in Lhasa. In the early days of Lhasa, a big wall surrounded a cluster of temples. As there were many holy objects in the temples, Lhasa people would circumambulate outside the wall, sometimes making full prostrations and usually reciting prayers. A person seated along this wall trying to meditate was interrupted by a person circumambulating who asked, "What are you doing?"

The sitting man replied, "I am meditating on patience." The circumambulating man teased him by saying, "Oh, you are meditating on patience? How about you eat *ka-ka*?"

The struggling meditator stopped his meditation and retaliated with, "You eat *ka-ka*!"

You can see how fragile our patience is. What began as a virtuous effort to meditate on patience can be easily destroyed by just a few words.

The perfection of perseverance

Perseverance is the energy and joy in performing continuous virtuous actions. It is extremely useful to be aware of the benefits of perseverance and the shortcomings of not having it. The practice of perseverance is fundamental to avoiding suffering, and through it we receive both ordinary and transcendental realizations. Perseverance is the best cause for the complete attainment of all virtue. As it says in the teachings, "If we have great energy, great perseverance, and do not get upset, there is nothing we cannot achieve." Both humans and nonhumans are pleased to help the energetic person, and thus such a person receives realizations quickly, produces results day and night, and retains knowledge. Spontaneous perseverance makes life meaningful, whether that life is long or short.

How quickly we attain enlightenment also depends on perseverance, because it keeps us from life's distractions, laziness, and sleep. Buddha said, "The lazy person is far from enlightenment. He does not practice the six perfections from generosity to wisdom and does not work for others."

Therefore if we fall under the control of laziness, we cannot fulfill our chances of success in ordinary work or in Dharma practice.

There are three kinds of perseverance:

1. *Armor-like perseverance* is the mind that is happy to engage in virtue and strive toward enlightenment for the sake of extinguishing the suffering of even one sentient being, even if that means being in the hell realms a million times the number of three countless, great eons. The person who possesses such perseverance finds nothing too difficult and is never discouraged from helping others. Generating this thought of perseverance just once quickly accumulates infinite merits and purifies unimaginably great obscurations. It is said, "Because sinfulness is avoided there is no suffering. Because skillful work is done for sentient beings with wisdom in the evolution of karma, there is no unhappiness."

2. *Perseverance in collecting merit* is the second kind of perseverance. Collecting merit is done through constantly engaging in meritorious actions and through making offerings and purification. The Buddha persevered for three countless eons in serving sentient beings, and by doing this collected vast amounts of merit. All good qualities come with practicing perseverance. This doesn't mean trying hard just for one or two months or for two years, as this won't lead to continuity of the practice. Without continuity, mind will become weaker and weaker and we may even stop the practice entirely. Through perseverance coupled with virtue we can complete the accumulation of merit, the merit of method, and the merit of wisdom, which cause the Buddha's physical body and the Buddha's enlightened mind.

3. In the third kind of perseverance, the *perseverance of working for other sentient beings*, the practitioner perseveres in all aspects of the bodhisattva's conduct, motivated solely by the wish to benefit sentient beings.

To activate perseverance we need to overcome the three kinds of laziness that hinder our progress on the path. The first of these is the laziness of putting off practice by thinking we will always have enough time. The remedy for this is to meditate strongly and with deep feeling on the fact that our human rebirth decays very quickly and that it is extremely difficult to win another human rebirth after death. This meditation creates the urgency to practice.

The second manner of laziness arises from being attached to worldly concerns and being under their control. We cling to samsaric pleasures solely for the comforts of this life, which include objects of the five senses, sleep, receiving respect, idle chatter, work such as farming, business, or travel. From a Dharma point of view, all of these activities are the opposite of perseverance in Dharma. The remedy is to meditate on the fact that Dharma practice is the source of infinite happiness in current and future lives and is the method of decreasing misery.

The third and last is the laziness of discouragement when we think "Buddhahood means the complete cessation of every single defect and the complete accumulation of all knowledge. There are too many levels of realization to achieve, too many different practices and things to study. How can someone like me be capable of attaining buddhahood?" The surfacing of discouraging thoughts like these can cause us to give up bodhicitta.

The remedy is to think how awakened beings past and present did not achieve the path by already being enlightened. They achieved enlightenment through perseverance. Let them be our role models to inspire us to possess such energy.

A soldier should not drop his weapon, but will pick it up instantly if he does, driven by the fear of death. In the same way, we should not drop our vigilance, but should instantly pick it up if we do, for fear of breaking the precepts and the immense suffering that would cause. By persevering in this way, we will not feel upset when meeting difficulties and attaining release will become easy.

The scriptures reveal how Guru Shakyamuni Buddha became enlightened before Maitreya Buddha. The reason is that Guru Shakyamuni Buddha's compassion was much stronger than Maitreya's compassion.

At one time there were two brother bodhisattvas living in Nepal. While walking through the forest on their way home, the brothers came across a mother tiger and her four cubs who were dying of hunger. But the two brothers had no food to offer them.

Unable to bear their suffering, with great compassion Guru Shakyamuni Buddha soon returned to the tiger family and offered his own flesh as food for them, saving their lives. He then prayed the tiger family would be his disciples in the next life. And so it happened that the five tigers became the Buddha's first five disciples. From this you can see that how quickly we achieve enlightenment depends on how strong our compassion is.

The perfection of concentration

Meditative concentration is the king that rules the mind. The paramita or perfection of concentration is shamatha, also called calm abiding. We can achieve this nine-level concentration only after abandoning the scattering thoughts and sinking thoughts I mentioned earlier. But just attaining shamatha is not enough to liberate us from samsara. We also need to complete the perfection of wisdom that realizes ultimate truth.

The perfection of wisdom

The direct remedy to ignorance is accomplishing the wisdom of shunyata, that is, realizing emptiness. Since beginningless samsaric lives we have perceived the "I" as existing by itself, completely independent, not depending on any part of the body and mind. This perception has been intuitively there from the time we were born and is there all the time, day and night. Because of this perception we see the "I" as highly important and central, but this is a wrong view. Developing the wisdom that sees emptiness directly can cut through this wrong view, releasing us from samsara.

But achieving full enlightenment also depends on equal cultivation of bodhicitta, the altruistic mind. There is an inextricable relationship between cultivating the perfection of concentration and the perfection of wisdom.

PATHS OF THE TWO VEHICLES AND THREE YANAS

To better understand how Guru Shakyamuni Buddha taught according to the mental dispositions of his disciples, we can refer to the terms "the two vehicles" and the "three yanas."

For those beings whose goal is the cessation of suffering, overcoming samsara, and achieving the sorrowless state of liberation, the Buddha gave teachings that included karma, refuge, the twelve links, suffering, its causes, and the antidote to suffering. This is sometimes referred to as the Hinayana or Small Vehicle path, also cited as, though not synonymous with, the Theravada.

For those with an altruistic mindset and the karma to practice bodhicitta, which means working for the welfare of all sentient beings and leading them to enlightenment, Guru Shakyamuni Buddha revealed the Mahayana path. It contains the same foundational teachings as in the Hinayana path but includes added and extensive teachings on the altruistic mind of bodhicitta.

The Mahayana path consists of the sutra path and the tantra path

The sutra path or *paramitayana* is a causal path, guiding us to create positive causes for attaining enlightenment. However, the sutra path requires us to accumulate merit for three countless great eons to achieve enlightenment. Therefore, although the sutra path is an undisputed method to attain enlightenment, it is slow. This means the numberless sentient beings who rely on us to teach them the Dharma and to lead them to liberation and then full enlightenment must wait and suffer for many eons until we attain enlightenment to help them. Therefore we should work toward achieving enlightenment more quickly so that beings won't suffer for so many eons. This is where the tantra path comes in.

The tantra path is called the quick path to enlightenment. Tantra practice offers a way to achieve enlightenment within one lifetime instead of three countless great eons. The tantra path also is known as the secret mantra or Vajrayana. Tantra is not just about taking initiations and ritual practice. To succeed, the tantra practitioner must have unshakeable refuge in the Three Jewels and ideally must achieve realization of the renunciation of samsara, bodhicitta, and the wisdom realizing emptiness. But we can practice tantra correctly if we have studied and have some feeling of renunciation, the altruistic aspiration to liberate all sentient beings, and an understanding of the absence of inherent existence, even if we're short of fully realizing them. Based on these three, tantra can direct us and guide us to liberation from samsara and toward enlightenment.

But going through the motions of practicing tantra is useless to us if we don't understand the sutra teachings on death, impermanence, refuge, guru devotion, renunciation, bodhicitta, and emptiness.

The Buddha taught four classes of tantra according to the ability of disciples. They are the *kriya* or action tantra, the performance or *carya* tantra, the yoga tantra, and the *maha anuttara* yoga tantra, which is also called the *highest yoga tantra*. This fourth category of highest yoga tantra enables us to achieve the peerless happiness of full enlightenment in just one lifetime during this degenerate age.

The kriya and carya tantras emphasize outer practices such as keeping the body clean and abstaining from certain "black" foods, including meat, onion, and garlic. The principle here is that keeping the body clean without polluting it helps clarify the mind.

Inner practices are emphasized in the second two categories of yoga tantra and highest yoga tantra. These tantras cease the gross mind and actualize the clear light mind to meditate on emptiness, on the wisdom of nondual bliss and emptiness, like a bomb that destroys attachment, delusions, the dualistic view, and the subtle dualistic view. The highest yoga tantra contains a special practice called the *clear light meditation*, which ceases the gross mind. This is important because gross mind does not go to enlightenment; what goes to enlightenment is only the extremely subtle mind.

The clear light mind, the extremely subtle mind that directly realizes emptiness, is the direct cause of the Buddha's wisdom body or dharmakaya. The purified, extremely subtle inner wind or illusory body is the direct cause of the rupakaya, the Buddha's form body. Therefore we need to achieve both the dharmakaya and the rupakaya to benefit numberless sentient beings. The method to actualize the clear light and illusory bodies is not taught in the lower tantras and appears only in the highest yoga tantra. That is why one needs to eventually practice the highest yoga tantra.

We can achieve enlightenment within one lifetime if, as a foundation, we realize the four noble truths and we practice any category of tantra. The highest yoga tantra is special because it offers more developed and sophisticated meditative methods to the practitioner.

The scriptures speak of one thousand buddhas descending to earth in this fortunate eon. Guru Shakyamuni Buddha was the fourth of the thousand buddhas. The scriptures say that only three of these thousand buddhas will teach tantra: the fourth buddha, Guru Shakymuni Buddha; the eleventh buddha, the embodiment of Je Tsongkhapa; and the last buddha, who promised to teach everything the buddhas before him taught.

None of the other buddhas will teach the tantras, not because they lack the knowledge but because sentient beings of their eras won't have the merit or karma to receive the tantra teachings. How fortunate we are to live in this age when Guru Shakyamuni Buddha descended and revealed the tantra teachings.

Here I want to emphasize again that the basis of tantra practice is the complete Buddhist teachings: refuge in the Three Jewels, guru devotion, morality, renunciation of samsara, bodhicitta, cultivation of wisdom realizing emptiness, the six perfections, and the entire sutra path.

Without these it is simply not possible to practice tantra properly. This point must be very clearly understood.

Now we can see why meditation is so important, why the development of the mind is so important, why the development of compassion is so important. The ultimate goal of practicing the Dharma is not only for our own happiness but also for the happiness of all sentient beings. Therefore the purpose is not narrow but vast, like the infinite sky.

Guru Shakyamuni Buddha gave teachings to suit different levels of beings, which resulted in the Hinayana and Mahayana paths—the Sutrayana and Vajrayana teachings coming within the Mahayana path. That is what is meant by the three yanas or three spiritual pathways within the two vehicles.

Common aspects of the three yanas: Method and wisdom

All Buddhist paths are based on method and wisdom, whether Hinayana or Mahayana.

In the Hinayana Vehicle we develop the wisdom realizing emptiness as the remedy to cut off ignorance, coupled with moral conduct and the renunciation of samsara, which are collectively called *method*. We end suffering and attain nirvana by cultivating wisdom and method together. Just cultivating wisdom realizing emptiness is not sufficient; it must be coupled with method.

The Mahayana Vehicle also requires both wisdom and method.

In the sutra path we cultivate wisdom realizing emptiness just as in the Hinayana Vehicle. The Sutrayana method is more extensive than the Hinayana Vehicle method. The Sutrayana method is based on renunciation, morality, and bodhicitta, the altruistic mind of enlightenment. This bodhicitta is derived from generating the thought of loving-kindness, great compassion, and responsibility to free all beings from suffering.

Bodhicitta is not taught in the Hinayana path. With the altruistic attitude of bodhicitta we cultivate the six perfections of generosity, morality, patience, perseverance, concentration, and wisdom.

When we take stale, foul-smelling food out of a bowl, the bad smell tends to remain and linger in the bowl. Likewise, although the

Hinayana path eliminates the delusions that cause suffering and even the seeds of delusion, it doesn't completely remove the imprints of subtle obscurations left by subtle delusions, such as the mistaken conception of true existence. These subtle obscurations also must be totally removed.

This is why there are differences between the noble arhat and the fully enlightened buddha. Arhats have completely eliminated delusions by completing the method and wisdom of the Hinayana path. However, there yet remain in them the subtle obscurations, the subtle tendency to grasp at true existence, although they are completely free of the true cause of suffering,

The arhat has attained the lower nirvana or lesser liberation but not the great liberation, the great nirvana, otherwise called *enlightenment.* This latter state is the cessation of all delusions both gross and subtle, as well as their stains. Because of this limitation the arhat's understanding is not yet complete; there also remain limits in the ability to guide sentient beings.

By realizing the wisdom realizing emptiness coupled with the Mahayana path's skillful, extensive method of bodhicitta, we can eliminate even the subtle obscurations. Just as the reflection in a dust-covered mirror becomes clearer the more you clean the mirror, when there is not the slightest stain of obscuration left realizations become complete.

Accomplishing the Great Vehicle path may look hopeless now. But through effort we can completely purify our stream of consciousness from delusions, their seeds, and even the subtle smell of dualistic views. At that time, all realizations are complete and the stream of consciousness becomes omniscient. This omniscience is called dharmakaya. This is the great liberation, enlightenment.

When our stream of consciousness becomes omniscient there are no mistakes at all. We will be able to see every single being's different level of karma and will possess complete understanding of how to guide sentient beings. We will be able to reveal the teachings through the holy body, holy speech, and holy mind in a way suited to the mental dispositions of different sentient beings. This is the perfected combination of method and wisdom.

Likewise in the tantra aspect of the Mahayana path, method and wisdom are practiced together. In Vajrayana the wisdom realizing emptiness is much more refined. It is developed in conjunction with bodhicitta, with a method that is much more skillful than the method taught in the sutra and paramita teachings. With Vajrayana we can stop the delusions and their subtle imprints more quickly than in the paramita path.

These three yanas or pathways of the Hinayana, Sutrayana, and Vajrayana all support us in purifying delusions and accumulating merits. Actualizing them in the mind is the main purification. The stream of consciousness that was temporarily obscured is separated from the deluded obscurations, resulting in wisdom.

To achieve this we have to create the cause of merit and remove all the obstacles that interfere with attaining those realizations. For this, method is required. This means the combined practice of method and wisdom is crucial in all the vehicles.

ANECDOTES FROM THE LIFE OF KYABJE LAMA ZOPA RINPOCHE

Advice to a mother

We sat down to eat at a Whole Foods supermarket in the United States. A number of shoppers came up to Rinpoche, asking questions. One woman said to Rinpoche, "I have eight children. What advice can you give me?"

Rinpoche replied, "Ordinary education is important, but more important is the education for a good heart." She seemed to understand and thanked Rinpoche and went on her way.

Beyond the stroke

It has been two years since Rinpoche had the stroke. The stroke happened gradually over several days, and things kept getting worse, and even after he arrived at the hospital the stroke seemed to continue for several days. It got to the stage where Rinpoche could hardly move. It was a serious stroke. He just lay there, and it was very hard to know what to do.

Yet Rinpoche took absolutely no interest in his body. He never asked the doctor how he was, or what he should do, or what his chances were, or whether he would be OK. He did not seem to have the slightest concern about his critical condition. During his entire time at the hospital, Rinpoche focused on prayers for the sick people there. He even did a little fundraising for the Christian hospital during the latter part of his stay.

Nothing has changed much over the past two years. Rinpoche's lifestyle continues, and his prayers and concerns for the welfare of others continues, an attitude that is hard for most people to relate to. He lives now as he did prior to the stroke, with no worldly interest, with everything for others. He has no interest in sleep or in any worldly benefit.

Generosity on the streets of New York

While in New York City to attend His Holiness the Dalai Lama's teachings, Rinpoche and Roger needed a taxi to get to the venue. So they stood on opposite sides of the street, each trying to hail a cab. Ven. Roger wasn't having any success, but when he looked over he saw Rinpoche getting taxis . . . except he kept giving them to other people waiting!

Still prostrating despite the body

Rinpoche stood with his hands in the mudra of prostration before a very large thangka of Avalokiteshvara, the deity of compassion. Since the stroke, prostrations are very difficult for Rinpoche, yet he perseveres.

Rinpoche gradually leaned forward before the image of Avalokiteshvara, slowly going to the ground. His stronger left arm reached for the ground, his fingers contacted the floor. Gradually Rinpoche put weight on the arm as his body leaned forward cautiously. The left knee moved toward the ground and made contact. Now came the hard part: the right arm reached out to touch the ground while Rinpoche tried to spread his fingers so they landed open and stretched out on the floor.

I was feeling anxious because when Rinpoche's head goes lower than his waist he can feel dizzy, and that's a little dangerous after a stroke.

Gradually Rinpoche lowered his body forward awkwardly, always the left side taking most of the weight. Watching Rinpoche making this kind of effort is very moving. I can see others feeling likewise and getting emotional. The whole hall is very quiet while Rinpoche makes such an effort to do a full-length prostration to all the buddhas.

Rinpoche is now stretched full length on the floor, although he can't yet straighten his right arm. The process is slow but done with great, great determination. Now the really hard part: Rinpoche gets up alone, as he won't let anyone help! Rinpoche has developed a technique as he gradually rises, whereby he shifts his weight over several stages, including finally to the stage where he has to take the weight from his arms and be on his legs. That is most difficult. It's quite tense watching this part, and I can see some observing students holding their breaths.

Rinpoche is hesitating now as he has to make a huge effort to go from kneeling to his feet. He does so and then straightens his body and is standing. His hands slowly come to his heart in the mudra of prostration in front of Avalokiteshvara.

5 : LIVING IN AWARENESS
OF THE FOUR NOBLE TRUTHS

DAILY REFLECTIONS ON THE FOUR
NOBLE TRUTHS

THE FIRST NOBLE TRUTH reveals that the nature of samsara is suffering. The second noble truth shows the causes of suffering are delusion and karma. The third noble truth of cessation says the end of suffering is definitely possible, and the fourth noble truth shows how to accomplish this. The Dharma path targets the poisonous roots of all suffering and vigorously eliminates them.

Therefore we should spend a few minutes each day—whether at home or while we are out, driving to work, returning from work, under the shower, shopping, anywhere—reflecting on the subjects of the four noble truths. These subjects include impermanence and death, precious human rebirth, devotion to the guru, the sufferings of samsara, taking refuge in the Three Jewels, karma and the twelve links, how delusions function and their antidotes, renouncing samsara, developing the good heart, cultivating bodhicitta, and cultivating the wisdom realizing emptiness.

We can unhook ourselves from clinging to this life's concerns just by remembering impermanence and death. Suddenly we find enjoyment in life! By applying the antidotes to delusions and by fortifying this with meditation, we can stop the dissatisfied mind. This immediately brings enjoyment in the heart and peace. More than that, we near the goal of enlightenment, securing not only our happiness but also the happiness of everyone, of countless sentient beings.

Merely knowing the teachings of the path is not sufficient. What we actually *do* with Dharma teachings we have received is far more important. Just having Dharma knowledge is like planting a seed in the earth and leaving it. We need to nourish the Dharma seed with meditation, doing virtue, purifying negativities, and engaging in practices that support our progress on the path. These include the purification practice of the four opponent powers, prostrations to the thirty-five buddhas, performing the seven limb practices, and making mandala offerings. Buttressed by the motivation to benefit all beings, these practices bring the blessings of the guru buddha into our minds and, like rainfall and sunshine, nourish the spiritual seed in sprouting and growing.

Transforming Problems into the Spiritual Path

By practicing thought transformation we can transform problems into spiritual cultivation and can convert adversity into happiness. We can transform bad conditions into favorable conditions, powerfully turning problems and difficulties into the path to enlightenment. Thought transformation converts negative circumstances into positive ones through analysis and through the view.

Transforming negative situations through analysis

When a disease infects our body, causing unpleasant symptoms like fever, this fever is beneficial because, rather than the disease festering inside us unnoticed and creating more harm, it alerts us to a problem inside our body. Likewise when a snake in the jungle bites us, even though it is painful to cut away skin around the bite, the cutting is beneficial, as this could save our lives. Likewise it is said suffering is the broom that cleans away negative karmas and obscurations.

Therefore when trouble or sickness strikes, use this analysis: The negative karmas that I have committed in the past, the results of which I definitely have to experience, have now ripened on this body. If this did not happen now, I would experience even greater hardship later, including the horrors of inconceivable lifetimes in the lower realms.

We don't experience anything that was not caused by our past actions, just as a tomato does not suddenly appear in midair. There are causes and conditions behind the appearance of tomatoes. Likewise all our troubles have an origin: our own negative minds that motivated negative actions, causing the results we now experience. Acknowledging our role in creating the problems we face helps us cope with a better attitude. In this way, we do not get upset or depressed about difficult situations.

This is the Mahayana thought transformation practice. As the mind understands that it is responsible for a problem, it seeks a solution that does not involve blaming others. If we are having problems with a colleague, that colleague is only a condition and not the cause of our problems. If it were not this colleague, there would be some other person or circumstance appearing to us, seemingly creating difficulties for us. So it is wholly inappropriate to point to one person or one thing as the troublemaker. The real troublemaker is our own past negative action. By thinking this way, external hindrances no longer disturb us, and we are able to continue our lives and Dharma practice. This is how problems can be transformed into nutrition for our spiritual practice.

Transforming negative situations through the view
When problems arise, we have the habit of getting mentally jammed up. No matter what tough circumstances confront us, always think, "This is a favorable, beneficial condition." First see the advantages problems bring, including finishing past negative karmas and strengthening our minds. Once we can see the benefit of problems we will label them as "useful" and face them with a buoyant mind. This happiness depends on understanding the benefits of problems and cultivating a mental attitude that says, "This is not a problem. It brings benefits to my practice." We are not fooling ourselves. We are simply not giving into our habit of negatively interpreting our experiences.

This brings us to the second aspect of the view, which is that suffering and happiness come from our minds. There is not the slightest atom of misery or happiness existing from its own side. The misery or happiness that appears to be real and permanent is in fact totally empty. Unhappiness is caused by how our thoughts label experience. Happiness and suffering are actually empty, mere mental labels on the bases of persons or situations.

When we mentally label difficulties as "problems" and "interferences" they paralyze us, upset us, and we suffer. This is because we believe our own mental labels. Once we have labeled the situation a "problem," it appears to us as real and tangible. But it is not. Because this "problem" is merely imputed to a particular circumstance by thought, it is not truly existent but is completely empty. The understanding that the seemingly existent "I" is merely a mental label on the base of aggregates and does not inherently exist can also be applied to problems. As our minds have conjured the problem, the solution lies in how we view the problem and deal with it.

We can train our minds to see advantages in all problems and to realize problems are merely a mental construct. For problems to subside, we need to stop dwelling on their shortcomings and look at their usefulness instead. Whether a life situation is wonderful or not depends on the way our minds interpret it. We can choose to label a person, thing, or situation as "wonderful" or a "problem." The choice depends completely on our minds, on our interpretations of the object and circumstances.

For example, if we repeatedly think of the shortcomings of sense objects, no matter how much our possessions and wealth increase, we enjoy them while realistically seeing their limitations. However, if we focus only on the benefits of sense objects, this deceives us into thinking they are permanent and into ignoring how they trap us in samsara. Whether something is positive or negative depends on the mind.

Training in Mahayana thought transformation makes our minds adaptive, nimble, and light. Happiness and courage arise from seeing the benefit of difficult circumstances, and we can flexibly accomplish much. We are not easily disturbed by crises, and people feel comforted by our company. Wise people who see that all happiness and misery depend on the mind seek happiness from within their own minds and not from anything external. Mind possesses all the causes of happiness.

We can test this with thought transformation practice, particularly as it uses hardship as steps on the path to enlightenment. Give it a try.

Any happiness we feel comes from our own minds. From the small pleasure of a cool breeze when we feel hot up to sublime enlightenment, all happiness comes from our own minds. The thoughts within our minds cause our happiness and suffering, so we should seek happiness from our minds. This is the essential point of the Dharma. Thought transformation training is the clearest and most skillful way to bring about happiness from within our own minds.

When someone is angry with us, our compassion and skillful response can emerge if we remember the suffering nature of samsara, how delusions traumatize every living being and drive us to do all sorts of things. In this way, we can feel loving-kindness from our hearts, seeing everyone as someone to be cherished.

Using thought transformation we can see that "difficult" person as someone unbelievably precious and kind. This difficult person becomes the most precious treasure in our lives, more precious than millions of dollars or mountains of diamonds. Why? Because this person presents us with the perfect opportunity to practice thought transformation, bringing us inner peace and a step closer to enlightenment. No matter what harm someone does to us in body, speech, and mind, use thought transformation to see how incredibly beneficial that difficulty is for the development of our minds. This will uplift us.

When we practice Mahayana thought transformation, no living being or nonliving thing can truly injure us. Even when we are dying, thought transformation practice is hugely beneficial, for instance through tonglen, the bodhicitta meditation of exchanging self for others. A person who dies with the thought of cherishing other living beings is self-supporting. If we die while doing tonglen practice, our minds will be stable and comfortable, and it would be impossible for us to be born in the lower realms.

The foolish ones seek happiness from the external world, running around and keeping themselves busy with that expectation. If we seek

happiness from the outside, we have no freedom because we have sur-
rendered to the control of external conditions, making life always appear
unpredictable and problematic. We will never be completely satisfied.

We can therefore see very clearly that it does not matter how others
behave toward us or what they think of us. What we think is a problem
actually comes from our own minds. What we think is joyful also comes
from our own minds. We are the sole author of our own happiness.

Purifying Negativities

Vajrasattva four opponent powers practice

Even though we may commit only a small negative action, the fact that
karma expands means the results of any negative action double, triple,
and multiply without end. Over time, the small atom of a misdeed
becomes the size of the whole planet! This is a serious matter.

Even nonbelievers who do not accept any religion or faith system,
who merely want freedom from the problems of this life, can find the
ultimate answer to their wishes through overcoming afflictive thoughts
and purifying the negativities of mind that cause all their problems.

Our ability to attain enlightenment depends on removing all negative
karma, delusions, and obscurations. If these remain the mind cannot
be transformed and thus cannot achieve realizations of the path. This is
why the practice of purification, such as the Vajrasattva four opponent
powers practice, is so essential.

The Vajrasattva four opponent powers practice purifies all forms of
negative karmas and obscurations. Vajrasattva is the purification-related
aspect of the Buddha.

The four opponent powers are:

1. The power of regret (recollecting our mistaken actions and seeing
   their disadvantages and how they create future suffering)
2. The power of reliance (reaffirming our refuge in the Three Jewels)
3. The power of the remedy (reciting prayers to request blessings,
   purify our mind, and strengthen our virtues)

4. The power of the promise (generating the intention not to commit the mistaken action again for a defined period of time)

To start, it is useful to recollect our mistaken actions so we can analyze their disadvantages and then generate the intent not to repeat those actions. This is called the power of regret, which is *not* about guilt. Instead it is about recognizing having done something harmful, the disadvantages of having done so, and wishing not to do it again.

For example, if we mistakenly drink poison and realize we have done so, we will recognize our mistake and will deeply regret it. This will spur us to take the antidote and to be much more careful in the future. In the same way, through the power of regret we recollect the negative actions we have done, regret them, and take action to purify them.

The power of reliance is reminding ourselves of the qualities of the Buddha, Dharma, and Sangha to guide us from error as we reflect on our negative actions. It is also extremely beneficial to remember the Buddha's teachings on nonharm, morality, and the renunciation of samsara.

We then apply the remedy by reciting the Vajrasattva mantra, either the long version or short version, "Om Vajrasattva Hum," twenty-one times or more. While reciting the mantra we visualize all our negative karma in the form of black liquid coal and dark smoke leaving our bodies and flowing into the ground. At the same time pure white nectar from Vajrasattva fills our entire body, like milk being poured into a vessel. We imagine all negative karmas completely purified from our minds, and our physical bodies becoming clean and clear like pure crystal. This is the power of remedy.

The next step of the promise is vital. Make a strong determination, "I will immediately purify those negative karmas that I can. In addition I will purify slowly, gradually, but steadily those that I am unable to purify easily." Regarding delusions we are most vulnerable to—these could be anger, attachment, or pride—resolve to avoid committing that particular negative action for a specified period of time. We could set the time frame as one hour, one week, or one month.

Making the resolution and fulfilling it brings a mountain of benefits. Even a very short period of restraint is worthwhile because it helps us gain a hold over our minds and accomplishes our promise. Fulfilling the commitment helps us avoid the harmful results of that negative action. At the end of this practice we should mentally dissolve Vajrasattva into light and absorb Vajrasattva into our hearts. Then imagine that body, speech, and mind have been blessed by Vajrasattva, the embodiment of all the buddhas.

The thirty-five buddhas practice

When the thirty-five buddhas were bodhisattvas cultivating the path, they prayed to benefit sentient beings by helping them purify their negative karma and defilements. When the bodhisattvas achieved enlightenment they achieved the Buddha's ten qualities or powers, one of which is the power of prayer. Their names thus have the curative and supportive power of their past prayers. Sentient beings who recite those names purify eons of negative karma and are thus able to avert the harmful consequences that would otherwise have followed.

The late Serkong Dorje Chang Rinpoche was a highly realized lama with amazing clairvoyance. He was able to see through anyone who came to see him. He would know exactly what that person had done in the past and what they were going to do. Rinpoche could even see clearly the dreams a person had. I myself experienced this with Rinpoche, and it was rather startling, kind of shocking, that someone else could know me so profoundly. Thus those who knew Rinpoche were very careful never to tell him any lies because Rinpoche would always know.

Sometimes people would come to Rinpoche and ask for observations and advice. One day a Tibetan man came to him about how to succeed in his business or something like that. But before responding to the man's questions, Rinpoche suddenly said, "Oh, you have killed a human being!" The Tibetan man was completely shaken and very embarrassed, and he dared not repeat his question. Rinpoche then advised him, "You must do prostrations and confession to the thirty-five buddhas." This shows how powerful this practice is, as it can remedy even the terrible karma of killing a human being.

A daily practice: The seven-limb prayer

Progress on the spiritual path depends on purifying negativities and accumulating merit. But this is difficult because of the strong delusions in our minds and the fact that our virtues are often weak while our negativities are perfect. The seven-limb practice, based on the Seven-Limb Prayer, is a simple yet powerful method that purifies negative karma and accumulates positive karma:

> Reverently I prostrate with my body, speech, and mind
>   and present clouds of every type of offering.
> I confess all my negative actions accumulated since
>   beginningless time
> and rejoice in the merits of all holy and ordinary beings.
> Please remain until samsara ends and turn the wheel of Dharma
>   for the sake of sentient beings.
> I dedicate the virtues of myself and others to the great
>   enlightenment.

We begin with visualizing Guru Shakyamuni Buddha, inseparable from our gurus, in front of us and then read the prayer while reflecting on the meaning and effect of each line or limb, which are as follows:

Prostrations. We imagine numerous emanations of our body, enough to cover the entire earth. All these bodies go down into full prostration, laying the entire body flat on the ground before the Buddha. This effort collects extensive merits and purifies a vast amount of negative karma.

Offerings. We visualize as extensively as possible offering light, flowers, incense, perfumes, food, music, and any other offerings to the Buddha. There is no limit to our visualizations, so we can fill the skies with beautiful mental offerings!

Confession. Here we should think, "I am confessing individually all the negative karmas committed with my body, speech, and mind." In this way, we can purify all negative karmas, including broken vows and any heavy negative karmas done in relation to our gurus.

Rejoice. Rejoicing in the virtues of others is the easiest way to accumulate merit. Therefore rejoice in the works of the buddhas and bodhisattvas, as well as the virtues of ordinary beings. This overcomes jealousy and is the easiest way of generating unimaginable skies of merit. Simply be happy at the good deeds of others.

Requesting the guru to have a stable life. The guru is our guide on the unmistaken path, so we visualize offering the guru a beautifully crafted golden throne supported by eight snow lions, adorned with jewels and double vajras. We mentally offer as many thrones to the guru as we can.

Requesting to turn the wheel of Dharma. We visualize offering a thousand-spoked dharmachakra or Dharma wheel so the teachings that secure the welfare of all beings can flourish and never decline.

Dedication. Having done all the virtuous actions and visualizations above, we then offer our merit toward the enlightenment of all sentient beings and "seal" the dedication with emptiness. We do this by thinking, "Due to all the past, present, and future merits collected by me, by numberless sentient beings, and by all the buddhas and bodhisattvas (who are all empty from their own side), may I alone (who is also empty from my own side) achieve enlightenment (which am empty from its own side) and lead all sentient beings (who are empty from their own side) to enlightenment (which is also empty from its own side)."

THE PRACTICE OF THE FIVE POWERS AT THE TIME OF DEATH

By familiarizing ourselves with these five powers during our lives, and in particular practicing them at the delicate time of death, we will be assured of a happy mind. The five powers are:

1. *Power of attitude/determination.* Every morning we should think: "The purpose of my life is to free everyone from suffering and its causes and to bring happiness to them. Therefore from now on until my death, whether this year, this week, or even today, I will avoid coming under

the control of self-cherishing. Instead I will practice cherishing others. I am going to practice the altruistic intention of bodhicitta, and even when I die and enter the intermediate stage I am not going to separate from this good heart of altruism. I will never separate from this resolve to benefit others."

Motivate in this way each morning and try to live the rest of each day with the same motivation. If we habitually set up an intention like this, we will be able to uphold this altruism all the time, even at the time of our deaths. This intention will infuse our lives and deaths with gentle courage, making them instead pleasant journeys that benefit ourselves and other sentient beings.

2. *The power of the white seed.* Creating merit should be done without conditions. When we know death is imminent we should utilize our possessions as generosity for other beings, for poor people, or for anyone who needs help. The primary method for generating extensive merit is to cultivate bodhicitta, this good heart that cherishes all sentient beings and seeks to bring them to the highest happiness of enlightenment. It is very important not to cling to people or possessions as we approach death. Clinging is what makes death difficult and terrifying as we are separated from our objects of attachment.

Two things make us afraid of death. The first is clinging to our own bodies, possessions, and loved ones. The solution is to not grasp at them at the time of death. Instead give freedom to ourselves at death, because death can be an easy, comfortable, and even happy time if we give up anxious clinging. Be as generous as we can to benefit the poor and sick, make offerings to holy objects and other living beings, and dedicate this generosity for the happiness and enlightenment of all beings. Doing so offers great release to our minds.

The second cause of the fear of death is knowing we have done some unwholesome actions like harming ourselves and others with the negative, self-cherishing thoughts of anger, attachment, and pride. These unwholesome actions tend to arise in the mind at the time of death and bring so much unease in the heart. If we wish a peaceful death without worry or fear about what will happen then and beyond, waste no time to purify negative deeds and their imprints, starting right now. Purifying negativities and warmly wishing all beings to gain ultimate happiness makes death something like going for a picnic or a holiday with a carefree mind free of fear and doubt.

3. *The power of repudiation.* Apart from confessing our negative actions and doing purification practices, repudiation of negativities includes retaking broken vows or simply rejecting the ego, which essentially is the self-cherishing attitude. This means that when a problem arises in our lives, whether it is cancer, AIDS, relationship difficulties, financial loss, or any form of trouble, we should immediately think how all problems originate from self-cherishing.

We must direct our energy toward destroying our self-cherishing attitude. Without the inner enemy of self-cherishing there would be no outer harms coming at us. So we should reflect and mentally bombard the self-cherishing mind with the thought, "My self-cherishing attitude has brought about dissatisfaction and problems." We should think about how the self-cherishing attitude gives free reign to our attachments—our anger, pride, and jealousy—to act out in ways that harm us and others. We should continue this reflection and meditate on it as best we can.

4. *The power of prayer.* We should recite prayers with the bodhicitta motivation and strongly dedicate our prayers and all the virtues we have done toward the happiness and enlightenment of all sentient beings. We should keep the heart warm and always hold close to the heart the welfare of all living beings.

5. *The power of familiarity or training.* Regularly holding the altruistic thought throughout our lives, and especially at the time of death, is an excellent way of using death as a spiritual path. We can generate compassion and think of all beings who are dying and having great distress owing to impending death. We can think, "How wonderful if they can all be free from suffering and its causes and all have happiness and its causes. I dedicate all my merits to them." Whatever we think, say, or do, whether we are in a healthy condition or not, we should do it with the bodhicitta motivation.

When the moment of death is near some people lay their bodies down on their beds, some die seated in the meditation position, some lie down in what is called the lion's position. For the lion's pose you lie down on your right side, resting your head on your right hand. Use your fifth and smallest finger to gently close the right nostril. You should keep your two legs stretched out, with the left hand lying along the stretched-out body. You can try to do this on your own or, if you cannot, you can ask others to help position your body this way.

This is the position Guru Shakyamuni Buddha adopted when he showed the aspect of passing away, which was itself a teaching on impermanence and death. Lying in this special position becomes a form of protection for the mind and helps one die with a positive thought and without anger, attachment, jealousy, or any such disturbing thoughts. Dying with a positive thought definitely helps us secure a better rebirth. The positive thought activates positive karma that has been accumulated in our mindstreams.

We need to begin our training now if we are to handle death well and accomplish Dharma practice at the time of death. Practice the five powers every day—they will help us know when we are about to die. Outer, inner, and secret signs, including dreams and physical indications, will tell us when death nears. If we train in the five powers every day, life as well as the moment of death becomes peaceful, comfortable, and light.

ANECDOTES FROM THE LIFE OF KYABJE LAMA ZOPA RINPOCHE

Himalayan frogs and mani

After completing a *nyung ne* (fasting retreat) at his retreat center in Lawudo, Nepal, Rinpoche visited Lama Dorje's place (located between Lawudo and Lukla). Several monks accompanied Rinpoche. Rinpoche received many requests to visit homes, from the village in Namche Bazaar down to those in Lukla, a long distance away. We journeyed entirely on foot and it took us three days and three nights of trekking with little rest or sleep. All the way Rinpoche would give teachings, do pujas, confer blessings, give consultations, consecrate altars and holy objects, circumambulate stupas, and offer prostrations to the thirty-five buddhas and to all the mountain *chortens* (stupas) and stones that had *Om mani padme hum* carved into them.

Of course Rinpoche's blessings were not only for humans but for animals too, ranging from the ox-like dzo to frogs and ants. The treks between villages were done at night, as the days were filled with Dharma activities within the villages. One late night it rained, making the air freezing cold and the ground muddy, but that didn't stop Rinpoche from performing an extensive Lama Choepa puja in the rain from midnight until dawn.

On this journey we would hear frogs croaking in the dark wilderness. Rinpoche would stop to recite prayers to the frogs. Rinpoche was tireless but we monks were worn out. It got to the point where we would dread the sound of any more frogs because that meant yet another stop for prayers! The exhausted monks would lean against each other's back to catch a few seconds of sleep. At times it would appear as if Rinpoche were giving teachings to the frogs, but in fact the teachings were primarily for us monks, although we were simply too tired to hear them.

I recall hearing only the first few lines of one of Rinpoche's talks and then being awakened by a loud cough from Rinpoche at the end of his teaching. Keeping up with this living Buddha even for twenty-four hours was no easy task. Although it was physically exhausting, it was also mentally inspiring and joyful.

The inner meaning of rest

Rinpoche and I are scheduled to fly to Nepal for Kopan Monastery's November meditation course. Rinpoche has been on an extensive international teaching tour, which began in the late 1980s (when Rinpoche's main guru, Lama Yeshe, passed away) and hasn't stopped since. The tour has gone on and on, from one center to another, from one continent to another, with barely two or three days between centers. The years of touring have been grueling, with hard days and nights that never end, so days and nights merge and weekends don't exist.

I always asked Rinpoche to consider some rest, to take just one day off to rest, if only a few hours at night. But Rinpoche always ignored my pleas. After some years, I asked Rinpoche, "What does rest mean to you? He replied, "Abiding in virtue."

After that I think I gave up on the rest issue. The phrase that immediately and vividly arose in my mind was, "So THIS is the bodhisattva's way of life!"

GLOSSARY

aggregate. The association of body and mind. A person consists of five aggregates: form, feeling, discrimination, compositional factors/karmic imprints, and consciousness.

arhat. Lit. "foe destroyer." A being who, having ceased his or her karma and delusions, is completely free from all suffering and its causes and has achieved liberation from cyclic existence.

arya. Lit. "noble." One who has realized the wisdom of emptiness.

Atisha Lama Dipankara Shrijnana (982–1054). The renowned Indian master who went to Tibet in 1042 to help in the revival of Buddhism and who established the Kadam tradition. His *Lamp for the Path to Enlightenment* was the first lamrim text.

attachment. A disturbing thought that exaggerates the positive qualities of an object and wishes to possess it. One of the six root delusions.

bhumi. Lit. "stage" or "ground." Bodhisattvas must traverse ten bhumis on their journey to enlightenment, the first reached through the direct perception of emptiness.

bodhicitta. The altruistic determination to achieve full enlightenment in order to free all sentient beings from suffering and bring them to enlightenment.

bodhisattva. One who possesses bodhicitta.

bodhisattva vows. The vows taken when one enters the bodhisattva path.

Buddhadharma. The teachings of the Buddha.

Buddhist. One who has taken refuge in the Three Jewels—Buddha, Dharma, and Sangha—and who accepts the philosophical world view of the four seals: all composite phenomena are impermanent, all contaminated phenomena are in the nature of suffering, all things and events are devoid of self-existence, and nirvana is true peace.

causative phenomena. Things that come about in dependence on causes and conditions; includes all objects experienced by the senses as well as the mind itself.

central channel. The channel or nadi that runs from the crown of the head to the secret chakra. It is the major energy channel of the vajra body, visualized as a hollow tube of light in front of the spine.

clear light. Very subtle mind. This subtlest state of mind occurs naturally at death and through successful tantric practice and is used by practitioners to realize emptiness.

compounded phenomena. Phenomena that arise due to causes and conditions.

conventional bodhicitta. The altruistic mind of enlightenment; a mental primary consciousness holding the two aspirations of wishing to benefit all sentient beings and wishing to attain enlightenment in order to do this.

conventional truth. As opposed to ultimate truth, which is the understanding of the ultimate nature of reality or emptiness, conventional truth is what is true to the valid conventional consciousness. See also *two truths.*

cyclic existence. The beginningless, recurring cycle of death and rebirth under the control of delusion and karma and fraught with suffering. See also *samsara.*

delusions. The disturbing negative thoughts, or minds, that cause suffering and negative karma. The three main delusions or three poisons are ignorance, attachment, and anger.

demigod. A being in the god realm who enjoys greater comfort and pleasure than human beings but who suffers from intense jealousy and quarreling.

dependent origination. Also called dependent arising, this describes the way the self and phenomena exist conventionally as relative and interdependent. They come into existence in dependence on causes and conditions, on their parts, and most subtly on the mind imputing or labeling them.

desire realm. One of the three realms of samsara, comprising the hell beings, hungry ghosts, animals, humans, demigods, and the six lower classes of gods. Beings in this realm are preoccupied with desire for objects of the six senses.

Dharamsala. A village in the northwest of India, in the state of Himachal Pradesh, the home of His Holiness the Dalai Lama and the Tibetan government in exile.

Dharma. In general Dharma describes spiritual teachings, and more specifically the teachings of the Buddha, which protect from suffering and lead to liberation and full enlightenment. Dharma is also described as "that which overcomes delusions."

dharmakaya. The truth body of a buddha, the blissful omniscient mind of a buddha, and the result of the wisdom side of the path. Dharmakaya can be divided into the wisdom body and the nature body.

dualistic view. The ignorant view characteristic of the unenlightened mind, in which all things are falsely conceived to have concrete self-existence. To such a view the appearance of an object is mixed with the false image of its being independent or self-existent, thereby leading to further dualistic views concerning subject and object and self and other.

eight freedoms. These eight are the defining features of the perfect human rebirth: freedom from birth as a hell being, hungry ghost, animal, long-life god, when no buddha has descended, in a place where there are no Dharma teachings, with defective mental or physical faculties, or as a heretic holding wrong views.

eight Mahayana precepts. One-day vows to abandon killing, stealing, lying, sexual contact, taking intoxicants, sitting on high seats or beds, eating at the wrong time, and singing, dancing, and wearing perfumes and jewelry.

eight types of suffering. Also known as the sufferings of humans. The suffering of birth, old age, illness, death, encountering what is unpleasant, separation from what is pleasant, not getting what you want, and the five aggregates.

eight worldly dharmas. The worldly concerns that generally motivate the actions of ordinary beings: wanting gain and not wanting loss, wanting to be happy and not wanting to be unhappy, wanting praise

and not wanting criticism, and wanting a good reputation and not
wanting a bad reputation.

emptiness. The absence of inherent, true existence. Ultimately every phenomenon is empty of existing truly or from its own side.

enlightenment. This is called full awakening, or buddhahood, or omniscience. Enlightenment is the ultimate goal of a Mahayana Buddhist,
attained when all limitations have been removed from the mind and
one's positive potential has been completely and perfectly realized.
It is a state characterized by infinite compassion, wisdom, and skill.

eon. A world period, also called a kalpa—an inconceivably long period
of time. The life span of the universe is divided into four great eons,
which are themselves divided into twenty lesser eons.

eternalism. The belief in the inherent existence of things, as opposed to
nihilism. It is one of the two extremes.

form realm. The second of samsara's three realms, which contains sev-
enteen classes of gods.

formless realm. The highest of samsara's three realms, which has four
classes of gods involved in formless meditations. The four meditative
levels attained in this realm are: limitless sky, limitless consciousness,
nothingness, and neither existence nor nonexistence (also called the
peak of samsara).

four immeasurables. Also known as the four immeasurable thoughts or
the four sublime attitudes, these are four states of mind or aspirations:
loving-kindness, compassion, sympathetic joy, and equanimity.

four noble truths. The subject of the Buddha's first turning of the wheel
of Dharma: suffering, the origin of suffering, the cessation of suffering, and the path leading to the cessation of suffering.

gelong. A fully ordained Buddhist monk, also called a bhikshu.

Gelug. One of the four main traditions of Tibetan Buddhism, it was
founded by Lama Tsongkhapa in the early fifteenth century and has
been propagated by such illustrious masters as the successive Dalai
Lamas and Panchen Lamas.

Gelugpa. A follower of the Gelug tradition.

god. A rebirth in a state within samsara of luxury and much pleasure.

guru. Lit. "heavy," as in heavy with Dharma knowledge. A spiritual teacher or master.

guru devotion. The practice of devotion to the guru with thought and with action.

guru yoga. The fundamental tantric practice whereby one's guru is seen as identical to the buddhas, one's personal meditational deity, and the essential nature of one's own mind.

hearer. A Hinayana practitioner who strives for nirvana on the basis of listening to teachings from a teacher.

higher realms. The higher realms comprise the more fortunate rebirths as a human, god, or demigod.

highest yoga tantra. The fourth and supreme division of tantric practice, sometimes called *maha anuttara* yoga tantra. It consists of the generation and completion stages. Through this practice one can attain full enlightenment within one lifetime.

Hinayana. Lit. "Small Vehicle." The path of the arhats, whose goal is nirvana, or personal liberation from samsara. The term *Theravada* is often preferred, although it is not fully synonymous.

hungry ghost. Also known as pretas, these abide in the three lower realms of the six classes of samsaric beings. Hungry ghosts experience the greatest sufferings of hunger and thirst.

ignorance. A mental factor that obscures the mind and prevents it from seeing the way in which things exist in reality. There are basically two types of ignorance: ignorance of karma and ignorance of ultimate truth. Ignorance is the fundamental delusion from which all other delusions arise.

impermanence. The gross and subtle levels of the transience of phenomena.

imprints. The seeds, or potentials, left on the mind by positive or negative actions of body, speech, and mind.

inherent (or intrinsic) existence. What phenomena are empty of; the object of negation, or refutation. From the viewpoint of ignorance, phenomena appear to exist independently, in and of themselves.

karma. Lit. "action." The working of cause and effect, whereby positive actions produce happiness and negative actions produce suffering.

lamrim. The graduated path to enlightenment. A presentation of Shakyamuni Buddha's teachings as a step-by-step training of a disciple to achieve enlightenment.

liberation. The state of complete freedom from samsara; the goal of a practitioner seeking his or her own escape from suffering.

lineage lama. A spiritual teacher who is in the line of direct guru-disciple transmission of teachings, from Buddha to the teachers of the present day.

loving-kindness. The wish for others to have happiness and its causes.

lower realms. The three realms of cyclic existence with the most suffering: the hell, hungry ghost, and animal realms.

Mahayana. Lit. "Great Vehicle." Mahayana is the path of the bodhisattvas, those seeking enlightenment in order to liberate all other beings.

Maitreya. The next buddha after Shakyamuni Buddha and the fifth of the thousand buddhas of this present world age.

Manjushri. The bodhisattva (or buddha) of wisdom. Recipient of the wisdom lineage of Shakyamuni Buddha's teachings, which he passed on to Nagarjuna.

merit. Positive imprints left on the mind by virtuous or Dharma actions, merit is the principal cause of happiness. The merit of virtue, when coupled with the merit of wisdom, eventually results in rupakaya, the Buddha's form.

merit field or field of accumulation. The visualized or actual holy beings in relation to whom one accumulates merit by going for refuge and making offerings, and to whom one prays or makes requests for special purposes.

method. All aspects of the path to enlightenment other than those related to emptiness. Method is primarily associated with the development of loving-kindness, compassion, and bodhicitta.

Middle Way. The philosophy presented in Shakyamuni Buddha's Prajnaparamita Sutras and elucidated by Nagarjuna, which is that all phenomena are dependent arisings, thereby avoiding the mistaken extremes of self-existence and nonexistence, or eternalism and nihilism. Also called Madhyamaka.

Milarepa (1040–1123). Tibet's great yogi, who achieved enlightenment in his lifetime under the tutelage of his guru, Marpa, who was a contemporary of Atisha. One of the founding fathers of the Kagyü school.

mind. Synonymous with consciousness and sentience and defined as that which is "clear and knowing." Mind is a formless entity that has the ability to perceive objects.

Nagarjuna. The great second-century Indian philosopher and tantric adept who propounded the Madhyamaka philosophy of emptiness. He is one of six great Indian scholars known as the six ornaments.

Nalanda. A Mahayana Buddhist monastic university founded in the fifth century in north India, not far from Bodhgaya. Nalanda served as a major source of the Buddhist teachings that spread to Tibet.

Naropa (1016–1100). The Indian Buddhist master and meditator who, by the practice of meditative disciplines, attained miraculous powers. A disciple of Tilopa and the guru of Marpa and Maitripa; transmitted many tantric lineages, including the renowned Six Yogas of Naropa.

nihilism. The doctrine that nothing exists, as opposed to eternalism. Nihilism contends there is no cause-and-effect to actions and no past and future lives.

nirmanakaya. The emanation body of a buddha that manifests in a variety of forms for and perceivable by sentient beings.

nyung ne. A two-day Avalokiteshvara retreat that requires fasting, prostrations, and silence.

object of negation. The object that seemingly appears to be inherently existing.

obscurations. Also known as obstructions, they hinder the attainment of liberation and enlightenment.

om mani padme hum. Also called the *mani,* this is the mantra of Avalokiteshvara, the buddha of compassion.

oral transmission. The verbal transmission of a teaching, meditation practice, or mantra from guru to disciple, the guru having received the transmission in an unbroken lineage from the original source.

perfect human rebirth. The rare human state, qualified by eight freedoms and ten richnesses, that is the ideal condition for practicing the Dharma and attaining enlightenment.

perfections. The main practices of a bodhisattva are the six perfections. On the basis of bodhicitta a bodhisattva practices the six perfections of generosity, morality, patience, joyous perseverance, concentration, and wisdom.

pervasive compounding suffering. The most subtle of the three types of suffering, it refers to the nature of the five aggregates contaminated by karma and delusions.

preliminary practices. The practices, also called *ngondro*, that prepare the mind for successful tantric meditation by removing hindrances and accumulating merit. These practices are found in all schools of Tibetan Buddhism and are usually done 100,000 times each. The four main practices are recitation of the refuge formula, mandala offerings, prostrations, and Vajrasattva mantra recitation.

puja. Lit. "offering." A religious prayer ceremony.

pure land. A pure land of a buddha is a place where there is no suffering. In some, but not all, pure lands, after taking birth, the practitioner receives teachings directly from the buddha of that pure land, actualizes the rest of the path, and then becomes enlightened.

real I. The I that seemingly appears to exist from its own side without depending on anything such as causes and conditions, parts, or the mind's imputation. It is the object to be refuted. See also *object of negation.*

refuge. Heartfelt reliance on the Buddha, Dharma, and Sangha for guidance on the path to liberation and enlightenment.

Rinpoche. Lit. "precious one." Generally a title given to a lama who has intentionally taken rebirth in a human body to continue helping others. It is also a respectful title used for one's own lama.

root guru. The teacher who has had the greatest influence on a particular disciple's entering or following the spiritual path.

rupakaya. The form body of a fully enlightened being. The result of the complete and perfect accumulation of merit.

sadhana. Step-by-step instructions for practicing the meditations related to a particular meditational deity.

sambhogakaya. Called the enjoyment body, the form in which the enlightened mind appears in order to benefit highly realized bodhisattvas.

samsara. Cyclic existence, or samsara, refers to the six realms of conditioned existence or suffering. These are the lower realms of the hell beings, hungry ghosts, and animals, and the upper realms of the humans, demigods, and gods.

samten. The first of the four levels of calm-abiding meditation.

Sangha. Absolute Sangha are those who have directly realized emptiness; relative Sangha are ordained monks and nuns. Also used loosely to refer to a lay Dharma community or members of a Dharma center.

self-grasping. The mind of ignorance that believes in an inherently existent self, which leads to self-cherishing.

self-cherishing. The self-centered attitude of considering one's own happiness to be more important than the happiness and well-being of others. This is the primary obstacle to realizing bodhicitta and thus enlightenment.

Shakyamuni Buddha (ca. 563–483 B.C.E.). The founder of the present Buddhadharma. The fourth of the one thousand founding buddhas of this present world age, Shakyamuni Buddha was born a prince of the Shakya clan in north India. He taught the sutra and tantra paths to liberation and full enlightenment.

shamatha. Meditation to attain the state of concentration or calm abiding.

Shantideva (ca. 685–763). The great Indian bodhisattva who wrote *A Guide to the Bodhisattva's Way of Life*, one of the essential Mahayana texts.

shunyata. The direct realization of emptiness.

six perfections. On the basis of bodhicitta a bodhisattva practices the six perfections: generosity, morality, patience, enthusiastic perseverance, concentration, and wisdom.

stupa. A reliquary, also called a chorten, symbolic of the Buddha's mind.

suffering of change. What is normally regarded as pleasure, but which because of its transitory nature sooner or later turns into suffering.

suffering of pain. Also called the suffering of suffering. The commonly recognized suffering experiences of pain, discomfort, and unhappiness.

sutra. The open discourses of Shakyamuni Buddha; a scriptural text containing teachings and practices.

tantra. Also called Vajrayana, Mantrayana, or Tantrayana, these are the secret or esoteric teachings of the Buddha. Tantric practices generally include identifying oneself as a fully enlightened deity in order to transform one's own impure states of body, speech, and mind into the pure states of that enlightened being.

tantric vows. Vows taken by tantric practitioners.

ten nonvirtuous actions. The three nonvirtues of body are killing, stealing, and sexual misconduct; the four nonvirtues of speech are lying, speaking harshly, slandering, and gossiping; the three of mind are covetousness, ill will, and wrong views.

Theravada. The Way of the Elders. One of the eighteen schools into which the Hinayana split not long after Shakyamuni Buddha's death. Theravada is prevalent in Thailand, Sri Lanka, and Burma, and is well-represented in the West.

thought transformation. Also known as mind training or *lo-jong*, this is a powerful approach to developing bodhicitta, whereby the mind is trained to use all situations, both happy and unhappy, to destroy self-cherishing and self-grasping.

three higher trainings. Ethics, concentration, and wisdom.

three poisons. Ignorance, attachment, and anger.

three realms. The desire, form, and formless realms.

tonglen. The meditation practice of generating bodhicitta by taking on the suffering of others and giving them happiness.

two truths. The two ways of relating to phenomena, as conventional or all-obscuring truth understood by a worldly mind and as ultimate truth understood by a mind engaged in ultimate analysis.

ultimate truth. One of the two truths, the other being conventional truth. It is the understanding of the ultimate nature of things and events as being empty of inherent existence, also known as emptiness.

upper realms. The three higher realms in samsara of humans, demigods, and gods.

Vajrasattva. A male meditational deity symbolizing the inherent purity of all buddhas, Vajrasattva is the basis for a major tantric purification practice for removing obstacles created by negative karma and the breaking of vows.

Vajrayana. The Adamantine Vehicle, and is also called Tantrayana or Mantrayana.

vipassana. The higher seeing or special insight into emptiness.

wisdom. Refers to levels of insight into the nature of reality, and ultimately refers to the wisdom realizing emptiness, which frees beings from cyclic existence and eventually brings them to enlightenment.

Yama. The lord of death, seen on the Wheel of Life.

yana. Lit. "vehicle." A spiritual path that takes you from where you are to where you want to be.

Yeshe, Lama (1935–84). Born and educated in Tibet, Lama Yeshe fled to India, where he met his chief disciple, Lama Zopa Rinpoche. They began teaching Westerners at Kopan Monastery in 1969 and founded the Foundation for the Preservation of the Mahayana Tradition (FPMT) in 1975.

yoga. Lit. "work." Yoga also means "to yoke." This refers to the spiritual discipline to which one yokes oneself in order to achieve enlightenment.

yogi. A highly realized meditator.

Zopa Rinpoche, Kyabje Lama Thubten (b. 1946). Born in Thangme, near Mount Everest, and recognized as the reincarnation of the Lawudo Lama, Lama Zopa Rinpoche became the heart disciple of Lama Thubten Yeshe. Lama Zopa is now Spiritual Director of the Foundation for the Preservation of the Mahayana Tradition (FPMT).

BIBLIOGRAPHY

SUTRAS

Four Noble Truths Sutra (Setting the Wheel of Dharma in Motion) (*Dhammacakkappavattana Sutta*). In *The Connected Discourses of the Buddha: A Translation of the Saṃyutta Nikāya*, translated by Bhikkhu Bodhi, 1843–47. Boston: Wisdom Publications, 2000.

Essence of the Earth Sutra. *Dasacakraksitigarbha Sutra*. *'Dus pa chen po las sa'i snying pa'ikhor lo bcu po'i mdo.*

Laying Out the Stalks Sutra. *Gandavyuhastra*. *Ldong po mkod pa'i mdo.*

INDIAN AND TIBETAN WORKS IN TRANSLATION

His Holiness the Dalai Lama. *Essence of the Heart Sutra: The Dalai Lama's Heart of Wisdom Teachings*. Translated and edited by Geshe Thupten Jinpa. Boston: Wisdom Publications, 2005.

Pabongka Rinpoche. *Liberation in the Palm of Your Hand*. Translated by Michael Richards. Boston: Wisdom Publications, 1991, 2006.

Shantideva. *A Guide to the Bodhisattva's Way of Life* (*Bodhisattvacaryavatara, Jang chub sem pä chö pa la jug pa*). Translated by Stephen Batchelor. Dharamsala, India: Library of Tibetan Works and Archives, 1987.

Tsongkhapa. "The Foundation of All Good Qualities" (*Yön ten shir gyur ma*). In *Essential Buddhist Prayers: An FPMT Prayer Book*, vol. 1, *Basic Prayers and Practices*, 139–41. Portland, OR: FPMT, 2009.

———. *The Great Treatise on the Path to Enlightenment* (*Lam Rim Chen Mo*). 3 vols. Translated by the Lamrim Chenmo Translation Committee. Ithaca, NY: Snow Lion Publications, 2000–2004.

English-Language texts

Sopa, Geshe Lhundub. *Steps on the Path to Enlightenment.* 3 vols. Boston: Wisdom Publications, 2004, 2005, 2008.

Tsering, Geshe Tashi. *Buddhist Psychology.* Boston: Wisdom Publications, 2006.

———. *The Four Noble Truths.* Boston: Wisdom Publications, 2005.

Zopa Rinpoche, Lama. *The Door to Satisfaction: The Heart Advice of a Tibetan Buddhist Master.* Boston: Wisdom Publications, 2001.

———. *Heart of the Path: Seeing the Guru as Buddha.* Boston: Lama Yeshe Wisdom Archive, 2009.

———. *How to Practice Dharma: Teachings on the Eight Worldly Dharmas.* Boston: Lama Yeshe Wisdom Archive, 2012.

INDEX

ABOUT THE AUTHOR

L AMA ZOPA RINPOCHE is one of the most internationally renowned masters of Tibetan Buddhism, working and teaching ceaselessly on almost every continent.

He is the spiritual director and cofounder of the Foundation for the Preservation of the Mahayana Tradition (FPMT), an international network of Buddhist projects, including monasteries in six countries and meditation centers in over thirty; health and nutrition clinics, and clinics specializing in the treatment of leprosy and polio; as well as hospices, schools, publishing activities, and prison outreach projects worldwide.

Lama Zopa Rinpoche is the author of numerous books, including *Transforming Problems into Happiness, Ultimate Healing, The Door to Satisfaction, How to Be Happy, Wholesome Fear, Wisdom Energy*, and *Dear Lama Zopa* from Wisdom Publications.

WHAT TO READ NEXT
FROM WISDOM PUBLICATIONS

··

BOOKS BY LAMA ZOPA RINPOCHE

How to Be Happy

"Rinpoche works with determination and great sincerity in the service of Buddha's teachings and sentient beings."
—His Holiness the Dalai Lama

Ultimate Healing
The Power of Compassion

"This truly is an awesome book."—Lillian Too

Transforming Problems into Happiness
Foreword by His Holiness the Dalai Lama

"A masterfully brief statement of Buddhist teachings on the nature of humanity and human suffering. . . . This book should be read as the words of a wise, loving parent."—*Utne Reader*

How to Enjoy Death
Preparing to Meet Life's Final Challenge without Fear

A beautifully-crafted limited edition!

About Wisdom Publications

Wisdom Publications is the leading publisher of classic and contemporary Buddhist books and practical works on mindfulness. To learn more about us or to explore our other books, please visit our website at wisdompubs.org or contact us at the address below.

Wisdom Publications
199 Elm Street
Somerville, MA 02144 USA

We are a 501(c)(3) organization, and donations in support of our mission are tax deductible.

Wisdom Publications is affiliated with the Foundation for the Preservation of the Mahayana Tradition (FPMT).